D0952065

AN OUTDOOR LIFE BOOK

Complete Guide to GAME FISH

A Field Book of Fresh- and Saltwater Species

by Byron Dalrymple

Drawings by Douglas Allen

OUTDOOR LIFE BOOKS

 VAN NOSTRAND REINHOLD COMPANY

New York   Cincinnati   Toronto
London   Melbourne

Library of Congress Catalog Card Number: 80-8780
ISBN: 0-442-21978-4

Manufactured in the United States of America

To my family, who have seldom allowed me to go fishing more than once a day, and under no circumstances more than 366 days a year.

Contents

Introduction

Many fishing books are billed, not always accurately, as packed with new and startling information. No such claim is made here. The intent of this book was not newness, but rather to bring together as concisely as possible, and with the easiest possible reference, as many of the basic facts about fish and fishing in the United States as might be packed between its covers.

One of the unfortunate deficiencies in fishing literature for the great mass of anglers, the author has long felt, lies in its specialization. The average fisherman who wishes to know the fundamentals about a particular fish or how to catch it must search through a welter of publications and then may not discover what he wishes to know. In addition, almost all modern fishing literature deals only with the scattering of most popular species. There are stacks of books about the "common fish of lake and stream" or the "common fish of the seashore." It is these "common" ones about which most fishermen already know at least something. It is the "uncommon" ones about which they are most likely to have questions that find no answers. To be sure, there are solid scientific references, but to the average angler one peek inside such books is too discouraging.

Thus it was decided to bring together here all of the hook-and-line species of both fresh and salt water, the common and the uncommon, and to show step by step their family relationships and how to identify each with at least fair accuracy but without the use of complicated scientific means. Since there are already many books about how to set up and use various kinds of tackle, this one assumes that the reader already knows the rudiments. Nonetheless, an angler from the East, traveling to the West, or vice versa, may not be well informed about the best methods to use to go about catching some species with which he has had no experience. And so, along with the description, range, and general facts about each species, there is material concerning the tackle and methods most commonly used and most successful in catching it.

What does this fish or that fish look like? Where does it live? What are its habits? How can it be caught? These are the basic questions most asked by anglers. All, it is hoped, are answered here, about all the species that can even remotely be considered game species.

To make reference easy and quick without any confusion, the book is divided into two parts, Freshwater Game Fish and Saltwater Game Fish. And each species, usually with subspecies if any, is covered separately, so that by a glance at the table of contents you may simply turn to the page where the fish you are interested in is listed. Its relatives in each instance are covered nearby. The excellent drawings by Douglas Allen depicting a great many of the species describe far better than words the identifying details of their subjects.

It is the hope of the author that the many months of work put into this book may be translated into much enjoyment for those who refer to it, and that it may help them to a broader interest in and knowledge of the finny world around them.

Identification of Fish

To be a well informed angler one should know each fish from the other at a glance. With most of our more common species, this is not difficult. Yet it is surprising how many anglers lump all sunfish, for example, together, without any interest whatever in which is different from which. A great deal of renewed enjoyment in fishing can be gained from knowing what one is catching, even if it is simply the enjoyment of knowledge for its own sake.

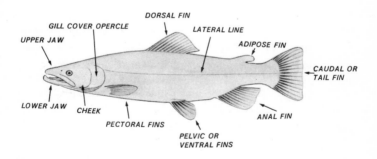

Parts of a Fish

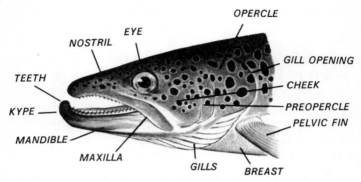

Parts of a Fish's Head

While most common species are easily separated and distinguished, it is not at all a simple matter to lay down explicit directions, easily recalled and applied, for distinguishing some of the others. To complicate matters, it takes science a long, long time to gather information that will allow suspected facts to become substantiated. The waters of the world are vast, money and opportunity for concentrated research limited, and the problems to be concluded all but numberless. But of course this is not the layman's affair. What he wishes to do is pick up a book, look at the name of a fish, check its scientific name perhaps, and know what is what.

However, not only are many of the questions still not answered, but scientists, like other human beings, have difficulty agreeing among themselves. Thus, a fish that one may choose to call by one name, and place in a certain family, another may feel he has good reason to classify differently. There are organizations, principally the American Fisheries Society, which try to compromise

Heterocercal tail fin of the sturgeon.

Heterocercal tail fin of the alligator gar.

Homocercal tail fin of the smallmouth bass.

Fishes have either heterocercal or homocercal tail fins. Ancient fishes like the sturgeon and the gar have heterocercal fins in which the vertebral column extends into the upper part of the fin. A heterocercal fin may have an elongated upper lobe, like that of the sturgeon, or may be symmetrical, like that of the gar. Modern fishes like the smallmouth bass have homocercal tail fins in which there is no spinal extension.

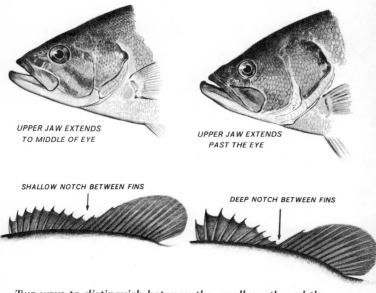

UPPER JAW EXTENDS
TO MIDDLE OF EYE

UPPER JAW EXTENDS
PAST THE EYE

SHALLOW NOTCH BETWEEN FINS

DEEP NOTCH BETWEEN FINS

Two ways to distinguish between the smallmouth and the largemouth bass are shown here. In the smallmouth, the upper jaw extends only to the middle of the eye; in the largemouth the jaw extends beyond the eye. The smallmouth has a shallow notch between its dorsal fins; the largemouth has a deep notch.

these difficulties. All told, everyone involved does a pretty good job. That does not mean, however, that a reference book published a few years ago will necessarily agree all the way through with one published more recently. Indeed you may find that three different reference books give three different scientific names for a fish, and usually the common names are even more numerous and confusing.

Thus, if you have occasion to check the names, particularly the scientific names, in this book with those in some others, you may find perplexing differences. You may wonder who is right. If the other reference is older, no doubt both are right. Scientists often change scientific names in light of new knowledge, or when it is discovered that one name preceded another. Or two mildly similar fish, for example, thought a few years ago to be two distinct species, may be found by long study to be identical, or at least differing only superficially and not enough to command species status. One is deleted.

The scientific names used here have been carefully checked, and are those currently recognized by the American Fisheries Society. Common names have been selected to come as close as possible to making things easy for the greatest number of readers. Purposely left out are detailed lists of the hosts of colloquial names used here and there for various fish. A few are noted where this seems necessary. Although the American Fisheries Society also officially recognizes only certain common names, we have not followed their list in all instances. Some of their selections, we feel, are questionable simply because fishermen just do not use them, and undoubtedly never will.

It is not possible even in the best scientific references to so meticulously relate identifying physical characteristics that the angler actively fishing can simply flip a page and know the identity of an obscure species. In such instances, perhaps dissection, scale counts and other painstaking research projects may be mandatory. However, the purpose here has been to select only those characteristics that might be used quickly and easily in identifying the fish caught. A bit of study of the relationships of fishes, plus attention to the illustrations, will help further.

The Future of American Fishing

Anglers are inclined to reminisce wistfully about the "good old days." To be sure, they *were* good. But all things are relative to the time in which one lives. Certainly brook trout fishing over its native range in the last century was far better than today. The Michigan grayling, once supremely abundant, has long been extinct. But largemouth-bass fishing of decades past cannot even remotely compare with what is available today. The advent of hundreds of huge impoundments—regardless of their necessity—is solely responsible for making the largemouth, by numbers of interested anglers and fish caught, the most important sport fish ever to take a hook anywhere in the world. The rainbow trout, once extremely range restricted, has been successfully transplanted almost throughout the entire nation.

Indeed, enlightened fish management, in tune with our times, has led us to a thorough knowledge of how to control undesirables and how to enhance potential with desirables. If you search this book you will discover that hybrid sunfishes, for example, open a whole new world to pond-fishing panfish enthusiasts—and only the surface of this vast field has been scratched. Crosses of numerous closely related species—the black basses, white and striped bass are examples—show promise as "new" game fish. Anadromous fish from the West Coast, the salmons, have made unbelievable angling news in the Great Lakes Region. Other saltwater species—for example, the striped bass—have become common, and provide high drama, thousands of miles from their native homes. Walleyes, smallmouth bass, pike, all "northerners," are now found almost everywhere in the U.S., even in the southwestern desert.

So, we not only trade around with our native fishes, establishing species where they'd not have been dreamed of years ago, but we substitute saltwater varieties for fresh and make them work. Yet this is only a beginning, and the future is still more exciting. Biologists along the Gulf of Mexico are slowly learning how to raise and propagate saltwater fishes—thought impossible a few years ago— such as sea trout, drum, channel bass, and even shrimp. Mariculture—the science of producing "crops from the sea" in a kind of farming environment—is just possibly the most dramatic means for the future of feeding nations, as well as producing new recreation.

And again we are only starting. It is predictable that American sport fishing in coming decades may have a wholly new face, and perhaps an even more exciting one than in the past, good as it was. Biologists are presently taking a world-wide view. Just as the Chinese pheasant in its way revolutionized upland bird hunting in this country, introduced exotic fishes may do likewise, and thereby vastly change in the long future the picture this book presents, at this time, of angling recreation in the U.S.

The South American *pavon* or peacock bass, of several species, are being studied as possible imports into certain of our waters, have even been hatchery raised and stocked in a few. They are beautiful, big, and as game fish sensational. So is the huge Nile perch of Africa. The reason for experiments with them is the growing number of electro-power plants in this country that are warming their impounded cooling-lake waters past the point where native species can survive in present quantities. Some of the exotics tolerate high temperatures—but cannot survive temperatures, say, below 60 degrees. Thus, they may be controlled by temperature management, act as large predators on undesirables difficult to control, and meanwhile fill niches in our expanding and ever-more-complicated water and angling pictures that are desirable.

Conceivably, even with lessons such as the introduced carp behind us, we may also make a few errors. During the 1970s controversy was severe in parts of the South and Southwest about transplants of the white amur, a large member of the carp group from Asia that presumably feeds so avidly on vegetation that it could clean lakes of undesirable infestations of noxious aquatics. Many biologists fear the worst if the white amur gets out of control, which it already may have. Others see it as a savior of certain southern waters, and a dynamic game fish as well.

Fortunately, fisheries scientists are far more cautious about introductions than they used to be. The errors they've made to date are far overshadowed by rousing successes on the side of the desirables. The future? Contrary to the doomsayers, we are not in an age that is about to see the demise of sport fishing. We are instead on the threshold of a perhaps radically changed but infinitely more exciting and varied period as compared to "the good old days."

part I

Freshwater Game Fish

Largemouth Bass

Micropterus salmoides

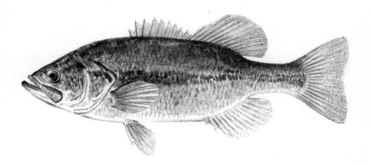

This chunky, voracious fish of varying shades of green, black, and bronze is unquestionably the most popular American freshwater game fish. It is native to or stocked in every state, and is found in southern Canada and Mexico. It is for almost everyone a "backyard" variety, of a size to instill pride, and is at home in all moderately warm waters from weedy ponds to vast impoundments, and slow streams large and small.

Moreover, it is a marauder, ready to gobble up anything that moves. Because of this temperament, it strikes almost any bait—nightcrawlers, frogs, minnows, mice—or such artificial lures as flies, plugs, spoons, and spinning jigs.

Its strike is generally a smashing blow, especially when the fish are feeding on the surface. The largemouth is famous for its wild surface-feeding sprees. These usually occur early or late in the day, or at night, but may start suddenly at any time around the clock. Where it is legally allowed, largemouths are much fished at night. Outsize specimens, difficult to fool by day, often strike with abandon when darkness cloaks danger.

When not surface feeding, these bass are usually catchable at specific depths from a foot or two down to 30, or occasionally 50, feet. The precise level is important. They lie where water temperature is most congenial. When deep, and still willing—which they will be at varying periods—some will fight bulldog, below-surface battles. Most will come surfaceward, a good many leap in showers of flying spray from one to a half-dozen times. This habit of hurling itself end over end in frantic battle is an attribute that originally won high honors for the largemouth.

Largemouths weigh to 20-odd pounds. Fish of 8 or 10 are not uncommon in the South, but 1 to 4 is average anywhere. These are the best jumpers.

The fact that, experienced or not, anybody can catch largemouths, adds to their popularity. But their slam-bang temperament is in one way a drawback. It lulls the tyro into believing he is doing fine, when by ardent application and observation of this impulsive fish he might catch more, and larger, fish.

Here is a species primarily of weedbeds and dropoffs. Often these bass feed in reed-filled waters barely covering their backs. Habitually they cruise shorelines, and among lily pads and other vegetation.

Weedless lures cast among lily pads, so they rustle across the pads and gurgle in tiny patches of water, get awesome smashes. Floating fly-rod bass bugs dropped into openings among pads and other vegetation, allowed to lie a bit, then twitched teasingly, or cast upon a pad and "crawled" off and let lie, account for scores of good fish. The usual method, regardless of lure, is to ease slowly, quietly along the shore by boat, and cast shoreward.

In the large impoundments so numerous and popular today with bass fishermen, weedbeds are not always abundantly present. Fishing over the dropoffs in these impoundments, especially in hot weather, gets startling results. With spinning or plug rod, and a quick-sinking lure such as a wobbling spoon, casts are made from shallow to deep water. The lure is allowed to sink to bottom, after a moment raised with a quick, hard, sweeping lift of the rod. The reel is now worked furiously. Rhythmic short jerks of the rod tip meanwhile impart erratic action. Especially where largemouths habitually feed on gizzard shad, this is a killing method.

Bait fishermen hook a nightcrawler through the head, cast it among weeds or over weed beds, or let it sink deep and retrieve slowly. Some place a spinner ahead of the crawler. Plastic worms work so well that nowadays they have almost replaced the real thing. Commercially packed pork rind works as well as crawlers. The method is almost surefire.

Southerners hook a large shiner through back or lips, use no sinker, but place a small bobber seldom over 3 feet above the shiner. This rig is cast to the edge of floating beds of vegetation. When a bass takes, it runs, sometimes far back under the floating weeds. When it stops, the angler gently tightens line to get direction, then sets the hook.

Many anglers troll for largemouths. It is a good method

for locating fish. The depth at which the lure runs, however, is important, and should be changed if no hits materialize. Drifting with the bait or lure overside is also popular.

The successful largemouth angler never forgets that these are *cover* fish. Logs, floating or sunk, stumps, debris, rocks, solid beds of weeds all will hide fish, unless temperature heights have driven them deep. Slow fishing also aids success. Largemouths strike savagely and impulsively, but commonly need coaxing. Letting a lure lie long, casting to the same spot over and over, making slow, erratic retrieves, are good tricks.

These bass have mouths in keeping with their name. Moderately sizable and strong hooks with a deep, broad bite are best for them. Because of weed handicap, leaders and lines should be stronger than necessary to land the fish, to avoid breaking off. In most waters a limp-nylon 6-pound level leader works well. Fly rods of "bass weight," that is, with solid action, to handle heavy bugs and lines, are best. Forward-taper fly lines make the best bug lines. Spinning lines of 6- and 8-pound test are generally used, plug lines to 12, or even 20 where weeds are very heavy. Soft-action spinning and plug rods are not good in heavy weeds, but are fine elsewhere. Lure color is not as important as many fanatics believe, except when it is desirable to closely imitate some specific food.

No net is needed for bass (either largemouth or smallmouth) if the following procedure is used: wear the fish out, bring it close, reach the left hand carefully under water, quickly, firmly seize the fish's lower jaw, thumb inside mouth, fingers outside. Bend the jaw down and lift. The fish will remain immobile.

There are several relatives of the largemouth that are confusing to fishermen. The spotted bass and its subspecies, the redeye bass and the Suwannee bass stand somewhere between the largemouth and the smallmouth, but may be closer to the smallmouth, and will be covered with that species. Scientists presently agree that the extra-large bass for which Florida lakes are renowned have enough differing physiological characteristics to be named as a subspecies. It is called *Micropterus salmoides floridanus* (in some references *Huro s.f.*). This refers to those king-sized specimens fairly common in Florida of 10 to 20 pounds. The number of rows of scales both above and below the lateral line are greater, and the scale count along the lateral line is greater, than in the northern largemouth bass.

There has been much interest in this bass over recent years, for use in transplants and in cross breeding. California has established it in a number of lakes of the southern part of that state, and some astonishing specimens have been caught, weighing from 17 to more than 20 pounds. Some Californians believe a new record will eventually be set there. Texas has widely stocked and established this "super-bass" and has also experimented with hybrids of it and specimens from certain Texas lakes where bass consistently grow to large size. The infusion of the Florida bass strain into the Texas bass population has already resulted in smashing the Texas state record, which had stood for thirty-seven years. Fisheries people are doubtful that the Florida subspecies of largemouth will be useful outside of the southernmost states, but it well may revolutionize bass fishing in numerous southern lakes in future, so far as maximum size is concerned.

Although largemouths are everywhere abundant, here are a few examples of the most famous largemouth fishing locations: Florida lakes and streams; impoundments of Tennessee, Kentucky, Missouri, Arkansas, Mississippi, Georgia, Oklahoma, Texas, New Mexico; border impoundments of Arizona-Nevada; southern California lakes.

Broadly speaking, May and November are the best southern bass months, June and September the best farther north. Good bass fishing is available around the year in the South, where most states never have closed seasons, and throughout most of the open season in the North and West.

It should be mentioned here that many books give the scientific name of the largemouth black bass as *Huro salmoides.* During the past half century the scientific name of this fish has been changed several times. In 1926 the ichthyologist Hubbs placed it in the genus *Huro*, separating it entirely from the former genus where it once was classified along with the smallmouth, and placing it as the only species in the new genus. The current listing of the American Fisheries Society does not recognize use of the genus name *Huro.*

There has long been much confusion among anglers as to which is a largemouth and which a smallmouth bass, especially since in some instances both are found in the same waters. Instructions on how to separate the two are given in the next section, where the smallmouth bass is covered.

Smallmouth Bass

Micropterus dolomieui

Although the smallmouth bass is the very closest kin of the largemouth, and on occasion is found in the same waters, it is so different in many ways that it seems totally unrelated. Not that it looks at a glance so different. In fact, as has been said, many anglers have difficulty distinguishing between the two. There is no need for this confusion.

When the two species are seen together, the smallmouth instantly shows up as a more chunky, close-coupled fish. It is invariably deeper vertically, and this makes the largemouth appear more elongated. The color patterns of all fish differ of course with habitat, temperature, and various other influences, but in general the largemouth bass appears to have a horizontal dark stripe (no matter how broken) along its side, while the smallmouth has vertical wavy bars or blotches, distinct or indistinct. The smallmouth is usually a paler green, or brassy, and even sometimes yellowish-gray or clay colored.

More specific identification can be arrived at by examination of the head. The upper jawbone, or maxillary, of the smallmouth reaches backward only to a position below the center of the eye. That of the largemouth extends past the rear margin of the eye. If there is still doubt, examination of the dorsal (back) fin will help further. The largemouth has the spiny and soft portions of the dorsal almost entirely separated by a deep cleft. In the smallmouth the two fin portions are very nearly continuous.

In many ways the smallmouth is a far flashier game fish than the largemouth. It usually makes many fine leaps and has tremendous tenacity. It might be called a "wilder" fish than the largemouth. By the same token it is more difficult to catch, far more whimsical. It is also less common than the largemouth.

Original smallmouth range was throughout New England and the Great Lakes area, including southern Canada, and southward to the rivers especially in Tennessee, Missouri, Arkansas, and eastern Oklahoma. The coming of numerous large impoundments to the Midsouth allowed the smallmouth to colonize abundantly in those that were suitable, as an example, Dale Hollow in Tennessee. Stocking over recent years has expanded the range to the West Coast and elsewhere.

California established smallmouths in certain waters. There is presently a striking smallmouth fishery that evolved from transplants, in portions of the Snake River where it borders Oregon and Idaho. The smallmouth, once thought able to survive only in the North, is now found in some surprising places. A wilderness stretch of Arizona's Black River has them. So do several lakes in Colorado. Texas has established excellent smallmouth fisheries in several lakes, particularly Canyon Reservoir on the Guadalupe River north of San Antonio. Texas biologists believe that year-round low-water temperature is not as important to the success of the smallmouth as is the steepness of lake shores. Interestingly, in New Mexico the smallmouth has successfully been established in portions of the Rio Grande, and has done so well in Ute Lake, an impoundment on the Canadian River, that state records of both largemouth and smallmouth were taken from there during the 1970s.

The smallmouth, a fish strictly of cold, clear water, of rocky shores and often of swift streams, is delicate to handle and locally restricted by the nature of its habitat preference. For the same reasons it is mainly a species of northern or moderate climates. It is not at all a fish of weedbeds or excessively warm water. It hides at the foot of submerged rock walls and among boulders, is inclined to lie deep and, in comparison to the largemouth, to feed on the surface very little.

In most smallmouth waters these fish eat minnows and crayfish in preference to any other foods, with the possible exception of large nymphs garnered from among the gravel on the shoals or in the riffles of fast streams. However, nightcrawlers, small frogs, and leeches are prime baits. This is not to say that smallmouths are never taken on the surface. But the consistently successful smallmouth angler will spend almost his entire fishing time using deep-running plugs or close-to-bottom metal flasher lures on his spinning rod, or streamer flies and nymphs on his fly rod, or bait right on or very near bottom.

On occasion, mainly toward evening, surface bugs and flies will get results, but not so commonly as with the largemouth, nor do smallmouths feed as avidly after dark as the largemouth. Whatever tackle is used, fishing must be done, on the whole, more carefully than for the largemouth, and a reasonably fine leader for fly fishing is a must for the larger specimens.

The smallmouth does not grow as large as the largemouth. Because it lives in colder water, and in a less lush domain, it has a shorter growing season and must work more actively to make its living. Nature has therefore fashioned the smallmouth as a hard, compact, nervous, and roving species. A smallmouth of 5 or 6 pounds is a good one, indeed. It grows somewhat larger. Specimens in the class from 9 to 11 pounds have been taken at the smallmouth-famous impoundments in Tennessee, but the usual average is from 1 1/2 to 3 pounds. The 14-pound Florida record of some years ago has now been discredited. The fish probably does not range there.

Here are a few of the more famous smallmouth fishing areas of the United States: Maine and portions of the other northern New England states; Ontario; parts of Manitoba; shorelines of the northern Great Lakes, especially lakes Michigan and Huron in their upper portions; specific impoundments of the Midsouth, such as Dale Hollow; certain Ozarks streams; a few rivers and lakes of the west coast from San Francisco northward.

The smallmouth angler should avoid for the most part

small ponds and lakes. Smallmouth bass seem to do best in large, deep lakes where they have plenty of space. Streams may not be especially large, but should have plenty of current and appear identical to many a good trout stream. In summer, water around 60 to 65 degrees seems to please the smallmouth best. Seek these fish at a depth where such temperatures exist, providing the water also has the other necessary requisites.

When baiting with a nightcrawler or plastic worm, the angler should place it on the hook so that it is stretched out. Then it is cast and crawled slowly along bottom and past rocks which form good hiding places. A crawler bunched on a hook will seldom be successful. When fishing along the Great Lakes where many anglers wade at times when the bass are inshore, it is possible to spot large submerged boulders beneath the clear water. By casting either bait or lure so that it works slowly past such a rock on the retrieve, and close to bottom, bass may invariably be taken. Often several modest-sized fish will be found using the same boulder for a hideout. Large smallmouths, however, are inclined to be solitary.

Along shores of the average lake, and likewise along stream courses, the shaded places will be the best spots to fish. Smallmouths like to keep cool and well hidden. Beneath overhanging trees, along a rocky ledge, on a shaded bend where a pool is formed but current swirls and eddies through—these are lairs of this shy but pugnacious fish.

Because the smallmouth is an extremely erratic customer, local fishing methods vary greatly. It behooves the visiting angler to listen and observe carefully what the successful locals are up to. This is even more important

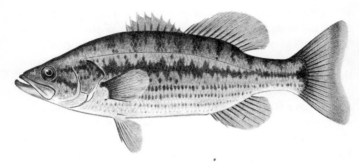

Spotted Bass

in smallmouth fishing than in trout fishing. Canadians in some areas know precisely how to fish a leech so that it is irresistible to the smallmouth. In Tennessee there are fabulously successful anglers who fish very deep at exact spots, and use a plug which they reel or troll at great speed. In some of the northern smallmouth streams, especially on toward fall, the well-sunk streamer fly works wonders.

Indeed, a part of the immensely provocative appeal of smallmouth angling is that this fish is such a moody and unpredictable creature. There are times, of course (mainly in spring and early summer, and occasionally in late fall), when it seems impossible to keep from catching them. Those are the times the enthusiast lives for, the times that make the long dry spells worthwhile, for the small-mouth is one of the gamest of the world's game fishes.

Scientists, and some fishermen, were aware for many years that there were specimens caught here and there neither easily identified as smallmouth or largemouth bass, but seemingly a little of each. In 1927 a new bass was named, first called the Kentucky bass because it was believed to exist only in that state. Later it was discovered to be really quite common over much of the South and on into Texas. Eventually it was called the spotted bass, and given the name *Micropterus punctulatus*.

The **spotted bass** has rather distinct diamond-shaped markings running along the sides, at least in most specimens. It is not easily identified by anglers, however, even when their string contains both spotted and the other basses. The mouth of the spotted bass is midway in size between that of largemouth and smallmouth. While the joint of the jaw is almost exacly below the center of the eye in the smallmouth, in the spotted bass it is a bit to the rear of that point, but not even with or beyond the rear of the eye.

In feeding habits the spotted bass resembles the smallmouth, but in the types of habitat it favors it stands between smallmouth and largemouth. This places it in modest temperatures, neither the cold spots relished by the smallmouth nor the warm waters the largemouth enjoys. Rocks intrigue it more than weeds, moving water more than still.

The spawning habits of this bass appear to be different from its relatives and it is also considered by fish culturists a more rugged species in many ways. It has become a very important game fish in its own right, and as time goes on may be handled for stocking purposes more than either of the others. In size it often runs small, or about like the average of the other species. It is thought not to grow as large as the largemouth, but recently in new impoundments, particularly Smith Lake in Alabama, some very large specimens have become quite common.

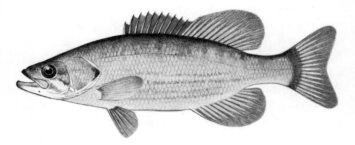

Redeye Bass

A new record of over 8 pounds has been established.

The **redeye bass** is another distinct species of recent scientific vintage. It was given full status about 1940. It is a relative of the smallmouth, and probably very close to the spotted bass. Its scientific name is *Micropterus coosae*. This is mainly a stream fish, in true smallmouth style, and is an inhabitant of the southeastern United States, most of the reports of it coming from Alabama, Georgia, and South Carolina. It is difficult to positively identify. Mouth size and position of the jaw joint will allow the amateur ichthyologist to come close, since they are about the same as in spotted bass. The side markings are faint bars rather than diamonds. It is doubtful if this fish grows on the average much larger than 2 pounds. It is a good game fish.

The **Suwannee bass** is still another smallmouth-spotted bass offshoot which has been given full species status. It is called *Micropterus notius*, and is known currently only from a small area of north Florida.

The spotted bass has two subspecies—the **Wichita spotted bass,** named from a single stream in the Wichita

Suwannee Bass

Mountains; and the **Alabama spotted bass,** native to the Alabama River system. Whether or not these should be elevated to the position of subspecies may be debated. Sometimes when a new fish is discovered, scientists call it a new species or subspecies when in reality it is nothing but a local race or phase. Many of these may need another million years before becoming different enough in their restricted environments to be called true species.

The spotted, redeye, and related basses are fished for by methods identical to those used for smallmouths. They will take surface flies, and, like the smallmouth, they also feed heavily on crayfish. They leap and fight with vigor, and can barely be distinguished at the end of a line from their illustrious cold-water relative.

Recently much interest has centered, in fisheries research, on hybridization of various species, among them the black basses. Hybrids of closely related varieties are usually tougher than either parent, grow faster, are commonly more aggressive, thus appealing to anglers because they are easily caught. Among the black basses, experiments with crosses have been numerous. Amusingly, one of the hybrids resulting from a smallmouth-largemouth cross was dubbed the "mean-mouth" bass. It proved so aggressive and voracious that fisheries people were dubious about stocking it. Black bass hybrids to fit specific habitat situations may be an important addition to future sport fishing.

Bluegill Sunfish

Lepomis macrochirus

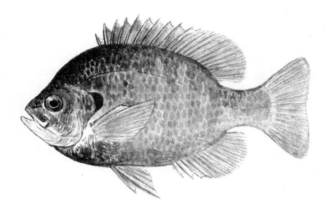

The bluegill and its relatives are probably, all things considered, the most well-loved of the smaller sport fishes. The black bass is our top game fish, with the various trouts second. But by numbers annually taken, by numbers of fishermen who angle for them, the various sunfishes, with the bluegill heading the list, unquestionably would force the larger game species into the background. These smaller species just about blanket the United States in range, and they are found in extreme abundance in all kinds of waters. In addition, they are perfectly willing to cooperate, good battlers for their size, and are excellent on the table. Nothing more could be asked of a fish.

The true sunfishes belong to the Centrarchidae, the same family to which large and smallmouth bass, crappies, and rock bass belong. But the sunfishes are a group by themselves. Because the bluegill is one of the largest of the lot, very widely distributed natively and stocked further, and because it will take a great variety of baits and lures, it is on the whole the most popular member of the group. When Southerners speak of fishing for "bream" or "brim," this is the fish to which they refer, unless they qualify the term so it points out some other member of the group. Throughout the entire eastern half of the United States the bluegill is represented almost everywhere. It ranges on into Texas and has been stocked in lakes on the west coast.

Bluegills are called "blue sunfish" in some areas. In others they may be called "perch" or "blue perch." This is true, for example, in portions of Texas. The name "perch" is perhaps more widely misused than any other fish name. Copperhead bream, blue bream, red-breasted bream are other names occasionally heard. Most of these are used in rural southern areas.

The color of this sprightly little fish differs greatly in different waters. It may run all the way from nearly black or purplish to dark brown, green, or silvery greenish. The vertical bars usually displayed may be lacking in older specimens. Males during breeding season are quite gaudy, the head and throat vivid aqua to blue, and the breast burnt orange or bright orange-red. The earflap, which all of the sunfishes have, is a good tag for quickly identifying any one of them with fair accuracy. The bluegill's earflap is rather squared at the back and is all black. In old specimens it may have a thin margin of white, but it never has any color.

Bluegills are mainly lake fish, although they are found

occasionally in slow streams. They like weedy lakes, where lily pads or other such aquatic vegetation grows. They travel as a rule in small, loose groups, cruising slowly along or hanging around a dock, a bay, a weedbed. They may be found in very shallow water, perhaps at depths of only a couple of feet on down to 10 or 15. Or, during summer when the surface temperature is warm, they may be down to 30 feet or more. Their habitat is in general very much the same as that of the largemouth bass. The bass-bluegill combination has often proved very successful when lakes are stocked, and bass fishermen using small lures invariably catch a few bluegills.

In size the bluegill runs from 4 to possibly 12 inches. Adult fish in a habitat conducive to sound growth usually average around 8 inches, with a few going to 10 and 11. Bluegills (and other sunfish) are built deep and compressed. When hooked they lay one flat side to the pull of the rod and run in swift circles. Much as bass anglers hate to admit it, the bluegill ounce for ounce easily outfights the bass.

Some of this sunfish's food is grubbed from the bottom, but much is also taken from the surface and near the surface. At various times, most usually toward evening, swarms of bluegills may be seen rising to take nymphs or surface insects. Thus the bluegill feeds in a manner to suit the taste of cane-pole bait fishermen as well as fly fishermen.

The bait angler offers bluegills just about anything handy in the area—crickets, angleworms, grasshoppers, grubs of various sorts. In certain areas, the catalpa worm, larva of a butterfly, is a sensational bait. Leeches and various nymphs also take bluegills regularly. There is nothing complicated about bait fishing for bluegills. A small hook is used, and preferably a very light sinker, just a split shot in most cases. The use of a leader or light monofil line will account for more large bluegills than will attaching the hook to a woven line. Once the proper depth is found, which may take a bit of experimenting, and the favorite hangout of the fish established, it is pretty much a matter of hauling them in. The fun is likely to be fast, too. Stillfishing is often best in summer, for bluegills will then congregate in deep holes or holes where bottom springs occur, and a great many can be caught in a hurry, sometimes in the middle of the day.

Fly fishermen sometimes use dry flies. But because such flies are easily dunked in lake fishing, a small cork-bodied bug, or so-called "popping bug," often with rubber legs that quiver, has found high favor. This is a true killer lure when the bluegills are rising, or in spring when the males are making nests preparatory to coaxing a female in to deposit her eggs.

Because bluegills are prolific, in most areas they may be fished during spawning season. Usually they spawn in colonies. In locations where they spawn in shallow water, the beds are easily seen in the shallows as clean, paler-colored circular patches perhaps a foot to eighteen inches across. When a bedding area is located, the popping-bug enthusiast either wades or fishes from a boat and casts over the beds.

The fish strike viciously and fight exceedingly well on the light tackle. The bug is simply cast, allowed to lie quietly for a few moments, then twitched. Often the strike comes while the bug is still. In some instances bluegills spawn deeper, 6 to 10 feet. Bedding areas are located by trial and error, often by drifting in a boat over clean, firm bottoms of sand or fine gravel, keeping bait or lure—most commonly the former—moving very slowly and right on bottom.

Small wet flies are also very good for bluegill fishing. Prior to spawning, and after spawning, they are especially effective. Color doesn't seem to be very important. In some areas a certain fly will be especially successful, in others another seems best. Local anglers usually know which is the "going fly" in their bailiwick. Bluegills can be taken on small plugs, on spinning lures, and on live minnows. By and large, however, bugs and flies, and the standard baits such as worms, grasshoppers, or crickets, are best. Flyfishing before or after spawning invariably produces the most action at dawn or in the evening. The fish often come up from deep water in summer to surface feed just at dusk, and until possibly ten o'clock at night. They are quick to sight a twitched bug at such times, and strike it with a bang.

In some lakes, trolling or drifting locates the fish and picks off the big ones. It should be done very slowly, with a worm and a small spinner, or, where bluegills run very large, with a whole nightcrawler on a hook but never in a bunch. It must be trailing naturally. Small pork rind is also effective. When a good spot is located, the spinning man can have high enjoyment by anchoring, rigging with a small shot and a hook and worm or pork rink, casting out, letting the bait sink and crawling it slowly along bottom, or reeling it slowly at whatever depth the fish are using.

The bluegill is a mainstay of the ice fishing fraternity in certain areas, especially in the Great Lakes Region.

Michigan, Wisconsin, northern Indiana, Illinois, and Ohio have thousands of winter bluegill enthusiasts. Smaller baits are used after ice forms. The fish are usually found in about 10 feet of water, near or over or in weedbeds. A short, limber ice-fishing rod, with a fine monofil line, tiny split shot and one of the popular ice-fishing baits such as meal worms—purchased easily at bait ranches—make up the rig. The fish generally stay close to bottom, bite rather weakly. Many anglers use a tiny bobber in the hole, the better to record the weak bite.

Ice flies are also popular for winter bluegills. In fact, the bluegill was responsible for invention of the ice fly. Nowadays this lure takes many forms, from tiny spidery lures to miniature jigging spoons. All are let down near bottom and jigged gently. They are extremely effective when properly used.

Most of the bluegill's immediate relatives have fairly similar habits and habitats, and commonly one or more species are caught while one is fishing for buegills. However, it is well to have at least a smattering of knowledge about a few of the more important species and their differences, for several are extremely popular small sport fish in their own right, in specific localities.

The **common sunfish,** *Lepomis gibbosus,* has a daub of red at the rear lower portion of the short, black, rounded earflap. The breast in males is likely to be brilliant yellow; the head usually has wavy aqua stripes. The body is usually green or brownish-green with orange spots. This is the "pumpkinseed," or "sunny," a very common variety in small lakes, weedy ponds, and slow streams from southern Canada to the Gulf and as far westward as western Montana. It is likely to be in shallow

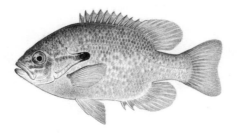

Yellowbreast Sunfish

water close to shore, and to take most of its food near or off bottom. Occasionally it is caught on flies, but mainly on bait. Size averages somewhat smaller than the bluegill.

The **yellowbreast sunfish,** *Lepomis auritus,* has an unmistakable earflap, very long, very narrow, often club-shaped, black, with blue tints at the forward portion. This species is sometimes called the long-eared sunfish, a confusing situation, because that probably should have been its name but unfortunately was officially given to another species. Southerners call this fish a yellowbelly or redbreast. The breast of the male is generally bright yellow or orange. The rest of the fish is rather dark, brown to green-black. There is some blue on the nose and about the eye. This is a good-sized sport fish running to 8 or 10 inches, most commonly (but not always) found in large rivers along the entire length of the east coast, and from the Great Lakes Region southward. It is also found in the Midsouth, eastward, and in Florida, Louisiana, and parts of Texas. It is taken much the same as the bluegill, but predominantly on bait.

The **longeared sunfish,** *Lepomis megalotis,* is a gaudy

Longeared Sunfish

species with numerous other regional names, the most common being "red-bellied bream." This fish ranges throughout the Mississippi Valley and eastward into the Carolinas and on to the Gulf. The Midsouth is its concentration point. It is of good size, although averaging perhaps a bit smaller than the previous (yellowbreast) species. Color varies in different habitats, but is usually orange and blue in wavy mottlings. The earflap is distinctive, very long, very broad, with a blue or red border. The iris of the eye also is a point of identification. It is red. The longear is a fish mainly of reasonably clean streams.

The **shellcracker,** or redear, *Lepomis microlophus*, at a maximum size is likely to run the largest of any of the true sunfishes. Specimens of 2 pounds are not uncommon. The main concentration of the shellcracker is in Florida, but the fish is also caught from lower Indiana to the Gulf, and westward into portions of Texas. The general color may vary from dark to pale greenish or yellowish green, with varied mottlings. The earflap is

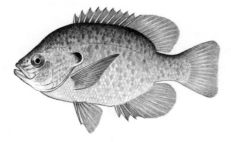

Shellcracker

rather short, but has an unmistakable red border at the
back. The odd one is caught on the surface, but the
shellcracker is predominantly a bottom feeder, living in
large rivers and in lakes, where its main food is crustaceans and small mollusks. These it crushes with paved
teeth that are at the back of the throat. Shellcrackers are
most often caught on worms, and usually in great abundance during brief periods when they are concentrated
in large groups preparing to make spawning beds. This
fish is the "chinquapin" of southern Louisiana.

There are a number of other true sunfish—the small
spotted sunfish or stumpknocker of the South, bronze
with dark speckles, found quite often precisely where its
name implies, near a stump; the **round sunfish,** a small
species of ponds and streams; the **green sunfish,** generally an inhabitant of ponds, creeks and small lakes. The
green sunfish, in almost all references, is spoken of as
"small." This is an instance of older faulty research. In
some midwestern and southern waters green sunfish
regularly grow to more than a pound.

The green sunfish, however, never was an especially important species until recently. Fisheries scientists know that in certain waters our most important sunfish, the bluegill, does not do well. In small lakes and ponds it also is so prolific that it quickly overpopulates and becomes stunted. Several hybrids have been tried, in attempts to solve these problems. One of the most successful is a male-green, female-redear (shellcracker) cross. This "manmade" sunfish produces a low number of females and each deposits a singularly small number of eggs, few fertile. Thus overpopulation and stunting are avoided. Further, this hybrid grows swiftly, is a fine scrapper, excellent eating, and grows under optimum conditions to 2 pounds or more.

Texas, which first produced this hybrid in quantity, went all-out with it as a perfect fish for stocking farm ponds, where overpopulation often occurs. Other states, and private hatcheries, across the South have been raising this hybrid and several others. Numerous sunfish combinations appear to have future use. The crosses, for example, of a particularly large strain of southeastern bluegill with a green sunfish, and also with the redear, have shown striking results in swift growth to large size. All such hybrids, however, appear to have their best future in private ponds where fish populations can be controlled. They must be stocked in a "clean" habitat, for they quickly recross with other available sunfish varieties, and eventually the desirable qualities of the hybrid are lost or swallowed by the conglomerate genetic pool.

White Crappie

Pomoxis annularis

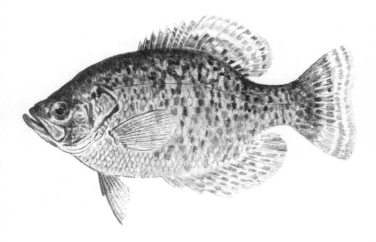

Fishermen seldom bother to distinguish between the white crappie and its twin the **black crappie,** *Pomoxis nigromaculatus.* Taken together as one fish, the crappie, which has the dubious distinction of having collected more colloquial names (fifty or more in all) than probably any other of our native fishes, has long been one of the most popular of the so-called "panfish."

The range of the white crappie is predominantly southern, that of the black variety the reverse. Each overlaps the other to such a degree that quite commonly both species are found in the same waters. From southern Canada down across the Great Lakes Region to the Gulf, and most of the area eastward, was the original crappie habitat. These fish have been so widely stocked, however, that they now range throughout most of the country. For example, Owyhee Reservoir in Oregon, many impoundments in New Mexico, and certain California lakes all furnish excellent crappie fishing.

Color is not a good key to identifying the two species, although the white crappie is paler than its counterpart. The white species is in general appearance somewhat longer and of less depth than the black. The white usually has six dorsal spines, the black seven or eight. This is not an infallible criterion. However, there is no especially important reason for keeping the two separated.

Both grow to about 3 pounds maximum, although larger specimens have been recorded. The average adult fish in most waters is much smaller, from a half pound to a pound. Many persons claim the crappie as the finest table fish of all the smaller species. Although crappies are good, their merit of first place is questionable.

Although the crappie is found in a great variety of waters—warm and weedy ponds, southern cypress bayous, large lakes, slow streams, and in both clear and murky waters—probably the mainstay of crappie fishing nowadays is in the big impoundments in various parts of the country. Kentucky and Tennessee, Texas, Kansas, Oklahoma, New Mexico, and Oregon all have amazing fishing for this species. During spawning time, which in Tennessee for example is about mid-April, literally thousands of persons catch tens of thousands of crappies, mainly by stillfishing with small minnows.

The reason the crappie has flourished in these large manmade lakes is that the exceedingly prolific little gizzard shad also is resident in most of the impoundments.

Crappies are predominantly predaceous. Their main food is small fish. The young shad is just made for them. However, all the best of the crappie fishing is by no means found only in the impoundments. For many years, as an example, the crappie has been known almost as the state fish of Minnesota, where scores of lakes abound with the species and where, in winter, it is the mainstay of the ice-angler's catch.

Crappies are not as game, generally speaking, as their cousins the sunfishes. Nor are they quite as interested in artificial lures. The method by which most crappies are taken is by live bait fishing, using minnows of an inch to an inch and a half long. The so-called "toughie minnow," a species of goldfish, is a great crappie killer in the Midsouth. It is most often used with a cane pole, eased down on a sinker and bobber rig beside a stump or into a patch of submerged willows.

That is the procedure of spring fishing. Later, after spawning, the fish retire to deeper water and are more difficult to find. Up near the dams, or in the protection of rocks in the tailraces of impoundment dams, crappies are regularly caught in great numbers all through the season by stillfishing with minnows. In natural lakes, anglers familiar with the water seek deep holes, as deep as 30 or 40 feet, generally near weedbeds or where snags and submerged stumps lie, and here they take many a good catch by stillfishing, even in midday.

In the main, however, crappie fishing picks up toward evening. On a summer evening from before dusk until well after dark and at times on into the night, crappies work upward and move into shallows to feed. One may see their rises dimple the water. These rises are not the solid boil of the surface-feeding bluegill, but are likely to be smaller and more gentle. A lure such as a small Flatfish, trolled slowly and near surface, will now catch scores of crappies. So will a wet fly or a popping bug cast to the rises.

In lakes with open shorelines, such as Owyhee in Oregon, spring crappies can literally be slaughtered by a small white streamer cast randomly and fished slowly. The same type of fishing will take them during an evening rise in summer. Light tackle should of course be used, and the fish must be handled gently and gingerly. The same caution is mandatory when stillfishing. The fish are easily torn free if roughly played. The crappie has a mouth that unfolds to fairly large size, but is paper-thin and exceedingly tender. In fact, one of the common names for the crappie is papermouth perch. Strawberry bass, calico bass, sago, grass bass are others. There is little point in mentioning more, for the list is so long.

During the winter, crappie fishing through the ice is likely to be best early in the season. Later on the fish change diet to very small organisms, and become all but impossible to intrigue. They are school fish (both summer and winter of course) so when one is caught very likely others are nearby. But the schools roam, and so when bites cease it is a good idea to change location. Although minnows are the standard bait both summer and winter, worms and other baits, even perch belly strips and small pork rinds, also work well.

In the Midsouth impoundments it was discovered some years ago that the crappie was extremely susceptible to small jigs. The leadhead, feathered, or hairdressed jig was born to and first used in saltwater. Small models, spoken of locally as "flies," were adapted to freshwater as spinning became popular. With light spin tackle a small jig was castable. These, in sizes of 1 to 2 inches overall length, chiefly in yellow and white, were cast along edges of button-willow stands in the Tennessee-Kentucky area, and bounced along. They proved sensationally productive especially in spring on schools of spawning crappies.

The "crappie jig" became so popular and successful that it is now standard as an artificial lure in many places. On impoundments where drowned timber is abundant, anglers often park a boat over a submerged treetop, let a small jig down vertically overside into the cover, dance it gently up and down, and catch crappies galore. Crappies will also strike all manner of small plugs, spoons, and spinners retrieved at moderate speeds through their hideouts.

Both the crappies are handsome fish, silvery with black and green mottlings. The fins are broad and jaunty, and the deep, severely compressed body with fins spread makes an ample catch a striking picture on a stringer.

Rock Bass

Ambloplites rupestris

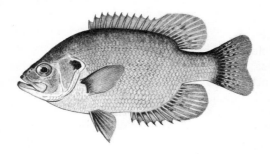

This fish is actually one of the sunfishes, not a true bass. It has six anal fin spines, instead of three like the other sunfishes. It is locally important, but by no means as important a species nationwide as, for example, the bluegill. However, rock bass are fun to catch, take all manner of baits and lures, are reasonably game, and fair on the table.

Rock bass are sometimes called "redeye," and quite commonly, especially in the South, "goggleeye" or "goggleeye perch." The eye is large, and in adults it is dark red. The general color pattern of the rock bass is bronze, or greenish bronze, with indistinct rows of small dark spots following the scale rows. Overlaying these are blotches of darker color with no firm pattern. In some waters rock bass may acquire a bluish cast.

The average rock bass is small, seldom over half a pound, but in certain waters they grow much larger. Commonly a specific lake or stream will be inhabited by rock bass of a pound, and a few waters contain specimens of over 2 pounds. The range of the fish follows a broad swath from southern Manitoba east to the Alleghenies and thence southward throughout all of the Great Lakes Region and the Mississippi Valley to the Gulf. It has also found its way into the East. Large lakes and streams, mainly clear and rocky or with gravel, appeal most to the rock bass. But it is also found in thousands of smaller lakes and ponds, sometimes where weeds and mud abound. In all such locations, because this fish prefers still pools or protected waters to open or fast areas, it is inclined to taste muddy, or to be host to numerous parasites.

The mouth of the rock bass is much larger than that of the other sunfishes. For this reason larger hooks can be used when fishing for it, and it will often successfully strike lures too large for other sunfishes. In fact, because rock bass feed a great deal on crawfish, minnows, and other fairly large food, they are inclined—especially the larger specimens—to strike large lures, even at times plugs meant for black bass.

Traditionally, the rock bass is a cane-pole fish brought to the skillet by use of worm or small crawfish. Thousands are caught that way by anglers young and old. Since the rock bass is not at all a moody fish, it often suffices to fill for the stillfisherman what would otherwise be an empty stringer. But anglers using artifical lures have found that rock bass are gullible where almost any method is concerned. They can be caught on wet flies fished slowly along a lake shore, especially over rocks or around lily pads or reed beds in the shallows. They will avidly strike small popping bugs meant for bluegills and bass. Ordinarily they hit best after dark, when the bluegills may have begun to slow down.

Perhaps the most deadly method for rock bass, besides bait, is the small or modest-sized spinning lure made up as a spinner and fly combination. The fly cannot be too gaudy. The lure should be fished at moderate speed near bottom. In places where large rock bass abound, small plugs and wobbling spoons also are excellent. In any large lake lacking heavy aquatic vegetation, a sunken brush pile will be the hangout for scores of rock bass. Fishing deep near such a brushpile will nearly always get results. In fact, owners of small lakes often sink brush-piles purposely to entice rock bass. Old sunken logs or debris in a stream likewise make good rock bass hideouts.

As a rule, early or late fishing takes the most rock bass. But deep fishing is often successful during midday, and in cool streams the fish may hit well at almost any time. On the hook they do not leap, nor do they fight as sprightly a battle as the doughty bluegill and its close relatives. The rock bass furnishes a simple struggle, and is quickly worn down. Large specimens, however, offer good sport.

Many anglers are not aware that rock bass can be taken through the ice. Here again, spotting sunken brush piles and such hideout locations before season will assist in finding the fish after ice has formed. The mayfly larva called a "wiggler," so prominent nowadays as a winter bait for numerous panfish, is an excellent bait for winter rock bass. Ordinarily the rock bass seems to bite best on sunny days in winter, and late in the season. There are no special tricks in this fishing. Once the fish are located, the bait is let down barely off bottom, and a rather weak bite announces the action.

All told, the rock bass has fallen into a niche as some-

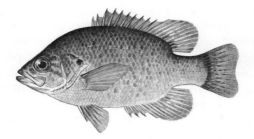

Warmouth Bass

thing of a fill-in fish, an understudy. It is not quite as desirable as most other species likely to be found in the same waters with it, but when the others grow sullen the dependable old rock bass often saves the day. And in a few locations where the others are not present, this species furnishes pleasant fishing by whatever method one may select.

The **warmouth bass,** or simply warmouth, *Chaenobryttus gulosus* (in some references *Chaenobryttus coronarius*), is another sunfish built very much like the rock bass and often also called "goggleeye" in the South. It ranges throughout the East, the Great Lakes and on to the Gulf, westward to the Rio Grande and north through portions of the plains states. It has been introduced on the west coast.

The warmouth varies widely in color, depending on the water where it is taken. In South Carolina rivers, for example, it may be bright greenish with orange fins. In streams such as the Guadalupe in Texas, it may turn up as a small fish streaked with bright blue along the jaws and with more aqua sprinkled over its sides. Mainly, however, the warmouth is bronze or greenish bronze, about like the rock bass, but it does not have the blotches characteristic of the rock bass. It is mottled with darker color but without noticeable pattern.

It has three anal spines, instead of the six of the rock bass. And it has a fairly prominent earflap showing more color than the rock bass. The breast may be yellow, orange, green, or blue. The size of the mouth, which is large like that of the rock bass, makes it easy to distinguish from the other sunfishes. In fact, for practical purposes, one needs only to distinguish between warmouth and rock bass. Neither can be easily confused with the various true sunfishes if the mouth size is well noted.

Most of the warmouths caught by anglers are taken in the South. And most of those purposely caught are collected by bait such as worms or small minnows and by cane-pole fishermen. However, the warmouth, like the rock bass, is quick to strike at all manner of lures, and no angler fishing lures of moderate size from flies to spinners to plugs in waters where warmouths occur is likely to go long unacquainted with the species.

The warmouth is fond of weedy locations, of sluggish streams, of quiet and often muddy areas of lakes. It may lie hidden under a submerged stump or log, and in most instances it is not especially good eating because its flesh is usually soft and muddy tasting. In addition, the warmouth appears to be fairly prolific and not hard pressed; for these reasons it is difficult to find spots where fish of consistently good size can be caught. Too often they are small, or stunted.

In other words, the warmouth is on the whole neither

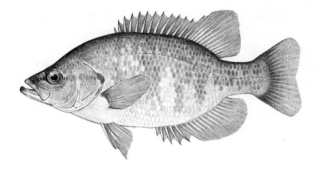

Sacramento Perch

a very important and popular species nor an especially desirable one. But it is so often caught in a mixed string that it deserves to be recognized.

The **Sacramento perch,** *Archoplites interruptus*, is a second relative of the rock bass, another large-mouthed member of the sunfish clan. In many ways it is a unique species. It is the only member of the bass-sunfish family (Centrarchidae) originally native to the country west of the Rockies. It is in fact the only warm-water species native to California. Scientists presume that the species is a leftover from ancient fauna that existed clear across the country before the western mountains were formed. The "perch" name is of course a misnomer. However, the Sacramento perch does have one habit in common with the true yellow perch: it does not build a nest as do the other sunfishes, or give much attention to eggs or young; it lays strings of eggs, draping them across submerged objects in the shallows much as does the yellow perch. The Sacramento perch is a rather good game fish. It grows commonly to a foot long and 1 1/2 to 2 pounds weight. Occasionally specimens approach 2 feet in length, and weigh 4 pounds or more. It was originally native only to a very restricted area, the Sacramento-San Joaquin river system. It is rather rare there now. It has been stocked elsewhere to some extent, but is abundant only in a few places. Clear Lake, California, is one. Walker Lake in Nevada is another. Because it fails to guard its eggs and young, it declined rapidly in its native habitat when species such as carp, catfish, and other spawn eaters were introduced. Late years, however, authorities have tried to manage it, and in places such as Walker Lake where no bass or other predaceous fish molest it, results have been gratifying. Experimental stocking has been done recently in several states. Nebraska has had quite good success with Sacramento perch in some of the rather alkaline waters of shallow lakes in the so-called Sandhills, in Cherry County, where native varieties do poorly. In Colorado this fish has been established in the Banner Lakes. It is likely to be handled more extensively, especially in alkaline waters marginal to indigenous varieties to which it is peculiarly able to adapt.

The general build of the Sacramento perch is an elongate sunfish shape. It is black to silver, in combination or almost wholly one or the other, with several irregular vertical bars on its sides. The prominence of these bars differs with the dark or pale color of each specimen. The gill cover has a dark spot. The scales are saw-toothed along the rear edge. These characteristics, plus the size, color, and restricted range of the fish, make it easy to identify.

Sacramento perch take numerous lures and baits, in

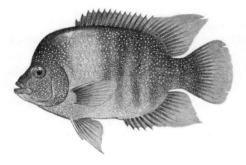

Rio Grande Perch

general about like all the sunfishes and the black basses. Large ones strike trolled wobblers and various deep-running lures. They can also be stillfished, and caught on wet flies sunk well down. A fair-sized lure is best, however, in order to intrigue the larger perch. Modest-sized plugs are a good bet. Since these are loose-school fish quite like other sunfishes, when a good one is hooked the angler should continue to work the vicinity.

Because the waters are few where Sacramento perch are found, only a handful of fishermen will ever know the species at the end of a line. For curious anglers, a pilgrimage to one of its haunts is worthwhile. On light tackle it battles very well. It is also excellent on the table.

The **Rio Grande perch** is possibly the least known of all sport-sized species within our latitudes. It is found in the United States only in portions of central and southern Texas, but is very common in streams below the border, in Mexico. It is neither a perch nor a sunfish, and is covered here with the large-mouthed sunfishes simply as a matter of convenience and because this curious species deserves at least some recognition. Oddly, almost no books dealing with American sport fishes even so much as mention the Rio Grande perch.

The larger specimens are almost round. The males have a steeply humped forehead. The fins are long and flowing, and the color of the fish may be anything from dark bluish-green to clay. Speckles of a lighter shade, sometimes white, cover the body. This pattern has evoked the name "guinea perch" among natives used to seeing the fish among others on their stringers.

The scientific name for this fish is *Cichlasoma cyano-guttatum* (older references *Herichthys cyanoguttatus*). It is a member of the Cichlid family common throughout the tropics. Although Rio Grande perch are usually small because of overcrowding in the streams that are their favorite habitat, where they have room and good feeding they grow to very substantial size. Fish of a pound are extremely common, those of 2 pounds or more not at all rare. These large ones will strike surface plugs and spinner-fly combinations readily. Wobbling spoons and other spinning lures are just as effective. Rio Grande perch also avidly take worms or minnows. In fact, so voracious are they that they will strike almost anything that moves, sometimes several of them attacking like miniature wolf packs.

Although this species is not especially prolific, it is not considered by Texas fisheries biologists a desirable species. The extremely small mouth is set with numerous sharp buck teeth, and the perch are vicious little monsters where other species are concerned. They commonly make group attacks on the nests of black bass and bluegills, seizing the spawn or the fry. They congregate in great numbers in the habitat most satisfactory to other game species, and so decimate these by destroying nests and fry that soon they monopolize the area. Then, scrounging for food until it becomes scarce, they continue to multiply and become stunted. Texas authorities have poisoned a good many stream sections in attempts to destroy the Rio Grande perch populations. Yet they are extremely tenacious and keep reappearing.

Notwithstanding these black marks, it must be said that Rio Grande perch of good size are veritable little demons on light tackle. They fight long and hard, and though they do not leap they easily outclass black bass for strength and stubborn determination. Numerous rivers of south Texas have good populations—the Guadalupe, the Llano, the San Marco, the Comal. Numerous streams in eastern Mexico also contain them. They are very game, very good eating, and they undoubtedly deserve much more attention by the roving angler than they have ever received.

The species is not likely to be transplanted outside its present range. It is neo-tropical, unable to survive water temperature below 49 degrees. Springs in Texas streams it inhabits provide over-wintering havens for survival during severe weather.

Several other members of the large Cichlid family have been introduced from time to time into the U.S. and have formed established populations. These are tilapia. Some have come from South America, some from Africa. Several of these are predominantly vegetation feeders, and have been experimented with as a control on aquatic weeds, as well as a sprightly panfish that grows swiftly and is prolific. Florida has tried tilapia. So has Arizona. Some populations, however, in both Arizona and Texas, were apparently unwittingly established, by release of aquarium specimens or by using tilapia minnows for bait. In Florida, tilapia did so well they became a nuisance and a problem in certain lakes. In some commercial fishing was encouraged, to help control them. Among fisheries people, the introduction is not considered desirable.

In canals around Yuma, Arizona, many are caught, of good size. Several power company lakes in Texas teem with blue tilapia. In both states several varieties weigh at maximum as much as 2 pounds. In Arizona a few lakes, of poor water quality, seem to be the perfect niche for tilapia. They are good eating, and sporty, although their feeding habits present an angler with difficulties. In some instances during spawning concentrations they are legally snagged. Tilapia are fishes of extremely warm waters. Most varieties die quickly at water temperature below 60 degrees. Thus their establishment is limited. Arizona has been experimenting with them as a possible sport and food fish in certain waters too warm for native varieties. In Texas the power company cooling basins furnish heated effluent in which tilapia survive low temperature periods in winter.

White Bass

Roccus chrysops

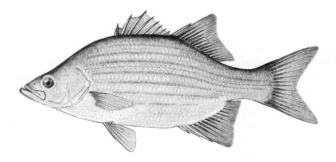

For many decades during the early fishing history of the United States, the white bass was an inconsequential, obscure species. But when the age of the large impoundments began, the white bass suddenly and rather surprisingly emerged as a kind of savior of fishing. It is a good scrapper, an excellent eating fish, an astonishingly prolific species, and a willing one much of the time. In addition, it is a school fish, which always makes for fast fishing action, and one whose favorite habitat is in large, open lakes, and streams of moderate current.

Thus it was a perfect species to quickly populate the impoundments, from Texas to Kentucky. Many of these vast new lakes were self-stocked by prolific gizzard shad. The white bass, also in many instances self-stocked from the streams on which the impoundments were made, is predominantly a minnow feeder. The gizzard shad fry and fingerlings were its natural food. It was thus well cared for, but most important it in turn helped to keep the shad population down.

The white bass belongs to the sea bass family. It is not related to the black bass. It and the yellow bass are the two freshwater representatives in this country of the Serranidae, or sea basses. The white perch is the third member of the group found in freshwater, although it is basically a fish of Atlantic coastal brackish waters. White bass average from 1/2 to 2 pounds, but may go as high as 3 and 4. They are silvery, with black or brown horizontal lines running along the body from head to tail.

The white bass can be distinguished from the yellow bass as follows: lines not broken, as in the yellow bass; lower jaw distinctly projects, while jaws of yellow bass are almost even; spiny and soft portions of dorsal fin separate, those of yellow bass joined at base. These rules are given because these two species occasionally are found in the same waters, and also sometimes are colored much alike. Both white and yellow bass are in some places called "barfish." "Striped bass," "striper," "streaks" are other names used for both, so name alone is not reliable identification.

Another confusion in identification presently is between the white bass and the landlocked saltwater striped bass, which is widely stocked and eminently successful nowadays in large lakes and some streams coast to coast. (*See* STRIPED BASS in the saltwater section, Part Two, for an account of this modern phenomenon.) In their normal habitat, striped bass make spawning runs into coastal freshwater streams, and are there also sometimes temporarily in an environment where white bass live. Both are found, for example, in the St. Lawrence. The two fish are of course closely related. Years ago scientists thought possibly the white bass was a freshwater form of the famed striper of the surf, a form anciently landlocked.

That idea is long discredited. The striped bass is a much longer fish, not as deep or compressed as the white bass. It also grows far larger. Positive identification can be made by counting the rays in the soft portion of the dorsal fin. The white bass has thirteen, the striped bass twelve. There is also present confusion at times in distinguishing between the white bass and the hybrid white-striped bass, which has for some years now been successfully stocked across the southern half of the country. An account of this fish will be found at the end of this chapter.

The range of the white bass is throughout the Mississippi system and on into Texas. Also, as mentioned, in the St. Lawrence area. It has also been stocked in numerous places. Some of the best of the white bass fishing occurs in Wisconsin (the run of the Wolf River is a good example), Kentucky (famous run on the Dix River), Tennessee, Missouri (Lake of the Ozarks), Oklahoma, and Texas. The spring spawning runs occur from late March through April and May, depending on latitude and weather. The fish move into streams emptying into the lakes where they live, and often far up them. Such runs draw hundreds of anglers.

During the runs the fish are taken on bait (usually small minnows), on streamer flies, spinners, small plugs, wobbling spoons, and jigs. Lures of modest size are best; those in yellow or white are very effective because they mimic rather closely the natural minnow food. Spoons and spinners in silver usually do better than gold. The rest of the tackle makes little difference. Fly rod, spinning rod, plug rod—all are useful. The mouths of small creeks emptying into larger rivers on which spawning runs are in progress make good places to cast. Also, every small obstacle such as a log, stump, tree root, or bit of debris along the spawning-stream bank may have a fish behind it.

White bass fishing is by no means confined to spawning runs. After spawning the fish return to cruise the open water of the lakes. They may lie deep, but usually come up to feed. At such times they rise in a school and slash into schools of small shad or other minnows, making a great surface commotion. This phenomenon can be seen at a distance by a watching angler. He then moves in close enough to cast along the edges of the school, trying not to frighten the fish. He may catch several. Then the school will submerge, only to come up again—perhaps close by, perhaps distantly. Another rush is made for more action. This is called jump-fishing and is a very popular method in summer in the big lakes of the Midsouth.

Surface-feeding orgies usually occur early or late in the day, or on overcast days. White bass are therefore considered a bit erratic in habits. Since they cruise widely, they seem more so. But they are not actually so very wary of bait or lure, and when located hungry can usually be caught. Some experienced southern anglers claim white bass like hot weather. During the very hottest, stillest days they go onto one of the impounds and fish over the dropoffs in deep water.

The deep places must be accurately located. The boat is anchored in, say, 6 to 10 feet of water; the casts are made over the edge into 50 feet. A long cast, perhaps with a spoon, is sailed out and allowed to sink until line is slack. After a moment it is raised with a jerk, and reeled furiously, with intermittent short jerks of the rod. This extremely swift retrieve mimics small-shad action, and is deadly.

White bass are active at night as well as by day. Some very fine fishing for them can be had after dark. Incidentally, the "bass" name should not lead anglers to fish for white bass along lake shorelines, except when schools happen to drive shad against a shore. They are fundamentally open-water fish (except of course during spawning runs). They do not hang out near or in weed-beds, but favor clean water of good depth. However, the swift water below the large impoundment dams often holds vast concentrations of these fish.

A curious characteristic of them is that when one is hooked quite often another, or others, will follow along as it is played in. If the first is brought up and unhooked quickly, and the lure tossed back, another will strike instantly. This is especially true when fly fishing with medium-sized streamer flies. These lures can be cast without frightening the fish.

All told the white bass is a very worthwhile game fish, and should be investigated by many more light-tackle anglers. It does not leap, but it's a rough little customer nonetheless.

Often found in the same impoundments nowadays is a king-sized version of the white bass, a hybrid of it and the striped bass. The original hybrids were produced by South Carolina fisheries biologists in 1965, a cross between a male white bass and a female striped bass. The idea spread swiftly. Today hybrids are annually stocked by millions in numerous states of the southern half of the U.S. Florida produced and uses what is called a "reciprocal" hybrid, the opposite cross, between a female white bass and a male striped bass.

The hybrids grow swiftly, are aggressive, attain weights of anywhere from 5 or 6 to as high as 18 pounds. Apparently the hybrids do not reproduce, and at any rate are incapable of producing more of the same. They are therefore a perfect fish for management purposes. Precise numbers can be placed in any lake, and the population can be allowed to run out or be assimilated into the white bass population if need be. The large size of the hybrid makes it a dynamic sport fish, as well as an efficient "policeman" to help keep overpopulous undesirable species in check. Although the striped bass far exceeds at maximum the size of the hybrids, the latter are so much easier for anglers to catch that they have become exceedingly popular.

Their habits are much the same as those of white bass. They run in schools, chop into surface-feeding schools of shad, move up into the tailwaters below dams. In general the same methods and techniques are used for them as for white bass, but with tackle proportionately heavier. In many areas live sunfish are highly successful as bait.

Where white bass, hybrids, and in some instances landlocked striped bass all inhabit the same impoundment, or are caught in an angler's general home area, correct identification is not easy. The striped bass is in body shape somewhat cylindrical and elongate. It is never as deep as either the white bass or hybrid. Its head is fairly large. The size at maturity of both hybrid and striped bass easily sets them apart from the white bass.

The dark lines along the sides are less distinct on white bass than on the other two, and those on the hybrid usually but not infallibly broken. The striper and white bass occasionally evidence broken lines. Size, broken lines, and the general body shape—the back distinctly arched and the head relatively small in white and hybrid—allow reasonably correct casual identification.

Yellow Bass

Roccus mississippiensis

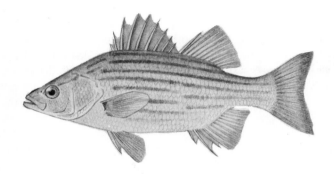

Covered to some extent in the preceding chapter, this fine little game fish belongs to the same family as the white bass. Superficially they are quite alike. Several ways to identify each are given under the white bass. Here is one more distinct identification characteristic: on the yellow bass the second spine of the anal fin is longer and thicker than the third; just the opposite is true of the white bass.

Yellow bass are almost always a definite brassy yellow. Sometimes they are really bright yellow. Especially before the fish is lifted from the water, its paired fins appear powder blue in color. The horizontal lines along the sides of this species are very sharply defined and very dark. They are broken erratically. Numerous scientific books have quoted each other for years in saying that the lines are broken only *below* the lateral line. This is not true. It may be true in one individual, while another on the same stringer may have every line above and below the lateral broken, and even some with boxlike designs where the interruptions occur. Another very curious characteristic is that any yellow bass selected at random, contrary to information in most scientific tomes, is likely to have left and right sides *marked unalike*.

In most habits and habitat preferences the yellow bass is quite similar to the white bass, and a study of foregoing pages about the white bass will also help the yellow bass angler. It prefers large lakes and rivers. It is most abundant throughout the Mississippi Valley, ranging from Minnesota to Tennessee and Louisiana, and westward into Texas. It is also present in Iowa. However, its abundance is a scattered one. A lake here, a stream there, offers good yellow bass fishing. But many others in the same area may not. Louisiana has good yellow bass fishing, mainly in the clear waters that empty into the Mississippi. In Tennessee, Arkansas, and Kentucky this fish is likely to be a small-sized nuisance, because for some reason it seldom grows as large here as its white relative.

Perhaps this is because it is so prolific. It becomes stunted, and a bait stealer. In a few waters yellow bass do grow to fair size, possibly of 2 pounds. Supposedly it grows to as much as 5. If so, certainly one of that size is rare. Most writers claim the average is 1 to 2 pounds. Even this is an exaggeration. Almost everywhere the yellow bass averages about like the bluegill, which is to say under a pound.

Iowa a few years ago had some of the best and most surefire yellow bass fishing in several of its none too plentiful lakes. Clear Lake was perhaps the classic example. Just because this fish is small it should not be written off. It is an excellent fighter when fished with light tackle. It does not leap but fights much like the various sunfishes. In Clear Lake it overproduced and became stunted. Muskies were planted to try to balance the population.

In a number of the waters inhabited by yellow bass they appear to be much more tolerant of weedbeds than are white bass. They cruise in schools through open areas, too, but many times they can be caught among reeds. Bait fishing for them is usually done with small minnows, fished very close to bottom. Drift fishing is a good way to take them, too. This requires the use of a sinker heavy enough to keep the bait down. The boat is allowed to drift with the wind.

Many yellow bass enthusiasts take along only enough bait to catch the first one. From this one they cut a small triangle of white skin and flesh from the throat. This they put on a small hook, cast out and retrieve slowly. It works as well as any artificial. A three-way swivel rig, sinker on one leader, bait on another, is a good way to operate. When the fish are cleaned, a few of these triangles are sliced off and kept in the refrigerator for the next time. Pork rind works just as well. The fish will also strike small spoons, spinners, and plugs.

Fly fishing for yellow bass is also very effective. This is especially true in spring, when they spawn. Spawning brings them inshore around rocky points and among reeds over sand and gravel. They swarm in large schools then, well concentrated, and the shallow water makes it possible to wade and fly fish for them if one wishes. A small streamer or wet fly is used. It should be fished slowly. Color is not very important, except to local fishermen who happen to have faith in some certain color.

The bass are willing to hit just about anything. If there are streams available for yellow bass in lakes to ascend for spawning, they will do so.

Because they are so often found on clear-water shoals and bars in both lakes and streams, they are sometimes locally called barfish in the South. In Tennessee some natives call them "jacks" or "yellowjacks," thoroughly confusing names since numerous other species (such as the chain pickerel) are also called "jack" by southerners. "Streaks," and "yellow perch" are other names used here and there where the species is most commonly found.

The yellow bass is very good eating, as well as good sport. It is a species undoubtedly deserving more acclaim, popularity, and management than it has had to date.

The yellow bass has been used to some extent in hybridization experiments. Fisheries biologists nowadays think in terms of filling every niche in any lake habitat. Because the yellow bass is a fish with inshore and weedbed proclivities, distinctly different from the open-water habits of the white bass, the idea was conceived of crossing it with the striped bass. It is hoped that the resultant hybrid might be a closer-to-shore species of substantial size. Striped bass females and yellow bass males have been crossed, and experiments have been recently in progress with a possible cross between a female hybrid white-striped bass and a male yellow bass. Some of the yellow bass crosses to date have resulted in extremely aggressive hybrids. Whether or not these fish will prove as popular and successful as the white-striper hybrid still remains to be seen.

White Perch

Roccus americanus

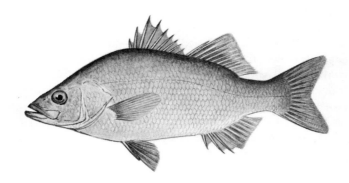

The white perch (in many references *Morone americana*) is neither fresh nor salt. Neither is it a perch. It is a bass, actually most accurately described as a saltwater bass. It is totally unrelated to the freshwater black basses and to the freshwater yellow perch. To make things more confusing, in the South the crappie is often locally called a "white perch."

Roccus americanus, however, is well known to its enthusiasts. It belongs to the large family Serranidae, the sea basses, most of whose members are marine species. The famous saltwater striped bass is probably the most illustrious member of this family. Two other species, the white bass and the yellow bass, are strictly freshwater fishes. This so-called white "perch" stands in-between. It is closely related to both yellow and white bass but is fundamentally a fish of brackish water, ranging along the Atlantic coast from South Carolina north to Nova Scotia. It is at home in saltwater, as well as in the brackish ponds, bays, and tidal waters that it favors most. And it is also perfectly at home, when need be, in freshwater.

It is anadromous, that is, it makes spawning runs up coastal streams. These usually occur in April and May. At various times it has become landlocked and has managed to do well in headwater lakes and ponds. Usually the freshwater specimens are smaller than those from brackish waters. Apparently it needs high salinity. The average fish, however, is not a large one. White perch up to a pound are the rule, although they may weigh as much as 3 or 4.

Because of its adaptation to freshwater lakes and ponds, some stocking has been done in New York State and New England with white perch. It is still a fish of restricted range. This does not dim its regional importance. When the spawning runs start, thousands of anglers gather to reap a veritable white perch harvest along the Atlantic coast.

Much of this fishing is with bait, such as worms, nymphs, or small minnows. Bait drifted on a loose line into deep holes is especially effective. However, white perch will also strike small lures. Spinner-fly combinations are quite popular for them. Small plugs and spoons also get results; so do various sunken flies.

The white perch is rather a shy fish, and like its close relatives likely to be erratic and moody, too. On occasion strikes come one after another. This spree may be followed by long periods when nothing gets results. Of course many species follow this same feast and famine routine, but it is accented in the case of the white perch.

Excepting the spring spawning runs, probably the best white perch fishing is to be found in brackish ponds formed by sandbars along the lower New England coast. In the inland lakes of the East, white perch often lie deep, at least during the day. Trolling takes a lot of these fish, sometimes at depths down to 50 feet or more. Quite commonly white perch seem more active at night than by day. They may even be in shoreside shallows after dark, chasing small minnows. Since they are school fish, like the white and yellow bass, and cruisers like those species also, the angler must find a school, fish it fast, then find another, unless he is fishing a small pond where the schools stay put.

Quite often white perch schools break the water surface, at dawn, or on dark days, or toward dusk. They are not always feeding when they do this, but when they are, the angler should make a quick but cautious approach with a boat, and cast along the edge of the moving school. This is similar to the technique used in the Midsouth of jump-fishing for white bass, and is covered in greater detail under that species.

White perch are not fish of the weedbeds. Again like their close relatives, they are more likely to be found over sand and gravel. They habitually feed deep, along the bottom, taking much insect food. This is especially true of the smaller specimens. The big white perch feed more actively on minnows.

The white perch is also called a silver perch, or sea perch. It is very silvery along the sides, greenish on the back. This describes the salt- and brackish-water fish. Freshwater individuals are usually darker, more olive colored. Young fish have indistinct stripes along the sides.

The only other species with which the white perch

might be confused are the white and the yellow bass. But since these two are not found, or at least are extremely uncommon if they have been stocked at all, in the home range of the white perch, there is little danger of confusion. Anyway, they are not difficult to set apart. Both yellow and white bass bear very distinct horizontal stripes along the sides; the white perch does not. The lower jaw of the white bass is definitely projecting, that of the yellow bass barely so, that of the white perch almost even with the upper. The mouth of the white perch is much smaller than that of its close genus-mate, the yellow bass.

On the whole, white perch are not tackle-smashing game fish. But they are good fighters and good fun. There is no need to use anything but the lightest of tackle for these panfish. It adds to their stature. Perhaps the very best part of white perch fishing is the aftermath of the eating. They are excellent.

Walleye

Stizostedion vitreum

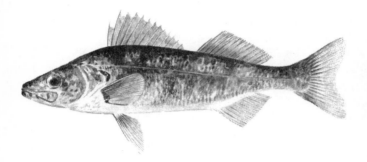

Enthusiasts of walleye fishing are likely to be a clannish lot, with only modest interest in other species. The walleye, walleyed pike, yellow pickerel, blue pickerel, jack salmon, dore, or pike-perch, as it is variously called, is not an especially sensational fighter. In fact, at times it battles very weakly. However, there is an appeal about walleye fishing that no other freshwater fishing has.

Often the very best of it is "bad weather" fishing, or after-dark fishing. This largest member of our freshwater perch family ("pike" and "pickerel" are complete misnomers) is a great lover of cold, clear, deep, large waters, both lakes and streams, and of dim light. Midsummer walleye fishing is seldom top-notch except in the depths, but during spring and fall, when the wind blows and rain or sleet whips the water surface, or when overcast, gusty days force many an angler to stay by the fire, the walleye angler is in his glory. Likewise in winter in the snow country, ice fishermen avidly go after walleyes, which are as likely to begin biting at 50 feet, or 5 feet, on a zero day as they are to refuse completely to cooperate.

The range of the walleye begins far north in Canada, from Great Slave Lake across to Labrador. It continues down through the Great Lakes regions, and far south through Tennessee and Alabama. At one time the Great Lakes were fabulous walleye havens. The fish are not as plentiful in the big lakes as they once were. Wisconsin and Minnesota are probably the two best northern walleye states. There are excellent individual walleye lakes and streams in Iowa, Missouri, Michigan, and New York. Just north of our borders, especially in Ontario, walleye enthusiasts literally swarm in spring. Farther south, Tennessee has become famous for its walleyes, especially at Dale Hollow Lake, where many exceedingly large specimens have been taken, usually in early spring.

There are of course numerous other excellent spots for walleyes. The Dakotas have many (as well as sauger— a relative of the walleye which will be discussed presently), and there are streams in Alabama and Kentucky where walleyes and saugers abound. In addition, there has been a great deal of interest among fisheries people over late years in extending the range of this predator fish into the West and Southwest. From stockings made experimentally twenty or more years ago in Oklahoma, that state has now introduced this fish to most of its major lakes. Texas has a prodigious and very successful walleye program in force, with many millions annually stocked all across the state. Walleyes have done well in a number of New Mexico and Arizona waters, and have established populations naturally in Arizona's Lake Mead and Utah's Lake Powell, apparently coming down the Colorado River.

In the Northwest the Columbia River system and lakes nearby have recently bloomed as walleye fisheries. Huge Fort Peck Reservoir in Montana, and several other Montana lakes, now have this fish in abundance. Several Wyoming reservoirs, Nebraska's Lake McConaughy, numerous others in Colorado, all have become excellent walleye waters. Although it was once believed that the walleye demanded deep, cold waters for survival, some waters to which transplants have been made successfully seem to at least partially discount the theory. For example, Texas has been able to establish substantial walleye populations not only in cold, deep Lake Meredith in the Panhandle, and comparable reservoirs, but in a variety of waters of widely differing habitats. A striking example of the latter is shallow Casa Blanca Lake in the hot area of the Mexican border near Laredo.

The walleye is a dark bronze to gold to yellowish fish, or it may be bronze to bluish, in either case with darker and patternless blotchings. The most striking physical attribute is the eye, which gives the appearance of having a film or cloud over it. Walleyes have strong fin spines and spiked gill covers, and therefore should be handled gingerly to avoid injury to one's hands. There is a black blotch on the membrane of the spinous portion of the dorsal fin. This is an important characteristic to assist in separating the walleye from its close relative, the sauger.

The average walleye weighs from 2 to 5 pounds. In especially good walleye waters, fish of 7 to 10 pounds are not rare, and the species grows to maximum weights over 20.

The walleye is a lurker in deep places, where it feeds almost entirely upon small fish and crayfish. It is also gregarious among its own kind. Where one is caught, others are almost certain to be present, and the troller will always mark well the spot where the first fish strikes. Here he is almost certain to clean up. Trolling is, in fact, one of the main methods of walleye fishing. Because walleyes stay in fairly deep water much of the time, a trolling rig can be got down to the proper depth and kept there. Trolling covers a great deal of water, thus quickly locating the fish. Then it is a simple matter to make runs back and forth over the area where they are lying, or to stillfish or cast there.

The type of bottom over which one fishes is exceedingly important in this angling. Walleyes seldom are found over mud. They like gravel, sand, or rock. They are seldom found in roiled water unless forced to be there. Some old hands at walleye fishing drift-fish with minnows, either in lake or large stream. This is a telling method. Others use crayfish or minnows on a dropper rig and cast from a boat, letting the bait down to bottom and leaving it there, or reeling ever so slowly, "crawling" the bait near bottom.

Oddly, although the walleye is ordinarily not a worm feeder, the nightcrawler is a killer bait for it, usually combined with a spinner. Some anglers use lures such as the popular Flatfish, which has hooks hung out at the sides, and on these hooks the angler drapes nightcrawlers, one on either side. He lets them trail well and trolls fairly deep, over bars and into the pockets formed by drop-offs, or through pools in a stream.

Of course, casting is also effective under many conditions. Spoons and plugs that run fairly deep are best. In spring when walleyes begin their spawning runs into shallow water where it is legal to fish them, casting is an excellent method. Also, later in the season, especially in northern areas such as Ontario, dozens of walleyes may be taken on wobbling spoons by casting into turbulent pools below rapids and working the lure through the eddies. The swift water below impoundment dams is also a good place to fish.

Although the walleye likes fairly low or at least very moderate water temperatures best, it will feed at 65 to 70 degrees, but is likely to roam widely in such waters. In some ways higher surface temperatures are a blessing to the accomplished walleye angler. This will concentrate the fish in the places where the water is cool. Or, it will cause them to feed mainly at night.

On occasion this night feeding gives rise to an excellent type of sport. The fish will sulk in deep holes all day, moving little and feeding hardly at all. Then as dusk draws down and the shallows inshore cool off, the walleyes will move up. Not into weeds, but usually over sand or gravel, or at the edges of weedbeds. Here minnows and other small fish will be lazing about in schools, and the walleye schools will glide in to slash them to bits. At such times an angler standing quietly in the water or sitting in a boat, casting either spoons or plugs, or even a streamer fly, can have rare sport. Sometimes, hooked in such shallows, walleyes will even jump. However, jumps are rare.

In fact, the walleye is basically a dogged fighter that gives up rather easily. Often one will strike and allow itself simply to be reeled in. It will then struggle a bit as it is netted. Nonetheless, in fast water an occasional fish will fight with surprising gusto. Regardless, the walleye will always be popular because it hits quite freely and can be taken by simple methods, and because it is one of the finest eating fish that swims. An interesting phenomenon walleye fishermen should watch for in specific lakes with heavy mayfly hatches is the evening rise. Walleyes can then be caught on bass bugs. This is a most unusual experience.

All told, the only real difficulty faced by the walleye fisherman is in finding the schools. A close study of temperature, of bottom contours, of daily vertical movements of the fish, in any given piece of water is of the highest importance for consistent success. Once the hangouts of early season (usually fairly shallow) and of mid-season (from moderate depths on down except toward evening) to late season (can be either) are located, the predator packs of fish can be counted on season after season to be right there at the proper time, provided water temperature is to their liking.

Because of these concentrations, walleye fishing differs vastly from, for example, bass fishing. Bass may be all along a shoreline. Walleyes will be in a few specific places as a rule. In addition, they have the odd habit of striking on occasion even when gorged from a feeding spree. But they will not rush after a lure at such times, nor will they often come up to one. The bait or lure must be brought to them. This means that depth is important. A lure almost scraping bottom may take fish while one running 2 feet above will not.

Practically everything said of the walleye may be said of the **sauger,** also called sand pike, or gray pike. This

Sauger

fish (*Stizostedion canadense*) is in general a small edition of the walleye. Usually it averages about 1 to 2 pounds, but may be much larger and therefore easily confused with the walleye. It is indeed not always a simple matter to distinguish between the two. The usual way is to note the membrane markings of the spiny dorsal. Instead of the dark blotch of the walleye, which in the sauger is completely lacking, this species has several rounded spots.

Sauger range generally duplicates that of the walleye. A number of widely separated areas have quite famous spring sauger runs. The river waters immediately below some of the Tennessee and Kentucky impoundment dams, and again in North Dakota, are examples. The sauger favors much the same habitat as the walleye, but will tolerate water heavily silted, or murky, whereas the walleye will not. The sauger in some areas is predominantly a stream fish. Feeding habits are much the same as those of the walleye, but if anything saugers stick to deeper waters than their larger relative.

There is a vaguely defined third variety recognized by

the American Fisheries Society which would probably be better off without subspecies status. This is the so-called **blue pike,** *Stizostedion vitreum glaucum.* Found chiefly in lakes Ontario and Erie, only the blue-gray color could possibly separate it, for the layman, from the walleye. It seldom grows larger than a couple of pounds and was long thought to be an immature specimen of the walleye.

Walleyes and saugers have gained their much deserved popularity because their school habits and predaceous gluttony have made them bonanza species many times for anglers whose days badly needed saving. Their lack of tenacity on the hook is overshadowed by the simplicity of their fishy souls, and their delectable qualities in the skillet.

Yellow Perch

Perca flavescens

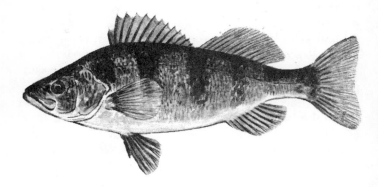

This member of that mixed group of small species generally and colloquially called the "panfish" holds a unique place in angling's hall of fame. It can hardly be said to be a fighter of any note whatever, and yet it is one of the best loved, most fished and therefore most popular of all our freshwater fishes. Part of this fame stems from the fact that the yellow perch is an exceedingly good table fish, and part from the ease with which it may be caught. The remainder no doubt arose from its tremendous abundance over a very wide range.

Originally the yellow perch was resident over eastern and central Canada and southward over the Dakotas, the Great Lakes region, and New England, with its extreme southern range reaching well into the Midsouth, from the Carolinas to Missouri and Kansas. However, stocking has placed it in many other areas, even to certain lakes of western Montana, in some of which it grows very large, and to the Pacific slope. Yellow perch are present also in a number of Arizona waters, in certain New Mexico lakes where, as in many other places they overpopulate, and from which in recent times surplus perch were transplanted to Lake Meredith in the Texas Panhandle.

The introduction of yellow perch to new waters is sometimes a mixed blessing. This is a species of quiet ponds, of streams without much current, and of lakes large and small. It is extremely prolific. Large adult females deposit as many as 50,000 or more eggs. Because perch are also predaceous, feeding avidly on small minnows, they complete with other species for food and, breeding swiftly, often monopolize a lake, with the result that they become stunted and worthless.

However, in proper habitat where they remain in balance, yellow perch grow to good size. A prime example: the Great Lakes. Here, especially in lakes Erie, Huron, and Michigan, the perch has for many years been an important commercial fish and also heavily fished for sport. Individuals weighing 1 and 2 pounds are not uncommon. They average much less than a pound, however, although specimens as large as 3 and 4 pounds have been caught.

The yellow perch belongs to the same family (Percidae) as the walleye and the sauger. It is often found in the same lakes and streams. This family contains in addition a number of small non-game species, the darters. Precisely what types of lakes yellow perch will most often be found in is difficult to say. They do well in a broad variety of waters: shallow, weedy lakes; lakes with many rocks and few weeds; lakes with gravel and sandy bottoms. And they are found in hundreds of small lakes as well as in large ones. Very generally, large lakes with only modest weed growth offer the largest perch.

The color of the perch is yellow to bronze to yellow-green, with dark vertical stripes. It is doubtful if it will be confused with any other freshwater species.

Probably 99 percent of all yellow perch caught are taken by stillfishing. Small minnows either dead or alive are the most popular bait, although worms work just as well at times. The tails of small crawfish are another excellent bet. So are "wigglers," the larvae of certain may-flies. There is nothing difficult about the method of bait fishing, and any tackle may be used. As a rule the old-line perch enthusiast sets up a rig with bell sinker on the bottom and with two dropper hooks spaced above it. He fishes with the sinker just touching bottom, which places the hooks about a foot and 2 feet above bottom.

At times perch are found in deep water, down as much as 50 feet, but they may be at various levels depending on temperature and feeding conditions. Thus, one must try until the proper level is found, or until the proper bottom depth is located. The bite as a rule is not especially strong. Nor is it uncommon to catch two at a time, for yellow perch are school fish. The schools hang compactly together, and are likely to be large. As a rule, when perch are biting and one is caught a whole limit can be taken right there. Each school generally contains fish of about the same size, schools of large fish hanging out in one locality, small ones in another.

Hooked, a perch struggles with fair tenacity, but briefly. Compared, for example, to the bluegill, it is not very game. Nonetheless, the bites come fast, limits, where they exist, are usually large, and the prospect of eating the sweet, white meat is so appealing that yellow perch fishing has a tremendous following.

Perch can be taken on artificial lures. They are susceptible to spinner-fly combinations, and to small, bright wobbling spoons. The weighted feathered jig is also good. On occasion perch are found rising to take mayflies or other insects and at such times they take a fly fairly well. Wet flies are in general much better than dry. On the whole, however, bait fishing is so fast and so successful that there is little point in bothering with artificials.

The best perch fishing in many areas comes in spring, during spawning time. This will be about April over most of the range of the fish. They will run literally by hundreds of thousands into slow streams or dredge ditches, bayous, bays and channels, and up creeks tributary to the larger lakes. Concentrated in such places, they bite weakly but hungrily, and hundreds of anglers congregate along the banks of the well-known spawning areas. In Michigan, for example, radio, T.V., and newspapers swiftly broadcast the good word when the perch run is on, and enthusiasts travel hundreds of miles to join the fun, and the "meat fishing." Many use small (1- to 2-inch) salted minnows for bait. These are easily carried and they work at this time about as well as live ones.

The yellow perch gets little respite from anglers around the year. Few places have a closed season because perch are so abundant. Since they also feed as voraciously in winter as in summer they have long been one of the top targets of the ice fisherman. The same methods suffice in winter as in summer. However, because perch fall easily for the charms of a flasher-type lure, the ice-jigging spoon, which goes by a variety of names depending on the locale, is very popular and effective. This is a narrow, weighted spoon with the hook brazed to the small end. It is let down and brought smartly up a few inches, then allowed to drop back, with this action repeated over and over. This causes it to dart and flutter. Schools of perch often surround such a lure, swarming at it. As fast as one is pulled up another is ready to vie with its buddies for a chance to get caught. When jigging is slow, a bait of a wiggler, or a perch eye placed on the hook of the jig, will often spark action.

In many ways the yellow perch may be said to be a meat-fisherman's fish. Nonetheless, the congenial fun of gathering the good eating is worth whatever stigma purist game fishermen may feel attaches to such endeavor. Because there is nothing in the least complicated or difficult about this fish, it is a kind of "everyman's" species.

Muskellunge

Esox masquinongy

Probably more freshwater anglers have spent more time catching fewer muskellunge than any other game fish. This is a fish of many moods, a great prize about which thousands of words have been written, most of them to little avail as far as catching it is concerned. The muskie is a challenge to anglers. It is one of our largest freshwater species, a fighter of unusual ability, and it is exceedingly whimsical.

This is the king-size member of the family Esocidae, which also contains the pike and the several pickerels. It is easily distinguished from others of the family by the lack of scales on the lower half of both the gill cover and the cheek. It is easily set apart from the pike by its markings, which are dark upon a lighter ground, as opposed to the light spots on dark ground for the pike. Overall color ranges from green to brownish to gray.

There has been a great deal of interest in recent years in the artificial propagation and stocking of muskellunge. Wisconsin, one of the foremost muskie states, has long been first in this. Muskellunge range takes in portions of Canada above the Great Lakes, as well as the Lake States and on down into Ohio and Tennessee. Lake Ontario and the St. Lawrence River are muskie havens. Muskellunge have been stocked, or are being stocked, in numerous other places. There are several subspecies, probably originally only races separated widely by geographical barriers.

Wisconsin has publicized its fine muskie fishing for many years and has many excellent lakes and streams. Lake St. Clair, out of Detroit, Michigan, is also famous for its muskellunge. There are numerous places in Ontario hardly explored as yet that may eventually beat the standard locations. In a few places it is legal to spear muskellunge through the ice. Several of the big lakes in the northern part of Michigan's Lower Peninsula have been popular for this unusual sport, notably Mullet Lake.

Muskellunge grow very large. Fish of 100 pounds have allegedly been caught in nets. Hook and line records over recent years have run in the sixties. In general, fish of 15 to 45 pounds are taken. Invariably each is a wild fighter, often leaping time after time and never quitting until exhausted. In this respect the muskie differs from its cousin the pike, which sometimes hardly fights at all.

The large size and the large, heavily toothed mouth of the muskellunge tell much about its habits. It is a most voracious and predaceous species, lying in wait and in hiding and then rushing out to smash or engulf its prey. It is a solitary fish. Experienced muskie men know it as most individualistic, too. A large specimen discovered by a certain log, or in a certain cove, will be there week after week as a rule, possibly year after year, and may react in a predictable pattern time after time—when it will indeed react at all!

Muskellunge like cold water, and it must be clear. Clean weedbeds or the quiet pools of rivers are their favored hangouts. Ordinarily they stay in fairly shallow water, feeding not more than 1 or 2 to 15 feet under the surface. During hot weather, which is seldom a good time for musky fishing, they go into deep water. By and large, spring and fall are considered the most productive times for the angler.

Needless to say, stout tackle is necessary in order to control this fish. And because the baits and lures used are invariably sizable and heavy, lightweight saltwater boat rods or stiff plug rods of modest length have long been the most popular. These serve both for casting and trolling, the two traditional methods of muskie fishing. Heavy nylon monofilament or wire leaders must be used.

Actually, there is a good bit of hunting connected with muskie fishing. An expert angler seeks his fish first, then sets about coaxing it to hit. Of course in trolling many muskellunge are located and caught at the same time, but in general the experienced muskie angler trolls very specifically. He knows beforehand where each fish hangs out. And they are not likely to be ganged up. Each muskellunge requires much food, and therefore a good deal of living space. For the newcomer to any muskellunge waters, a good local guide is just about as important as the tackle.

Large spoons and wobblers, with or without feathers or bucktails trailing, are traditional muskie lures. So are various large plugs, most of them of the diving or sinking variety. However, on occasion surface lures that dart and churn prove extremely attractive to muskellunge that are feeding near the surface. Casting such lures along the edges of weedbeds or through any open channels in the weedbeds of bays is standard procedure. The same goes for trolling. Areas where streams come into lakes are often good spots for muskie fishing. So are rock ledges, brush piles, or log jams.

It is possible to catch muskellunge during hot weather by going down after them with the standard lures but using metal line or a downrigger to get the lure down to 50 or more feet. The problem of course is to locate the fish. It is therefore advantageous whenever possible to know a lake thoroughly, and to fish one that has as small an area of deep water as possible. Such a lake narrows the gamble. Trolling should be fairly fast. So should the retrieve when plugging.

One of the most popular methods of muskie fishing, and a very productive one, is fishing with bait. The usual bait is a sucker about a foot long. Suckers are a favorite muskellunge food. Other anglers use dogfish minnows or shiners about half that size. The bait is sometimes stillfished, alive, with a float. Or it is cast, dead, rigged intricately to the hook. This latter method is used by experienced muskie fishermen, often when they have located a fish beforehand. They cast the bait to it and try to coax it into striking by an erratic retrieve.

Commonly a muskellunge will follow a bait or lure and roll at it, but refuse to take. Or, it may follow almost to the boat, then smash viciously just as the lure is about to be lifted from the water. When the fish take a live bait plenty of time must be allowed before the hook is set. Muskies will carry a sucker off some distance as a rule, then take their time getting ready to swallow it.

All told, muskellunge fishing is a difficult sport for the beginner. One who desires to make a hobby of it will do best to team up with an old hand or spend time with a top guide, learning the whims of this fish. These are many indeed, but the prize is worth the often long and tedious effort. The beginner must also realize that he is not likely, even with the best guidance, to take fish quickly, or in numbers. There are times when for reasons not well understood muskellunge go on striking sprees, but these are rare enough to be freak occurrences. As a rule the old hand considers one good fish a day, or even a week, an enviable record. Many addicts angle a whole season— or several of them!—for a single legal-sized muskie. Muskellunge fishing is one of those sports likely to totally mesmerize a susceptible angler—but he had best be a stubborn one!

Pike

Esox lucius

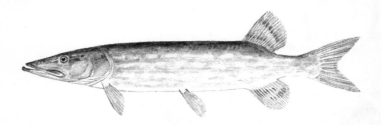

The long, ugly-mouthed pike has never had the standing as a game fish that it deserves. Called "snake" in disgust by many a northern trout angler, and accused of many depredations by certain conservationists, this fish has nonetheless always had a clan of admirers, most of whom would prefer to catch pike over all other species. Currently the pike is enjoying a better game reputation and better publicity, both of which are long overdue.

This is the fish often called "northern" or "northern pike," "great northern," and "jack" or "jackfish." None is a good name, for several reasons. Since there is only one pike species (the remainder of the family are true pickerel and muskellunge), there is no need to add to the name. And because many other fish are colloquially called "jack" and "jackfish," particularly the chain pickerel, close relative of the pike, any name other than "pike" only serves to confuse the beginner. It should be noted that especially in the South the native chain pickerel is invariably called a "jack." In Tennessee the muskellunge bears that local name. In Canada, especially in Manitoba and Saskatchewan, the pike is called "jack."

The pike is a lurker, a solitary fish, carnivorous in the extreme, a predator of the weedbeds. Like a long, lean cat it lies in wait for its prey, rather than actively hunting. Its alligator-like snout is studded with teeth. It lunges at fish large and small, seizing them and swallowing whole surprisingly large forage, even including ducklings and small muskrats. The fin arrangement of the pike is typical of the family, with the dorsal set far back and almost directly above the anal. There are no fin spines, only soft rays. The cheek is scaly only on its upper half, which separates the pike from the chain pickerel with which it might possibly be confused. However, although color patterns will differ slightly in various specimens, the typical pike has oval light spots on a darker ground, while the chain pickerel has very definite chain-link markings.

The average size of the pike depends a great deal on the water where it is caught. Some lakes or streams support a great many small pike, fish of 1 to 5 pounds. In some others, such as in scores of Canadian lakes, pike caught by sports fishermen may average 5 to 25 pounds. On the whole, a pike of 10 to 15 pounds is a good fish almost anywhere over the range. The maximum runs upwards of 50 pounds.

Pike are found in all of the world's northern waters. On this continent the original range was from Alaska to Canada's most eastern areas, thence southward across the northern portion of the United States from about the Dakotas to the St. Lawrence. Southernmost points were roughly into the Ohio Valley, and to Missouri and Nebraska. For some years now, however, range has been vastly broadened by transplant. Good pike populations are now established in several of the mountain states and far into the Southwest. Montana, Wyoming, Colorado, New Mexico, Arizona now claim this fish. So do Arkansas, Oklahoma, and Texas. Phenomenally swift growth occurs in the latter states.

Further, with the building of the immense reservoirs along the Missouri River from eastern Montana (Fort Peck) down across the Dakotas (Sakakawea, Oahe, Sharpe, Francis Case, Lewis & Clark) a tremendous pike fishery was established in wholly new territory. Undoubtedly the greatest amount of easily accessible pike fishing of top quality is still to be found in Ontario, Manitoba, and Saskatchewan. But emphasis has shifted noticeably to the Missouri River lakes, where a great many large fish—to 35 pounds or more—are taken. Over all of pike range, the habitat is rather similar: shallow, weedy lakes large and small, or shallow areas of deeper waters, such as bays; rivers of modest current that offer cover.

Because the fighting spirit or ability of pike appears to vary widely from locale to locale, this fish has been underestimated. In addition it is exceedingly erratic even in the same waters. One pike may smash a lure viciously, then allow itself to be led right to the boat without a struggle. Another may act identically until just as the gaff or net is put down, at which time it simply explodes into action. Still a third may strike and immediately go through a series of wild and beautiful leaps. Certainly this fish is capable of a rousing battle when hooked, and with fair regularity gives it.

Spring and fall are the best times for pike fishing because pike are rather sensitive to temperature changes.

It is not true, as many anglers have claimed for years, that pike will refuse to strike in summer because they are shedding their teeth. They are simply in deep water and not feeding avidly. By very slow fishing and the simultaneous jigging of a lure, right along bottom, they often can be cajoled.

However, when pike are in from 3 to 15 or 20 feet of water and feeding fairly close to the surface the sport is at its best. They are one of the most gullible species as far as artificial lures are concerned. Metal spoons of all kinds, sizes, and shapes are the standard pike lures. Plugs also work well. So do large streamer flies, if one wishes to try pike fishing with a fly rod. For fly fishing to work well the fish must be in water not much over 6 or 8 feet deep, and the fly must sink well. A sinking fly line can be used to great advantage. On spinning tackle, the metal flasher lures are excellent. The plug rod, however, has long been the old standby of the pike addict, and it is hard to beat. Short metal leaders should be used, or else hard monofil of substantial poundage test, for a pike's teeth can cut too-light or braided line as neatly as shears.

There is nothing especially tricky about catching pike on artificials. Many of the fish will lie right in the weedbeds whose tops show above water. But such places are difficult to fish, and sunken weedbeds often hold the largest fish. A lure that runs well down along the dropoff edge, or among the submerged tops of weeds that rise from beds 10 or 15 feet down, will intrigue many a big fellow. Such a fish will rocket from its lair and strike with a smashing blow.

Sinking lures such as the metal flashers and wobblers are especially good for pike because they are easy to fish at varying depths, depending on how the angler handles his rod, and the speed of retrieve. It is necessary of course to discover the depth at which the fish are lying. In summer they may be down 50 feet or more.

Trolling is traditional with many pike enthusiasts, but casting certainly is more sport. Trolling occasionally helps, however, in locating a particular hangout of the fish. Bait fishing is also a tried and true method. In fact, it sometimes works when pike cannot be induced to strike artificials. Although various baits such as frogs are used, the standard pike bait is a good-sized minnow. It can be anywhere from 3 to 10 inches long. An average of 5 inches is generally considered best. Suckers, shiners, chubs, young dogfish are all considered good. They seldom get results if dead or inactive.

Most bait fishermen use a float. They learn to give the pike plenty of time after it seizes the minnow, before the strike is made. Pike seize their prey crosswise, and are inclined to fiddle with it a long time. They seldom make long carrying runs with it, as does a bass, but rather take the float more or less straight down, as they sink lower in the water preparing to turn the prey and swallow it. All too often the inexperienced bait fisherman after pike gets excited and tries to set the hook too quickly.

Pike are among the top targets of the ice fisherman. They feed avidly all winter long. Minnows are the traditional bait. Most ice anglers prefer to use some form of tip-up, setting out several, where that is legal, then watching for the signal flags to fly as pike spring the traps. Others use handlines. Pike are also a favorite of spearmen during wintertime. In this sport a decoy minnow—alive or artificial—is let down into the ice hole on a length of monofil. The spearman sits inside a darkened shanty and waits for a pike, intrigued by the minnow, to enter the area. He then lets fly with the spear. This is a most dramatic pastime, although it is often criticized by summer anglers.

Because of the numerous forked bones scattered throughout the flesh of the pike, many anglers disdain the species as a table fish. It is true that small pike are difficult to eat, but large ones have correspondingly large bones. Consequently they are easy to remove after cooking. Fillets from a large pike are delicious. Because of its abundance throughout northern waters, its slam-bang strike and rough battle, its size and its general willingness, the pike properly should have a high place on our list of freshwater game fish.

Chain Pickerel

Esox niger

Sometimes pike fishermen incorrectly call their catch "pickerel." The walleye is also often thus misnamed. But when New Englanders speak of pickerel, they mean the fine little game fish called the chain pickerel because of the chain-link shaped markings on its sides. This handsome gold-tinged green fish with its dark lacings averages from 1 to 5 pounds in weight and may occasionally grow a bit larger. It is the largest of our true pickerels.

There are at least two more species: the **mud pickerel,** *Esox vermiculatus* (the so-called "grass pike" of the Midwest); and the **barred pickerel,** *Esox americanus*, which ranges the length of the east coast. Both of these fish are small, seldom over a foot to 15 inches in length. Neither is likely to be confused with the chain pickerel, because of the distinctive markings of the latter, and its larger size.

Originally the chain pickerel was native only east and south of the Alleghenies, but it has been stocked to some extent in other areas. The best pickerel fishing, however, is still to be found in the New England states, and south-

Mud Pickerel

ward through the quiet rivers of the Carolinas, the cypress sloughs of Georgia, and the slow creeks and weedy rivers of Florida. There is also excellent chain pickerel fishing on across the Deep South. In several Arkansas waters big pickerel—6 and 7 pounds—have been caught, and in Caddo Lake, in northeast Texas, shared with Louisiana, there is excellent pickerel fishing. Notably, this fish has been tried as a predator of modest size in small lakes in several places, to assist in holding down rough fish as well as furnishing sport. Nebraska has done substantial work with it in that regard.

Almost everything that has been said about the pike is true of the pickerel, except that the smaller size of this fish and its distribution throughout the South must be considered. It is a fish invariably of weedbeds and of weedy waters. It is a lurker, lying in wait and then rushing a short distance to seize its prey. It is predaceous, and feeds mainly on minnows and frogs. It is not a deepwater species, but is most often caught in the levels from surface down to about 10 feet. On occasion it may be taken in 20 feet of water, but this is probably about the limit.

In fishing for pickerel, light tackle should be emphasized. The pickerel is a good jumper when hooked on

Barred Pickerel

streamer flies and bucktails. A short wire leader can be used, but hard monofilament is just as good. Seldom will pickerel teeth cut it, although they will snip braided lines easily. The fly fisherman, using streamers or bucktails (white, yellow, yellow and red) fished slowly along the edges of the weeds or above weeds whose tops fail to reach the surface, will find the chain pickerel a sporty species. A very light plug rod with small lures is also a good outfit. Light spinning gear is better. Needless to say, weedless lures save much difficulty.

A wobbling spoon (weedless) with trailing pork rind strip is a standard lure for pickerel, when plug or spinning rod is used. In quiet southern cypress sloughs, hollow-faced chugger-type plugs that are cast, allowed to lie on the surface, then "chugged" with a short, sharp movement of the rod tip also do well.

A traditional method of pickerel fishing in the East is "skittering." This is accomplished usually with a cane pole, a line about as long as the pole, and a pork chunk or a frog as the bait. The lure is swung out over the weeds as the boat glides silently along, and then is drawn over the surface with smooth or erratic motion and much or little splashing, as the mood of the fish dictates. Spoons of various types can also be used in this manner, and a good spinning or plug man can successfully skitter with his normal tackle, by holding the rod high and reeling fairly swiftly.

Bait fishing with minnows or frogs is just as effective for chain pickerel as for pike. Modest-sized minnows hook the fish better than large ones. The fishing is done exactly as for pike, and the pickerel take the bait, and should be hooked in the same manner. Both pike and pickerel often appear to strike best on cloudy days. Neither, incidentally, is a nocturnal feeder.

The chain pickerel is a popular ice fish in New England. It is caught on minnows. Methods are in general exactly the same as for the pike. (Pike are thoroughly covered in the pages immediately preceding the chain pickerel.)

On the whole, outside New England where pickerel fishing in the ponds and streams has long been popular, this fish does not receive its just share of acclaim. In the southern portions of its range, the pickerel (here usually called "jack") too often is scorned by bass fishermen whose bait or lures it strikes. To be sure, it is only a fair table fish, but it is an excellent fighter, in many instances better than the black bass sharing its sloughs and ponds. For some time now Florida authorities have been urging fishermen in that state to give the pickerel more attention as a game fish. So have some other states. Wherever it is found, certainly this species repays investigation, especially by the light-tackle enthusiast looking for solid freshwater thrills.

Atlantic Salmon

Salmo salar

This swift, powerful salmon once ranged in quantity from about Delaware north, following its ancient habit of living in the sea but coming into freshwater rivers to spawn. Dams and pollution all but wiped out the Atlantic salmon in the United States. Today a few northeastern streams have reestablished salmon runs, but sport fishing for Atlantic salmon is almost entirely confined to the east coast of Canada. There it still draws many of the world's elite flyfishermen, and many a tyro determined to experience at least once the startling runs and high leaps of this fine game fish whose numbers have slowly declined.

Some years ago the landlocked form of the Atlantic salmon was stocked experimentally in a Michigan lake connecting to Lake Michigan. Nothing came of it. In recent years, however, with the astonishing success of the Pacific salmons in portions of the Great Lakes, further experiments with Atlantic salmon have been attempted, and occasionally one has been caught along the western

Lake Superior shore. So far the modest success has been far overshadowed by the attention to and the explosion of transplanted Pacific salmons. Whether or not Atlantic salmon will become established in the northern Great Lakes is at this time questionable.

When fresh in from the sea, the Atlantic salmon is bright silver and blue, with double-X and X-shaped spots scattered along its body, most of them above the lateral line. It may enter freshwater as much as six months prior to spawning. As it remains, it loses its brightness and its weight, becomes darker and sometimes acquires a pink-ish or reddish cast. These salmon do not die after spawn-ing, as most Pacific salmon do. Therefore salmon of various ages make spawning runs in the same streams.

Runs start in the spring and continue on through sum-mer and fall, when spawning begins. Each individual river gets its peak run as a rule at a different time, de-pending on water level. High water causes fish to rush in, low water keeps them waiting. The first fish in are usually those that have spent two years in saltwater. These will weigh from 10 to 15 pounds. A couple of weeks later those with one year at sea come in. These fish are called "grilse." A young salmon while in its parent stream, where it may stay for anywhere up to five years before going to sea, is called a "parr." Its sides are heavily marked with dark areas like those found on young rain-bow trout. These are called "parr marks" and easily iden-tify young fish.

The largest salmon, old ones that have spawned pre-viously, often come into the stream at about the same time as the grilse run, or a bit later. The average salmon caught by anglers will weigh from 10 to 20 pounds, but individuals grow much larger, to 40, 50, and on up past 75. Because they have fed in the sea, and had vast spaces to roam in, Atlantic salmon regardless of age and size are fabulously strong and swift. They are exceedingly difficult fish to handle, and possibly the most determined battlers of all fish taken in freshwater.

Oddly, they cease feeding when they enter freshwater, yet they can be induced to strike a lure. No one is sure why. Possibly it is because of their tenseness, their pent-up energy, as well as an impulsive urge now and then to forsake fasting. This situation created the classical lines along which Atlantic salmon fishing long ago developed. In comparison to the size of the fish, it was found necessary to offer small lures (flies), and because of the clear water and the intelligence of the fish, to attach the offerings to fine leaders. This in turn placed a further handicap upon the fisherman, forcing him to become skilled if he expected to hold and land his trophy. Even then, given skill and proper terminal tackle, which is little if any heavier than that used for trout, the angler still finds the Atlantic salmon a moody personality of erratic behavior, difficult in the extreme to induce. Add to this the fact that peak fishing seldom holds for more than a few days, a couple of weeks at best, and that the peak is almost impossible to predict even by thoroughly experienced guides right on the scene, and it is easy to understand the appeal of eastern salmon fishing.

Fishing is usually best when the fish are "bright," in other words, when they are fresh in. As they stay in freshwater they become, as salmon anglers say, "stale." Their interest in flies decreases as their energy ebbs. Fly fishing, it should be noted, is practically the only method by which Atlantic salmon may be fished. Wet flies are stock in trade, but dry flies are used to some extent during low-water periods. These fish could be taken on bait and by spinning, but because of their low population the flies-only method remains in effect. It is doubtful that salmon guides would have anything but contempt for an angler who chose to fish otherwise.

A guide, incidentally, is practically mandatory for any newcomer, or even for an experienced salmon angler who elects to try a new river. Because Atlantic salmon are not feeding as they progress upstream, their requirements differ from those of trout. While a trout will select a place that gives it food, safety, and comfort, the salmon needs only the last two. This dictates resting places differing often from those which the angler with only trout experience might visualize. The salmon selects a particular run because it is comfortable for him. Usually, however shallow it may be, it will have quick access to deep water and safety. Year after year salmon of different generations will select the same "lies," until these become well known to guides and experienced anglers on a given river. But the slightest rise or fall in the water level will change these spots drastically, making it necessary for the fish to switch positions. Thus it is necessary to hire a competent guide who has seen the stream at all seasons and knows where the fish will go when they move.

As a general rule, therefore, salmon "pools" are not what the trout angler thinks of as pools. They are more likely to be long runs with modest depth, usually with deeper areas nearby. Nor does the salmon choose, either while resting or fighting, the submerged log, the snag, the sunken brush. It has become, in the sea, a fish of open water. It stays in open water in freshwater, resting, and when hooked it fights in it, depending on strength and swiftness, not on cunning in fouling one's tackle.

There is a wide difference of opinion regarding salmon tackle, specifically the rod, which of course dictates the line and reel. Time was when heavy, two-handed rods of 14 feet or more were common. Nowadays most salmon anglers use a much lighter rod. Many tackle firms build the so-called "salmon rod," usually one of 9 feet and about 6 ounces, with an extra detachable butt of 6 inches that is slipped in place for a two-hand grip when a fish is on.

Flies for Atlantic salmon are not tied to represent insects of any specific variety, because of the salmon's fasting. They are a result of trial and error. Consequently a number of standard patterns have evolved that are consistent fish takers. Few Atlantic salmon fishermen experiment widely. They stick mainly to the proved patterns. Among the wets are the long-famed Jock Scott, the Silver Doctor, the Dusty Miller, the Black Dose. There are of course many others. Any good guide will have his favorites for a particular stream. Examples of well-known dry flies for salmon are the Cahills, the several Wulff flies (Grey, White) and the always effective bivisibles of several shades.

By comparison to trout flies, many standard salmon flies, especially the wets, are gaudy. The brightest of these are used on fresh-run fish, with patterns of more drab hue replacing them as the mood of the salmon becomes more somber with its continued stay in freshwater. Fly sizes range from about 1/0 down to as small as No. 14. Leaders correspond in fineness. The very small flies are usually necessary when dries are used during low water. Needless to say, backing line must be used on the reel. A hundred yards is none too much.

Some of the best salmon fishing invariably occurs when a rain breaks a dry spell. As the water rises the fish begin striking. Low water is a difficult time for salmon anglers.

There is nothing radically different in the manner of fly presentation between trout and Atlantic salmon angling, except the places where the casts are made. Traditional wet-fly technique—the fly cast across and allowed to float down—is standard. However, where in trouting a fly sunk deep is often mandatory, salmon seem to like a wet fly traveling not too far under the surface. Indeed, several methods have been worked out for causing the fly at times to cut the surface, leaving a wake. This trick, often accomplished by making a hitch or two around the head of the fly after it has been tied on, so that it does not ride evenly, has coaxed many a disinterested salmon into striking.

Because these fish are not feeding in freshwater, one must usually make a great many casts over the same fish to induce it. Rather often the fish may be seen, too. This of course requires a gingerly approach and meticulous and expert casting, so not to frighten it. If a salmon is seen lying in shallow water, but there is deep water as a safety haven nearby, it should be approached from the shallow side. Otherwise it may become wary and dart to the safety of the depths. The water nearest the angler is of course worked first, and the casts are made methodically down a pool—unless a particular fish has been spotted and one wishes to fish it. Sometimes dozens of casts are made before the salmon finally takes. Just as often it may refuse to budge.

One planning a first salmon fishing trip nowadays can line up a proper river by watching the eastern-Canada lodge ads in the outdoor magazines, or by contacting the travel bureaus in any one of Canada's Maritime Provinces. There is excellent salmon fishing in all of them. Labrador in general gets the least fishermen. There are opportunities, too, in both Iceland and Greenland for those who wish to venture that far.

All told, Atlantic salmon fishing is one of those experiences the serious angler can hardly afford to forego. The danger is, however, that once he has tasted it he will find himself an incurable addict. That can be a thrilling and delightful, but expensive, habit!

Landlocked Salmon

Salmo salar sebago

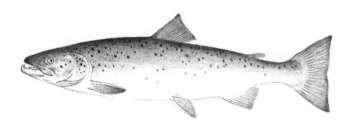

Many thousands of years ago, earth changes probably trapped spawning Atlantic salmon in freshwater, and thus produced the landlocked form of this fish. So closely does this subspecies resemble its ancient ancestors that only an expert could tell one from the other, even at times when looking at them side by side. The landlocked salmon does not grow as large as the sea-run type. Four or 5 pounds brackets most landlocks caught. Some go to 10. They are known to grow to 20 or 30; but this is most unusual. An average landlocked salmon therefore looks like a grilse. There may be a few more X-spots, and the tail may be larger in the landlocked form, also the scales and eyes.

Many, though not all, landlocked salmon descend lake outlets to spawn, then return to the home lake. Their spawning takes place in the fall. They feed much like the Atlantic salmon, living for the most part on fish. In fact, the predominant diet of the landlock is smelt. It is not known to have been native to lakes where smelt were also not in evidence, nor has it been to any extent successfully stocked where smelt were lacking. This gives rise to an interesting supposition: that the smelt were undoubtedly trapped in freshwater at the same time as the salmon, for the smelt in freshwater also were originally anadromous saltwater fish, that is, they came from the sea into coastal streams to spawn.

Probably because anglers are able to fish for landlocked salmon at times other than a spawning run; they are more easily caught than Atlantic salmon. They take a fly more readily because they are actively feeding at the time the fishing is done, whereas the Atlantic salmon is not feeding at all. Fly fishing is the traditional method, but the techniques are not quite like most fly fishing. Oddly, tradition alone is responsible for the fact that so many anglers think of the landlocked salmon as a fly fisherman's fish. The fact is, they will avidly strike spinning lures of numerous varieties, especially small wobbling spoons. In recent years spinning tackle has become popular for them. In fact, probably more landlocked salmon are caught on spinning lures than on flies, if for no reason other than the greater coverage of water afforded by spinning.

Before fly fishing became popular for landlocks, the stock method was trolling, usually deep trolling, often with heavy rod, metal line, and a string of outsized spoons behind which the bait, invariably smelt, was strung. This method is still used, and catches fish, both deep and shallow. It is successful in spring as well as during summer when the fish lie deep. But it is not very dramatic as far as sport is concerned. Nor is stillfishing deep with smelt, another method used by those who know the waters well and can pinpoint those lake holes

50 to a 100 feet deep where the salmon will be during warm weather.

The good fly fishing—in fact the best fishing of all kinds—occurs immediately after ice-out. At this time the forage smelt go inshore, swarming over shallow shoal waters, getting ready for their spring spawning run into the streams. The salmon follow the smelt. Water temperature is right for them, and the feed is there. Rocky points, stream mouths, submerged bars, modest shore-side depths where large boulders lie are all good places to find them. But since salmon are not actually school fish, one must keep on hunting even after the first fish is hooked.

Both trolling and casting are utilized by the fly angler, and one of the most successful methods is the use of both at once. The flies used most are streamers that attempt to represent the smelt in some fashion—the Green Ghost, Black Ghost, Gray Ghost, the Supervisor, the Edson Tiger, and many others. Such flies are trolled, the boatman rowing or running his motor in and out along the shoreline indentations and across the shallows off rocky points. Often two lines are put out, the one back some distance, the other right up close to the boat, even within 20 feet. Boats and motors do not seem to disturb the fish. They will often strike a fly almost in the prop wash, and many fishermen believe the action imparted by the wash is a help.

The nontrolling angler drifts or holds the boat over likely areas, casting and fishing the fly with smeltlike dartings out over ledges or among shoal rocks. But with two anglers working together, one rows or runs the motor and trolls, while the other casts toward shore, getting the fly just as close as he can. It is common on rough days for the fish to be right up in the shoreside surf. By using the combination of trolling and casting, much water is covered, and it is possible to get the cast fly to spots trolling cannot reach. Moreover, landlocked salmon have the odd habit of following the cast fly out toward deeper water without striking at it, whereupon they sometimes see one of the trolled flies and take it instead. Thus the combination method accounts for numerous fish.

Most landlocked salmon enthusiasts wish for a rough day, with a strong wind, regardless of its direction. For reasons known only to the salmon, they seem to strike much better if it is windy, and the tougher the gale, the better. The juts of land, and the white water right up over the rocks, are the really hot spots at such times. Whenever the salmon seem reluctant, whether in wind or calm, the old hand will hook a small smelt through the lips with the hook of his fly and troll with it. This seems always to be a most effective trick.

For casting flies, any good trout rod will do, but because of the bulky flies and the possibility of wind, it is best to use a forward-taper line and a leader with the heavy sections running well forward, both of which help drive the fly. It is also necessary to have adequate backing line on the fly reel. The landlocked salmon is as fine a fighter as its Atlantic ancestors. It makes leap after leap, and many long runs.

While midsummer is slow for this fishing, except by deep trolling or deep stillfishing, the brisk weather of fall and the spawning urge bring the salmon into the shallows again. September and early October are usually good, but not quite as predictable as the spring fishing.

Ouananiche

Because the landlocked salmon was first discovered years ago at Sebago Lake in Maine, it was named (scientifically) from that water. Transplants have not often been successful, but enough of them have been so they place the landlock now over much of New England and eastern Canada, clear to Labrador.

There is another Atlantic salmon subspecies, called the **ouananiche,** *Salmo salar ouananiche*, much like the landlocked salmon in appearance. This is a Canadian form, known mainly in Quebec. Although these are found where they have access to the sea, such as in rivers tributary to the Gulf of St. Lawrence, they do not carry out saltwater migrations. The ouananiche is smaller on the average than the landlocked salmon.

Landlocks are sometimes taken on surface flies, and do in fact feed on insects fairly often. The ouananiche feeds on the surface to a greater extent than the landlocked, and is therefore an excellent fish for the dry-fly caster. It also stays in streams more than the landlocked salmon, which lends it appeal as a fly caster's target. It is, in fact, a very famous light-tackle game fish.

Some of this fame has come to it because of its limited range, which is chiefly in Quebec's Lake St. John area. It has been stocked to some extent in other eastern Canadian localities.

The two forms of landlocked salmon are purposely discussed here as subspecies of the Atlantic salmon, because of their similar treatment in many references. Their environments and habits are different from the Atlantic salmon, there are at least minor differences in physical characteristics, and certainly all anglers think of them as completely different fish. However, most ichthyologists now believe that *sebago* and *ouananiche* do not deserve status as subspecies, but that the Atlantic salmon and the supposed subspecies are all identical. This theory simply lumps the Atlantic salmon of saltwater, the freshwater salmon that is truly landlocked, and the one that has access to the ocean but doesn't go, under one scientific species name, *Salmo salar*. The American Fisheries Society now subscribes to this usage.

Chinook Salmon

Oncorhynchus tshawytscha

This is the famous king, or tyee, salmon of the Pacific coast, the largest of the western salmons and one of our most highly respected game fish. Within its area the chinook is tremendously popular with resident fishermen, and with visiting anglers from all over the country who gather each year to add the king to their experience.

Chinooks of 30 or more pounds are spoken of, especially in their more northerly range, as tyee salmon, the word taken from an Indian expression meaning "chief." Smaller, younger individuals are known as "blackmouths." In some areas males two or three years old are called "jacks." All chinook salmon are silvery, with white belly and dark-blue back. The upper half of the body is stippled with small, dark spots, but in fresh-run fish these are often barely noticeable.

Like other salmon of saltwater, Pacific salmon spawn in freshwater streams. The young migrate at various ages to saltwater, return when mature to spawn, usually in the parent stream. Unlike Atlantic salmon, most Pacific

101

salmon die after spawning. But like their eastern relatives, the Pacific species progressively lose some of their brightness and fighting qualities after they enter freshwater.

The chinook is fished for both in salt- and freshwater. Since it grows to large size (over a hundred pounds, although those over 50 are seldom taken by sportsmen), fairly heavy tackle has in general been traditional. But during recent years, with the advent of spinning and its great popularity, salmon fishing along the west coast is changing in many ways.

Not only are methods and tackle seeing changes and innovations, but new fishing areas are constantly being discovered. For example, the chinook has long been known to range from southern California to northern Alaska, but not many were caught at the lower end of the range. During the last couple of decades, however, Monterey, California, became something of a salmon fishing center, and Morro Bay saw salmon taken. These fish have favorite ocean feeding areas, and the discovery of new grounds is a matter of exploration.

Unlike the Atlantic salmon, the chinook is not much as a fly fisherman's fish. Occasionally large streamers are used for it with some success, but other lures are more reliable. There is one exception. It must be remembered that these fish travel, in stream systems where it is possible, hundreds of miles inland. There are anglers far from the coast who eagerly await the appearance of salmon, and the word goes out from tributary to tributary when the first fish are seen or caught.

Fish so far inland rest or pass winter months in the pools and deep tail-runs. Here a good many are taken by expert anglers on flies. Numerous standard bright salmon patterns, some of them local, some from eastern originals, are used. In these same waters the fish will strike roe, or roe and spinner, or spinner and fly combinations. The jacks are particularly naive in the face of these inland methods. The thrill of taking salmon thus, far inland in fairly cramped waters, is unique.

In saltwater such as at Monterey Bay and off San Francisco and on north off the Oregon and Washington coasts and in the sounds and straits, chinooks are fished for by trolling. Frozen pilchard or other small fish is a standard bait. Various flashing spoons and metal wobblers are also used. Often bait and flasher, or dodger, as these are locally called, are used together. Commonly the bait is threaded on a metal pin with a locking device. A wire leader is attached, and to its other end sometimes a sinker release. Then comes the line, of heavy monofilament. Rod and reel are of medium weight, the reel a star drag, and, on most of the charter boats, the rods of glass. The sinker, which for deep fishing may weigh 1 or 2 pounds depending on the depth to which one must go to find the fish, is snapped onto the sinker release. Offshore in the bays the salmon will be anywhere from 20 to 75 feet deep. When fish are found, and one is hooked, its pull opens the sinker release. The lead is dropped and one plays the fish without it being handicapped by the weight—and pays the skipper for the dropped weight. Many skippers nowadays eliminate the dropped weight system by using a downrigger.

There are method variations, of course, up and down the coast. Fishing chinook in the streams or stream mouths during spawning runs is, however, totally different. The fish cease feeding upon entering freshwater.

They strike out of annoyance, or because of an instinctive urge. Because some fish go hundreds of miles upstream, and some go only short distances, the times of the runs in various streams differ widely, and many streams have runs going on at various intervals. Each stream has its best periods. Waves of fish come in with the tides, and each wave as a rule contains fish conforming fairly strictly to size. The famous Rogue River in Oregon, for example, begins furnishing good fish in April and reaches its peak (near the mouth) in early May. In other rivers, such as Vancouver's famed Campbell, peak fishing occurs during the first weeks of August.

The size of fish also differs somewhat with the seasons. This is particularly true in the bays where trolling is popular. In some, fish taken during April seldom run over 20 pounds and average some 8 to 12. Later on in summer fish of 40 are not uncommon.

In the streams nowadays saltwater spinning gear has become extremely popular. However, the standard light saltwater outfit is also much in evidence. Several methods are used, but one of the most popular is simply to anchor a boat at a proven spot in a good stream and let a large wobbling spoon down into the swift current. The current wafts the flashing lure back and forth, and eventually a passing salmon takes a crack at it. Some anglers lift and drop the lure so that it flutters. As a rule an anchor buoy is attached to the anchor chain. When a big fish is struck, the boat is set free and the angler put ashore to fight his fish, since he may have to follow it downstream.

"Mooching" and "stripping" or "spinning" (the name comes from the bait, not the tackle) are old and effective chinook fishing methods that are losing some ground nowadays. Or rather, they are being streamlined by modern anglers. Stripping or spinning is accomplished by using a cut herring for bait, cutting and hooking this slice of fish (called a "spinner") so it resembles in action a crippled fish when it is drifted into a tidal current and then stripped back in. Mooching is mainly a matter of trolling a flasher lure or a spinner bait so that it lifts and drops back, this accomplished by a pair of anglers in a rowboat or by the use of a small motor on the boat. By using standard modern spinning gear, however, both these methods are now somewhat fused and changed, for with it the bait or lure can be cast and handled most efficiently.

In fact, spinning lures have become popular and effective on chinooks. Plugs of various sorts, properly fished, take these salmon, too, and the large streamers formerly used by a few experts can now be handled well by spinning gear. Regardless of how caught, a chinook salmon is an awesomely strong fish. In saltwater it does not often leap, but when it does the jump is something to behold. In streams, especially smaller ones—many of which are being "discovered" as top-notch salmon hangouts—the water is shallow enough to force the fish to jump. In such waters the battle is especially wild. On the other hand, the strike of a salmon, even a large one, is not always a smashing blow. It may be telegraphed as a light tap. But once the fish knows it is hooked, it may make an astonishing run instantly.

For saltwater trolling, most anglers will need to go out on a charter boat, and thus will be guided, so to speak. Boats that furnish both tackle and bait at reasonable prices can be found throughout chinook range. Or, where a fisherman knows the water and is a capable boatman, skiffs can be rented for open-water trolling.

For the visitor it is also advisable to be guided on the streams during a run. The salmon lie in the pool heads or beneath ledges in deep runs, and travel through such places. A guide intimately familiar with the river can save much wasted time and effort. Also, because peak runs occur at such radically different times on different streams, it is best to plan carefully ahead of time when a trip will be made. Chamber of Commerce people in various towns, or lodge owners where reservations are desired, can furnish such information. As a very general rule, water from 55 to 65 degrees is needed for a good run, and early morning and evenings are the favored times, when most strikes seem to occur.

It is difficult to select the top spots for chinook fishing. There are many. Those already mentioned draw many anglers. Portland, Oregon, and surrounding area, most of the coastal streams up the entire Oregon, Washington, and British Columbia coasts are all popular at various seasons. Westport, Washington, is famous. Generally speaking, the Vancouver Island and Puget Sound region forms one of the most famous and productive salmon centers. A great deal of pinpoint information can be had from the travel bureaus and conservation agencies of the states and the province involved. And of course for those who may travel to Alaska, the same is true.

Probably the most sensational freshwater sport fishing story of the century is the astonishing phenomenon that began in the late 1960s, establishing salmon in portions of the Great Lakes, particularly in Lake Michigan and parts of Lake Huron. The coho or silver salmon (which see for details of this occurrence) was first tried, with amazing results. Then the larger chinook or king salmon was added. Numerous large specimens are now taken annually, far from their original home.

There are several other species of salmon native to the Pacific. With one exception (the silver or coho, dealt with in a following chapter) these are not considered especially game, not because they are incapable of a fight, but because they are not very large, compared to the king, and because they are never so very eager to take the hook. They are the dog (or chum) salmon averaging 6 to 10 pounds, the sockeye (red, blueback) salmon averaging 4 to 9 pounds, the humpback (or pink) salmon averaging 3 to 6 pounds. There is also the kokanee, a miniature form averaging 1 to 2 pounds, of freshwater.

The **dog salmon,** *Oncorhynchus keta*, is an important commercial fish. It is also caught in modest numbers by anglers, especially in the Puget Sound area. It ranges all along the coast from about San Francisco northward, but it is mainly populous off Alaska. It looks much like the chinook, but has no black spots on the back, nor on dorsal fin and tail, as does the chinook. During spawning, males have reddish (and sometimes also greenish) blotches on the side.

The **sockeye,** *Oncorhynchus nerka*, is a beautiful fish when spawning, for it turns dark red, with the foreparts often greenish. It is exceedingly important commercially, and ranges from Oregon throughout Alaska's coast. Although not much fished for purposely, it is occasionally caught by sports anglers. As a matter of fact, some experimentation done by big-game hunters who happened to have fly rods along seems to prove that the sockeye

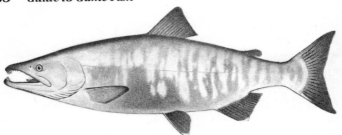

Dog Salmon

just may be more of a sport fish under certain conditions than its reputation indicates. It has been known to take flies fairly well, and is a very game fighter, as well as an extremely beautiful trophy and fine food salmon. Perhaps further trial and error may eventually tag this salmon as a "sleeper" in the game-fish world.

The **humpback,** *Oncorhynchus gorbuscha,* is undoubtedly the most valuable, commercially, of the Pacific salmons, even though it is small. This fish spawns only a short distance above saltwater. Its name derives from the distinct hump on the male's back during spawning time. Black spots on the back are larger than on the chinook. It ranges from California to Alaska, with most of its numbers northward. Humpbacks are eagerly sought in Puget Sound by sport fishermen. Runs do not occur every season. The humpback is not as predaceous as the other salmons, taking much insect as well as small-fish food. Over the past few years it has become far more popular as a sport fish than formerly.

Of the small salmons, the little **kokanee,** *Oncorhynchus nerka kennerlyi* (sometimes called silver trout in Washington), is perhaps the most interesting, and today the most important. This is a landlocked form of sockeye.

Sockeye Salmon

It is said in some places that the kokanee actually had access to saltwater but did not migrate. This may originally have been true, in its native range in British Columbia, Washington, Oregon, and Idaho, where for many years it has been popular with local fishermen.

The kokanee, under the name blueback or blueback salmon, names often used for the larger sockeye, was brought some years ago to Lake Pend Oreille, Idaho, and stocked primarily as food for the Kamloops rainbow trout also placed there. The kokanee, very fat and oily, was responsible it is said for the fantastic growth of the Kamloops. This trout, on its home grounds, habitually feeds where possible on the little salmon. But the small salmon also began slowly to make a name for themselves as game fish in their own right.

Soon kokanee were being raised for stocking in numerous lakes in the West, both natural and impounded. They began to appear in Montana and Wyoming, then Colorado. They were tried in Utah, more recently in New Mexico. They have been stocked even in some New England lakes, and now are being tried in the northern Great

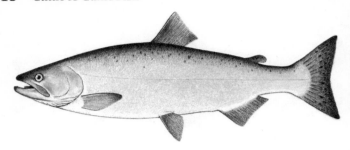

Humpback Salmon

Lakes. Where they have access to spawning streams, some successful spawning may take place. In many of the lakes both large and small it is doubtful that spawning is successful, but it has been found that the fish can be economically stocked as fry by millions and that they grow swiftly to furnish excellent sport.

In fact, as more has been learned about how to catch them, the kokanee has become tremendously popular. In due time it may well become, over a vast area of the United States, one of our most important game fish. It is already known in some places as a "bread and butter" fish for owners of fishing camps and other fishing resorts, for visitors catch it by thousands each season.

The kokanee is bright platinum or silver with blue or greenish back. Males turn red or orange at spawning time. The lower jaw of the kokanee is noticeably weak. This is because it is not a fully predaceous species, but feeds for the most part on minute plankton organisms and other very small forage. This presented difficulties to early experimenters in kokanee fishing. But it was soon learned that they would take small baits of various kinds, and that in particular they would strike very small lures.

Kokanee Salmon

Most kokanee are thus caught today by stillfishing or trolling.

The most successful method yet worked out is by trolling with a lead-cored line dyed different colors each 5 or 10 yards. A long nylon monofil leader is attached to the end of the line, and the lure used is a tiny wobbling spoon of very light weight. Some are made of plastic, in bright red, or white with a red dot. These utilize a single hook, not a gang hook. No sinker is used. The rod is held with the tip a constant distance above the water, and trolling is kept at a speed that places the point between two specific colors on the line right at surface. This places the lure at a precise depth. If no strikes materialize, one more color is brought up—or let down—until the depth at which the kokanee schools are lying has been discovered. From here on the angler knows exactly how to get his lure back to that exact depth without guesswork.

It was not realized until recent years that depth was the key. On any given day, under any specific condition of weather, apparently all the kokanee in a given body of water will be at almost exactly the same level. Once this is known, it is only a matter of moving until a school is located. Then the fisherman trolls back and forth over this area, catching fish after fish. This method originated in Montana, at Lake Mary Ronan west of Flathead Lake. It is proving successful elsewhere. However, casting with small lures also takes many kokanee each season.

The fish are fine fighters, often make many high, flashy leaps. They are also one of the finest of table fishes. Because they are generally fat, they are best filleted with the skin removed. This allows the fat along the lateral line to cook away. They are also delicious when smoked. In some places over recent years there has been a snagging or spearing season on kokanee during fall spawning runs, when streams are red with fish packed into them. Since the spawning kokanee, like their sea-going relatives, will die after attempted spawning, the feeling is that they may as well be utilized.

There is probably no doubt, as has been indicated, that kokanee is on its way to becoming over much of the country an exceedingly important species. This is one of the truly great stories of transplantation and blooming stature of a species originally thought to be rather inconsequential.

To avoid confusion, it should be stated that the American Fisheries Society does not recognize the kokanee as a subspecies of the sockeye, as has been done here (*O. nerka kennerlyi*), but only as a freshwater form that is identical. Older references considered it a subspecies, and its currently skyrocketing importance and spread of range may soon give it such status again.

Silver Salmon

Oncorhynchus kisutch

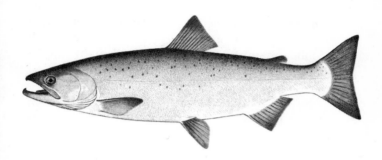

Because the silver salmon, or coho, is generally found closer to the surface than the king, strikes artificial lures more readily, and leaps wildly when hooked, it has long been extremely popular, particularly with light-tackle anglers.

The silver averages from 3 to 10 pounds, has a general maximum weight of possibly 18 pounds. A few individuals grow larger, to 25 or 30. It is a silvery fish with bluish back. There are small black spots along the back and on the upper portion of the tail. During spawning season the males become quite reddish, but this color changes quickly after they enter freshwater, and soon they are dark, almost black.

Throughout most of the chinook range the silver is also present. From Monterey, California, on to Alaska there are excellent runs of silvers in scores of streams, and there are hundreds of bays where they swarm at proper seasons. The Puget Sound region is one of the best locations. Here silvers may be taken almost the year around, if one carefully locates their feeding grounds during any specific time of year.

Spawning runs mainly occur later than runs of kings. For example, at Campbell River, B.C., so famous for its salmon fishing, the kings are at peak during August, the silvers follow them in. On California's Klamath, another famous salmon stream, the same is true.

By and large, therefore, the silver salmon is considered a fall fish. Almost all of the good chinook and steelhead streams up the north-California, Oregon, and Washington coasts have runs of silvers. The Smith in northern California, the Nehalem, Tillamook, Siletz, Suislaw, Umpqua, and scores of others in Oregon, the Columbia and the host of waters that cut up the entire Puget Sound area of Washington are all excellent locations.

Many of the silver salmon migrations, to be sure, begin as early as July, but peak runs almost everywhere are not underway until well into fall, from about mid-September through October and into November. Of course the good fishing for silvers is by no means restricted to the streams. The bays, and waters offshore from stream mouths, swarm with silver salmon during summer and fall. Clallam Bay in the Juan de Fuca Strait area is a good example, likewise the bays into which the various coastal rivers of Oregon flow.

Great hordes of silvers also follow schools of candlefish and herring, the chief food of the adult fish, into coves and other protected waters where they may gorge themselves. Because of this habit, especially in Puget Sound, silvers may be located and caught in spring as well as fall.

Many of the smaller salmon are found on such feeding

grounds in the region of the San Juan Islands during April and May, with larger fish cruising through during early summer. For one who wishes to make an extended fishing tour for silvers, the whole vast and complicated Puget Sound area is therefore a paradise. One needs only to go at practically any time of year, and then run down local information as to the whereabouts of fish. By and large, however, summer and fall will be the best times. Weather is almost certain to be cool, damp, and often foggy or rainy. Warm clothing is a must.

Much the same methods are used to catch silvers as for kings. But tackle can be lighter to match the size of the fish. The so-called "spinning" method, that is, fishing with a piece cut from a herring, "a spinner," is equally as effective for silvers as for kings. So is mooching, and trolling. But whereas a fairly heavy sinker might be needed for kings, which lie deep, a small sinker usually is adequate for silvers.

Probably one of the reasons the silver salmon fights so well is that it so often feeds near surface and is taken high in the water. One of the first items of coho behavior the tyro must learn, however, is their odd habit of appearing to be easily whipped. Quite often they will allow themselves to be reeled in close, then without warning there is an explosion that literally drenches the angler, and the run, with more wild leaps, is on. Because of this habit it is good fish insurance for the beginner to use a leader strong enough to stand the strain.

Trolling accounts for many silvers. So does casting with a variety of plugs, spinners, spoons, and spinning lures. In fact, nowadays spinning tackle is the outfit most perfectly suited to this fish. Lures that twirl or spin rather rapidly seem to have more appeal than slow wobblers. The reverse is often true for chinooks. From about 9 a.m. to late p.m. the fish will be well below the surface. Early and late they'll come up.

Probably the most dramatic method of taking silver salmon is with flies during those early and late hours. There is still much experimentation to be done in this field. Nonetheless, a great many silvers are taken thus each season in such prime spots as Cowichan Bay. Various streamers and bucktails are used. There is a pattern called the Coho, and it has several variations. The Polar Bear is another favorite. Blue, red, white, green in combinations are standard colors. The salmon come close to the surface at dawn and dusk to charge into packs of candlefish and other forage. They may be seen rolling at such times, and flies that represent to some extent the small food fish do a brisk business.

A reasonably sturdy fly rod is mandatory. The reel must be of large capacity, with plenty of backing line. A silver can take off a hundred yards of line in a single smoking run. Because the flies are bulky, a heavy forward-taper line is best for casting them. Or, one may use the trick employed by steelhead fishermen: a length of heavy fly line with monofilament or the newer small-diameter fly line, called "running line," behind it.

Fly fishing can be done simply by casting into fishy-appearing bays and coves, or by trolling a fly or fly-spinner until a hit occurs. The best plan, however, is to locate the feeding fish at dawn or evening, then bring the skiff close enough to reach the edge of the school with a long cast.

Trolling with streamers or bucktails, or with spinner

combinations, is a stock method for taking silver salmon when they gather at or near the stream mouths preparatory to making the upstream dash. This is surface trolling. The lure does not need to run deep. In areas where schools of chinooks and silvers are mixed, big surprises can occur.

One of the all-time great fisheries management successes has been the introduction of the silver salmon to the westernmost Great Lakes — Huron, Michigan, Superior — and its veritable explosion there, particularly in Lake Michigan. Some years ago the lake trout, a most important commercial and sport species in these waters, began to decline, chiefly due to lamprey depredations. The lakes were in serious difficulties. As the lamprey began to come under partial control after long and costly experimentation, a new menace appeared, an invasion of alewives via the Seaway from the Atlantic.

This small, bony fish found in these Great Lakes a perfect habitat, erupted by millions, threatening other species by crowding. Dieoffs along the shore left tons of alewives rotting for miles on beaches. Then imaginative Michigan fisheries personnel began thinking about a predator fish large enough and abundant enough to control the alewives. While many were claiming the Great Lakes "dead," these scientists were by no means ready to give up. They recognized in the seemingly useless alewife a prime forage source for some not-yet-determined food and game fish.

Silver salmon were tried. There were obviously not enough tributary rivers large enough to support completed spawning runs of consequence. But if the fish could successfully live out their cycle in these large bodies of water, eggs might be taken by millions and as one crop of adults died after their spawning attempt, another year-class would be ready to replace them.

Results were all but unbelievable. The small kokanee, landlocked form of the sockeye salmon, also had been stocked. But the explosion of fast-growing silvers totally overshadowed the smaller fish. Experiments had begun in 1966. By the late '60s and early '70s the chinook or king salmon had also been added. Both salmon grew fat, and swiftly, and to outsize proportions on their alewife diet. Meanwhile lake trout, ordinarily a slow-growing species, also made a husky comeback; "steelheads" (lake-run rainbow trout) grew larger than ever and more numerous. Tens of thousands of big salmon now are taken annually, most of the management difficulties have been ironed out, and the northern Great Lakes area is world renowned as a kind of second home of these Pacific salmons.

Interestingly, the success of the silver brought such swarms of anglers that a whole new series of industries has been born along the lakes. Marinas, boat builders, specially designed downriggers for trolling a bait or lure deep and releasing the line at the strike, so the fish is played without weight on the line, endless new lures designed for silvers, depth sounders—the silver has brought high drama and a great deal of money to the region. Granted, the king is larger, but one who catches a silver salmon undergoes a very special experience. Of all the western salmons this one comes closest to the Atlantic salmon in its relation to angling and its action on the hook. It is a much more dynamic game fish than the larger king.

Rainbow Trout

Salmo gairdneri

Because the rainbow introduces the trouts here, this is a good place to quickly review the trout species of the United States. Overall it is probably true that the rainbow is today and long has been our most popular trout. Although it was originally native only to the west slope of the Rockies, it has been so widely handled, and has proven so adaptable, that today there is rainbow trout fishing over a very great portion of the country. Hatcheries have even "built" fall-spawning varieties of this spring-spawning fish, in order to fill special needs.

The rainbow and its group, broadly speaking, are the only true American trouts. The famous steelhead trout is simply a sea-run form of the rainbow. The equally famous but range-restricted Kamloops trout is also simply a rainbow with habits differing slightly from the type species. The cutthroat trout native throughout much of the West is a separate species, but so closely allied to the rainbow that probably anciently it was but a race or off-shoot variety of rainbow—or it may have been just the other way around. The same is true of the gaudy golden trout, undoubtedly only a high-altitude rainbow that became different enough, because of isolation, to stand as a separate and distinct species. The Piute trout of a small, high western range is a subspecies of cutthroat. There are many other such isolated races of "cuts." There is also the Gila trout, *Salmo gilae*, a presently endangered species of the Gila River area of the Southwest.

There are also a great many races of rainbows. Scientists at one time were naming trout right and left, many from a single lake or stream in the West. Undoubtedly all of these "subspecies" were simply races of rainbows or cutthroats that had become a bit different in appearance, structure, or habits because of long isolation. At any rate, this large group of races, varieties, and subspecies of western trouts boils down to three main species: the rainbow, the cutthroat, the golden. Each of these will be given attention in some detail under its separate headings. The steelhead will get special attention here with the rainbow because though the fish carries the same scientific name, steelhead fishing differs radically from average rainbow trout fishing.

Interesting, indeed, and little realized by anglers, is the fact that all our native *true trouts* were originally westerners. The only other true trout we have is the brown or Loch Leven trout, a species introduced from across the Atlantic. It appears under a separate heading.

The other fishes we commonly call trout, including that much loved species the brookie, are not true trout, but chars. This is to some extent a technical matter, for of course a brook trout and a lake trout obviously have all the trout features. Still the two groups have many group distinctions. So perhaps it is most practical to say that our trout world can be split into two groups: the true trouts; the chars.

The easiest ways for the layman to set them apart are as follows. True trout, and salmon, have body markings darker than the general body color, in other words, dark markings on a lighter background. Chars generally have lighter markings on a darker background. Chars have very small scales. Some of them, such as the brookie, have such small ones that the fish often appear to be scaleless. True trout, and salmon, have larger, very noticeable scales. The paired fins and the anal fin of chars in general have leading edges of white backed up by black. This varies in degree from species to species. The teeth of true trout and chars differ somewhat, but this is again a technical item.

Here are the chars: brook trout; lake trout; Dolly Varden trout; Sunapee (or Sunapee golden) trout of a few New England lakes; Arctic char, or alpine trout, of far-northern water; Aurora trout, Quebec red, Maine blueback trout, all three of which are range-restricted chars closely related to the brook trout, if not simply races of it. The chars in general fight below-water battles, while the true trouts and the salmons are more inclined to leap.

Leaping is what has given the rainbow a preeminent place in the world of game fish. Hurling themselves out of the water is one of the things rainbow trout do best. This of course has brought them fame and popularity, but undoubtedly the main reason for their popularity is availability. The original stock for rainbows came from the McCloud River in California back in the 1880s.

Today the rainbow is found almost everywhere in the

mountain West, throughout the Great Lakes and the East, over much of Canada, in cold streams far southward into Georgia, in cold-water stretches below TVA and other dams in Tennessee, Arkansas, even Oklahoma and Texas. It is a kind of universal trout because it has proven that it can do well in a wide variety of habitats. It is now found in all manner of lakes shallow and deep, in streams large and small, in several of the Great Lakes, and in certain areas of saltwater. Like all trout, the rainbow demands cold, clean water, but it does put up with marginal conditions in many places.

The rainbow trout comes also in a variety of sizes, as well as locations. Steelheads of 18 to 20 pounds are not uncommon. The Kamloops rainbow of British Columbia grows larger still. That is the strain stocked in Lake Pend Oreille, Idaho, which some years ago became so famous. Here the fish grow fast and large because of the abundant presence of kokanee, or blueback salmon, fat forage fish upon which they gorge.

In numerous streams and lakes rainbows of 2 to 5 pounds arouse no special comment from anglers. This is more likely to be true in large western streams than east of the Mississippi, although many large eastern rainbows are caught. In general, however, it may be said that the average rainbow trout caught by the average angler is from 6 to 18 inches in length.

Although color differs widely in different waters, the general impression given by the rainbow is that of a gray-silver fish with olive to pale-greenish back, many black speckles over the head, upper body and upper fins, and with a striking swath of magenta running down each side. Some specimens are gaudily washed with this pink to red brush stroke, and in some it is only hinted at. Sea-run fish, or fish from large lakes such as the Great Lakes, caught on their runs into streams, are usually silvery, with little if any color and often few spots.

Rainbow trout strike hard as a rule, and fight a swift, headlong battle. They do not always leap, but usually do. There is so much legal-size stocking done nowadays that true wild fish are not always to be had. Hatchery fish, unless they have been in a wild state for some time, lack the spirit of a true wild resident. Water temperature, food quality, and many other influences cause rainbows in some places to fight better than in others.

Spring and fall are in general the most productive periods for rainbow fishing. From late April through June in the east and the lake country, from mid-June to mid-July in the western mountains the fish are actively feeding, and the fishing both on surface and below is ordinarily good. In September in all areas fishing is usually good again, although during fall, due to lessening of insect hatches, dry flies take second place to sunken lures.

The rainbow is a good dry-fly fish. The patterns it will take are legion. It is foolish to give advice on them here. The plain fact is, what will catch a rainbow in one place will usually catch a rainbow thousands of miles away. However, on every famous rainbow lake or stream, productive fly patterns differ because of local hatches, conditions, and angler usage. It is therefore wise for an angler to inquire as to patterns in general use where he proposes to fish.

Streamers, bucktails, numerous general wet flies and nymphs are proper rainbow lures. In fact, there are places where large rainbows feed hardly at all on the surface and must be fished, if one is to have reasonable success, with underwater lures. There are even certain streams where, notoriously, the large rainbows are almost never taken on anything but bait, or on such lures as small plugs, wobbling and flashing spoons, and spinners. The reverse is also true, in some places. Feeding habits dictate this. The ungainly strings of spinners several feet long, progressing downward from an immense blade to a small one just before the bait, are popular here and there for trolling for rainbows. Even small trout seem attracted to these preposterous contraptions. They do catch fish. They aren't much as far as sport goes.

As fine a fish as the rainbow is, it must be admitted that like all trout it is gullible for a stillfished bait, will take spawn, cut bait, live and dead minnows, and even corn and dough-balls. The top rainbow baits in most areas are nightcrawlers or angleworms.

Like all trout, the rainbow has definite feeding periods which may begin quite suddenly and end just as abruptly. There are occasional days, of course, when the trout appear to feed casually for hours on end. Early morning and late afternoon are favored periods. Most trout are caught then. On the other hand, on many a day of bright sun, and many another of downpour, trout will be found feeding avidly at high noon. On streams, the large fish are likely to be found in the deep pools or the deep, long glides. Smaller rainbows will feed in the shallow riffles.

When heavy insect hatches are on, very large fish commonly ease up from deep pools into flat but rather shallow stretches above, where food can easily be picked off, and where they may dart back to safety at the slightest hint of danger. The rainbow takes a great deal of insect food both from the surface and from stream and lake bottom. It also eats minnows and crustaceans. Here again is a reason for its great popularity: it is adaptable to almost every conceivable kind of fishing. Spinning lures are as deadly on rainbows as are flies. Large rainbows will even strike bass plugs and pike spoons.

For this reason it cannot be said that any outfit is *the* one. It is purely a matter of the angler's choice, related of course to the size of the fish likely to be taken in the particular water. For heavy rainbows in either lake or stream, backing line should be placed on the reel behind a fly line. Even with fish of 3 or 4 pounds it is not amiss, nor is a good supply of line on a spinning outfit.

Large rainbows are seldom easy to catch on flies, but for some reason seem to fall quite regularly to deep-fished metal spinning lures. However, nothing quite fits the rainbow so perfectly as a fly rod. The majority of anglers use wet flies and streamers. Where the water is exceedingly clear, a long leader tapered fine (9 feet at least and to no larger than 3X) is a must for dry-fly fishing. Dry-fly fishing for big rainbows anywhere requires that the leader sink well, and quickly. On a lake, a slight breeze to riffle the surface will greatly assist. In fishing a fly to rising fish, casting to the side, never directly over the fish, is a productive rule.

To sum up, anybody can catch rainbow trout. They are not the experts-only creatures much literature has attempted to have anglers believe. On the other hand, trout are trout, which is to say, erratic fish. Hundreds of volumes have been written about how to catch them. Obviously only a meager amount of fundamental information can be given here. Most pertinent of it all, where rainbows are concerned: the careful, observant, quiet, patient angler will usually have the fullest creel.

Probably no field of angling endeavor has been more carefully explored or more meticulously researched by its almost fanatic adherents than western steelhead fishing. The true **steelhead** is a native rainbow of the west slope of the Rockies that has access via stream to saltwater, and has when small run out to sea, spent considerable growing time there, and returned on a spawning run into freshwater. Scores of streams from California to Alaska are host to steelhead runs. Many, such as the Eel and Klamath in California, the Rogue and Umpqua in Oregon, are famous. A great many others, less well known, are actually just as good, and probably for the average angler some, especially the smaller streams, are better.

It will pay the prospective steelhead fisherman, therefore, to sit down with good west-coast maps and study them, then find out all he can from state and local sources about the runs of steelhead in streams not well publicized. Because steelhead are erratic in their runs, some entering certain streams in February and March, others being at peak during spring, summer, or fall, one must know which streams have which runs, and on which streams these runs are best. In some the trout enter during spring, migrate great distances, staying until they come to spawning maturity the next season.

One stream may have an excellent winter run of big fish, another a spring run of smaller fish, and so on. Of course, it must be realized that "small" is a comparative term where the steelhead is concerned. A modest-sized mature steelhead may still be a fish of 8 or more pounds. A good fish is certain to weigh 12 to 15, and many are still larger. They are also exceedingly strong, far stronger in fact than fish wholly of freshwater, and they are tremendously wild when hooked. Incidentally, steelheads do not die after spawning, as do the salmon whose life pattern they to some extent copy.

Rainbows that have grown to maturity in large lakes act much the same as sea-run trout. They seek out streams emptying into the lakes and move up them for spawning. Because of this habit, lake rainbows in the Great Lakes area and the East have come in past years to be called "steelheads" when caught during spawning runs in tributary streams or off stream mouths in their home lakes. The term may not be entirely correct, but the trout come close to matching their western sea-run relatives.

In a few areas such rainbows are taken as large as 18 pounds. In general the average is 3 to 7 or 8. They are good fighters, but most of them do not have the striking stamina and wildness of sea-run fish. There is presently one exception. In the northern Great Lakes area where silver and king salmon have been so successful (see SILVER SALMON for details), the steelhead has made a rather remarkable change. It, too, thrives on the same Great Lakes diet as the introduced salmons, grows larger than it once did, is more abundant, and a dynamic battler. In the streams here, and indeed in the lakes also, it is almost like a "new" trout. Many anglers have developed specialized methods of Great Lakes steelhead fishing. Streamer flies, bait, and varied metal lures are, however, the basic approaches, and in general steelheads east of the Mississippi are fished for about like large rainbow trout in lakes or streams anywhere.

Western steelheading differs substantially from its Great Lakes and eastern counterpart. A vast amount of specialized experimentation has been done in the West, and continues, particularly in fly patterns and in fly lines for long-distance casting, and even in rods. For example, the graphite rods introduced in the early '70s are lighter and stronger and more resilient than fiberglass, and have become a substantial help in this field as well as in many fishing endeavors. There are three main fishing methods currently in vogue for western steelheading: fly fishing; single-egg fishing; spinning.

Some steelheaders dote on dry flies. But these are restricted to summertime, when the streams are low and clear. Fairly large flies are generally used, with No. 8 a popular size. Patterns are in general copies of standard trout-fly patterns, with bushy flies often out front.

Wet flies are also used, with the weighted wet flies such as the famed Optics popular and effective. Streamers are also popular, most often at tidewater, where they are fished from anchored boats and allowed to work back and forth in the current in front of fish coming into mildly brackish waters.

Few steelhead anglers with any experience fish blindly. That is, they locate their fish before they begin casting. This is not as difficult as it may sound. Steelheads use the same pools, the same runs, the same submerged obstructions for protection and for resting water season after season. Anyone who is fairly good at reading stream character can soon locate good steelhead areas, but in most instances the newcomer can locate them by watching the crowd. Once a proper piece of water is located, the fish—assumed to be there—are then fished to.

In fishing all kinds of sinking flies, which is the most popular type of fly fishing for steelhead, long casts must be made, and the fly must be got well down. The cast is usually made (to the known lie of a fish) from almost directly across the stream, and a bit below. Some slack must be thrown, so that the fly sinks and rides the complicated currents naturally. Steelhead are exceedingly wary, and once their suspicions are aroused, they simply refuse to take, and must be rested for a time.

Specific ideas about tackle have grown up because of the particular demands of steelhead fishing. The rod must be strong. Many prefer 9 1/2 feet. Others claim shorter, lighter rods tire one less in distance casting from deep water where the angler may stand up to his armpits. Either three-dimensional lines in GAF or GBF must be used, or the newer idea of a short length of heavy fly line backed by monofil or small-diameter running line that it will carry. In either case, plenty of backing is a must, for a big steelhead cannot readily be stopped. And casts of 60 to 80 or more feet must be consistently attained on the larger streams. The double-haul casting process is used for distance. Most steelhead fly anglers demand that the line sink, and quickly, the better and more efficiently to take the fly deep down where the fish lie. They will seldom come up to it from any great distance. Fast-sinking fly lines have been developed for this work.

Single-egg fishing is a manner of fishing salmon eggs for steelhead. The usual method is to float a stream in a boat. A single salmon egg is placed on an inconspicuous hook, with just enough weight to get it down to bottom.

Then as the boat floats downstream the bait is literally bounced along the bottom. This is a most delicate operation, the how-to difficult if not impossible to describe. The best way to learn it—and it is very effective—is to be guided on the first few tries by one who is adept at it.

Spin fishermen take steelheads regularly on numerous of the standard spinning lures, from flasher-type wobbling spoons to various spinners. These lures are fished much like the flies, that is, across and slightly up, allowed to sink well and then retrieved in a downstream swing.

The space given to steelheading here has been awarded because this is an endeavor no angler should miss. At least once, every serious fisherman should experience western steelheading. Because it is a specialist's game, only the rudiments have been touched here, and then but lightly. For the beginner, or the tourist-angler, it is best to hire a good local guide. These are usually to be had on most of the well-known streams, and many a local fisherman can be persuaded in less famed areas to introduce a visitor to this heady sport.

The discussion of steelheading as "western" is not intended to detract from the "steelheading" known east of the Mississippi. Expert anglers have learned many tricks for taking large rainbows in the Great Lakes region and the East, when the fish swarm on upstream runs. A nightcrawler swirled on bottom so that it tumbles into a pool, a small plug of certain colors locally popular allowed to wiggle deep into runs, fishing with single salmon eggs, and many other methods are used. Fundamentally, however, the techniques used are simply those that have been found, in any specific location, most successful for catch-

Kamloops Trout

ing large rainbows. The sea-run steelhead of the West is quite a different fish, and even though the eastern "steelhead" is a grand fighter indeed, it is no doubt unfortunate that the name has been erroneously attached to it.

The **Kamloops trout,** or Kamloops rainbow, is a subspecies native predominantly to interior British Columbia. Apparently because its chief food is that small and very fat species of freshwater salmon, the kokanee, the Kamloops trout grows to unusual size and develops phenomenal strength. Fish of 30 to 40 pounds are not especially uncommon, and larger ones have been taken. In many waters of northeastern Washington and British Columbia, and in other places in the West where the Kamloops has been introduced, fishing methods for it differ very little from standard rainbow fishing techniques. Streamer flies work very well at times. On the whole, however, since the Kamloops angler is very often trying for an extremely big fish, trolling with kokanee salmon for bait, or with large deep-running plugs or spoons, and with heavy tackle—sometimes even with saltwater tackle—has become common practice.

There are a number of places, especially in British Columbia, that specialize in Kamloops fishing. These camps advertise as a rule in the outdoor magazines, or their addresses may be had from such sources as the Government Travel Bureau at Victoria, B.C. The prospective Kamloops fisherman can contact such places and find out what methods of fishing are favored in the area. There is some very spectacular fly fishing in some of the areas, and a chance at some tremendous trout, regardless of how one chooses to fish them.

Cutthroat Trout

Salmo clarki

The easiest way to get into an argument with a native western trout fisherman is to claim that the rainbow trout is a better fish than the cutthroat. Whenever westerners speak of "native" trout, or "mountain" trout, or "Rocky Mountain" trout, they usually mean their beloved "cuts," of which there are innumerable races scattered throughout the Rockies from California to Alaska. Of all our native trouts, the cutthroat has the largest original range.

The cutthroat is named from the twin slashes of red color on the underside of the lower jaw. Its scientific name honors Capt. Wm. Clark of the Lewis and Clark Expedition. Eastern trout anglers seeing this species for the first time might easily confuse it with the rainbow. But the cutthroat is not as compressed in the body section as the rainbow. It is thicker, more rounded. The forward portion of the body appears heavier than the rear half, while the rainbow appears about balanced in this respect. Because of its long jaws, the cutthroat seems

Piute Trout

to have a larger mouth. There are teeth on the base of
its tongue, which are lacking in the rainbow. The entire
body of the cutthroat is often heavily spotted with black
spots, and these cover the anal fin, while the anal fin of
the rainbow is unspotted.

Because of its heavy spotting, the cutthroat is often
called the black-spotted trout. However, there are endless
variations and many of these are locally named from a
single lake or stream where, in isolation for perhaps centuries, they have built up specialized characteristics of
coloring, sometimes with less spots, or few on the forward half of the body. The **Lake Tahoe trout,** the **Piute
trout,** the **Yellowstone trout,** the **Lake Crescent cutthroat** of Washington, the **Montana black-spotted trout**
are examples. Most of them have colorful gill covers and
a pinkish swath down the side. Others range from white
to yellow on the belly, and with spots heavier or lighter,
some of them with yellow spots. The simplest identification is that from which the trout takes its name: the
red markings under the lower jaw. Occasionally, especially in sea-run specimens, these may be extremely faint,
but ordinarily they are plainly in evidence. In a few lo-

Yellowstone Cutthroat

cations hybrids with rainbows have been stocked. These may still carry the red slashes.

There is a great range in size among cutthroats. In small, high mountain streams cuts may run only 6 to 10 inches. In Alaskan waters where they are exceedingly abundant and popular, trout of 12 to 24 inches are the rule. In certain lakes huge cuts have been caught, fish weighing anywhere form 20 to 40 pounds. The sea-run form along the Pacific coast is usually a fish of 1 to 4 pounds.

Probably the cutthroat best known to the greatest number of fishermen is the Yellowstone variety. This handsome fish, gaudily colored and at times even with the gullet a bold magenta shade, is the famed cutthroat of Yellowstone Lake. Tens of thousands of visitors to the Park have caught these fish, and the famed Fishing Bridge at the point where the Yellowstone River leaves the lake has seen cutthroats undoubtedly in the millions hauled over its rail. In numerous places in Yellowstone Lake, so abundant have these trout been over the years that in spring particularly limits can be caught at times in only a few minutes.

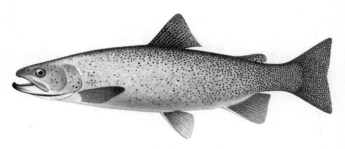

Montana Black-Spotted Trout

The cutthroat trout in whatever form is an excellent fighter. It generally fights an underwater battle, but a very strong one. Occasionally it leaps, but ordinarily it lacks the dash, the wild, hurtling abandon of the hooked rainbow. The argument among westerners is endless as to which fish fights best. There is never any argument about the quality of the cutthroat as an eating fish.

Although the cutthroat was found natively in all sorts of western waters from large torrential rivers to tiny creeks and beaver ponds at 10,000 feet, and again down on the coast feeding in saltwater, it was never as easy to handle and stock as the rainbow. It appeared hardy until taken over by the hatcheries. However, hardier cutthroat strains were eventually evolved, and stocking is now done in many western areas on a large scale. Nonetheless, the cutthroat still has not proved amenable to handling on such a broad scale as the rainbow.

Like the rainbow, the cutthroat is a spring spawner. In many ways it differs from the rainbow in habits, as for example in its favorite lies in the streams. The cutthroat is likely to be in places rather similar to those selected by eastern brook trout—near log or snag, in a deep hole beneath a cutbank. In other words, cuts are fish of somewhat quieter water, and indeed of a quieter disposition, than the rainbow, which likes the swift pulsating runs, the white water, and the sturdy riffles.

By and large, the cutthroat may be taken by the same methods used for rainbows. They rise well to dry flies during the early part of the season especially. But they favor wet flies perhaps on the whole more than surface flies, and they are inclined to be less selective at times than rainbows, taking many a gaudy fly that a rainbow might spurn. In fact, many anglers insist that streamers and bucktails for cuts carry at least some white, red, or yellow, or all three in combination. This, unfortunately, is no hard and fast rule. But broadly speaking, whether he uses flies or bait, the experienced rainbow fisherman will have no difficulty catching cuts, if he simply uses good trout sense.

In one respect the cutthroat seems quite different, and that is in its liking for flashing spoons and other comparable lures. In many an Oregon stream, for example, cuts of all sizes, even down to babies, will avidly go after a 2-inch brass wobbler with red and white stripes on the outside. Such wobblers, in all modest sizes, as well as innumerable spinning lures, account for hundreds of cutthroat trout.

The most unique facet of cutthroat fishing, and the main reason for giving this fish ample individual attention, is its love for saltwater. Throughout the entire length of cutthroat range, wherever these fish have access to saltwater they move from their parent streams out into it, and then return in due course to spawn. Yet there is a difference between the addiction of the cutthroat and that of the rainbow. Cuts do not fan out into the ocean depths, disappearing as do the steelheads. They cruise along the shores, usually not far from their home stream, or they hang about the bay or the broad brackish mouth of the stream.

Perhaps the movement of cutthroat trout to saltwater was originally brought about because the lower reaches of the torrential Pacific coastal streams are notoriously bleak forage grounds. Although to the visitor these near-tide-water stretches look beautiful and fishy, the truth is many of these streams can continuously support little fish life in their lower portions. For numerous reasons—raging floods, rock bottoms—they are nearly barren.

Thus, conceivably native trout populations may have anciently begun probing the salt coasts of necessity. At any rate, sea-run cuts grow fast, but they do not stay in the sea for long periods, as do the steelheads. Therefore, the usual weight will be from 1 to 5 pounds, with an average around 2 or 3.

While steelheads are not commonly caught in saltwater, sea-run cuts are taken in numbers in early spring along the beaches flanking the streams up which they will later travel. They can be caught on sunken flies, or on bait, or by trolling with either, usually in water of modest depth, seldom over 10 or 15 feet. The turning tides are the best fishing times. Trolling the bays into which the home streams flow also accounts for many of these fish. In saltwater or when later they come into the streams, they have lost color and spots like the steelhead. They are silvery, heavy, and very strong.

As summer wanes, the sea-run cuts begin to gather off

Harvest Trout

the stream mouths. By the time harvests are over and late-season rains begin to rise and cloud the rivers, the silvery saltwater cuts swarm into the lower reaches. Native anglers drop everything and go fishing, for this is the season of the famed **harvest trout.**

Out of the swift currents, in the quiet pools or where obstructions give protection and slow water, the silvery fish gang up to rest. And here they are taken by trolling with spinner and bait or fly, by stillfishing with bait, and by casting flies, usually wet flies or streamers. Where large boulders lie, in water that may look totally "dead," there are likely to be large resting harvest trout. And they will be ready to feed, because these lower waters are partially bereft of forage and the competition is severe. This, then, is the great difference between the steelhead and salmon, and the harvest trout or sea-run cutthroat. The steely and salmon do not feed after entering freshwater. The salmon eventually dies, the steelhead waits until after spawning to fatten up once more—but the harvest trout eats avidly all the way to the spawning grounds.

Occasionally these sea-run cuts can be found near the surface, or in shallow water where surface food is at hand. Then they will take dry flies, and the sport is most interesting. They seldom leap, but they fight doggedly.

Almost all west-coast streams have runs of so-called harvest trout. There are excellent runs all the way from northern California on up the Oregon and Washington coasts, and along Vancouver and northward. Because the trout are concentrated during this period, before spreading out into vast numbers of upstream tributaries to await spring spawning, harvest trouting is a phenomenon like nothing else in the world of trout fishing.

Golden Trout

Salmo agua-bonita

Of the large fraternity of trout fishermen, few have caught goldens. Unless this prized trophy can be induced by science to change its habits, not many will, because the golden in its celebrated original form and color exists only at western altitudes of 9,000 to 12,000 feet. The first goldens recorded were discovered in California's Volcano Creek, and the fish was called Volcano Creek trout. Later it was found in a number of streams and lakes in the high Sierra.

From this point on the golden was stocked here and there by campers and fishermen backpacking into the Sierra, and by state officials. Numerous small, high lakes of the area now have goldens, and so do their tributary waters. The fish was tried in other western lakes at and above the timberline. Some were successfully established in Washington and in Wyoming. In the high country of Wyoming's Wind River Mountains a number of lakes with goldens have now become popular with anglers on pack trips.

Most golden trout are not large. The high lakes do not have long summer growing periods, and food is of varied small insects and crustaceans. The water is very cold, weed growth all but nonexistent. Thus the fish in some of the streams and lakes are very small, in others grow to a maximum of about 1 1/2 to 2 pounds. In a few waters, however, goldens of 5 pounds or more are found. The record at present is about 11 pounds, for a Wyoming fish.

The appeal of the golden is partly in the difficulty of getting to where it lives, and partly in its startling colors. Typically goldens are olive along the back, crimson on gill cover and along a swath down the side, orange yellow to gold over much of the remainder of the body. The rear portion of the body just before the tail—the caudal peduncle—is often peppered with dark spots, and so is the dorsal fin. Head and upper portion of body may also be spotted. Markings and colorings differ extensively from lake to lake. Oddly, goldens reared at low altitudes are inclined to revert to rainbow-troutlike coloration and markings. They also cross with rainbows and lose identity. Thus the most distinctive attributes of this trout may be the results of isolation and altitude.

Goldens are not easy to catch. This is because of the clarity of the waters in which they live, and because they are so used to feeding on very minute creatures. They spawn about June, at which time they are inshore. This is about as early as one may get into golden trout territory anyway, because of snow. However, the trout are active all summer, and may be seen rising at some time nearly every day. This can be exasperating, especially since most waters (lakes) where there are golden trout do not have boats on them, or any way to get boats there except by horse or backpacking.

The fish can be caught stillfishing with bait such as salmon eggs or grubs, but this is not much sport after one has gone to some trouble to get to the fishing place. Spinning tackle has taken many goldens during recent seasons. Small spinners seem to do best, cast out and retrieved deep, over the edge of a steep drop-off.

Dry-fly fishing is an excellent way to catch golden trout, and is popular because it is such good sport. Flies used with success are usually small, seldom larger than No. 10 and more likely No. 14 or smaller. Dark flies representing midges are among the best. Other, larger flies heavily hackled are sometimes cast and allowed to lie for long periods inactive on the water. A trout eventually may come up and engulf the fly.

Wet flies also catch goldens. So do streamers and bucktails. In fact, the larger specimens are taken on such flies, or on spinning lures.

On the whole, however, goldens are likely to be erratic, and exasperating to the fisherman. It is not uncommon to pack into remote high water after goldens, and then to try every conceivable trick for several days without taking a single fish—meanwhile having to stare at big ones cruising or rising. One who sticks with it, however, is nearly always successful in due time.

To most trout enthusiasts the golden is more than a novelty. It is a dream that urges realization until a pilgrimage is made. The fish battle well, and are excellent eating. They will probably never be widely accessible. This also adds to the romance of them. The average angler who wishes to try for goldens should by all means depend on the services of an experienced guide, rather than attempting it, at least the first time, on his own.

Confusing occasionally to the layman is the fact that the Sunapee trout, a char related to the brook trout, is often called "golden trout" or "Sunapee golden." This is a fish of New England, far removed in all ways from the true golden trout. For further details on the Sunapee trout, see the section on brook trout.

There is one other most interesting "golden trout." This is usually called the West Virginia Centennial Golden. This variety originated from a single rainbow trout egg among thousands at a hatchery from which a gold-colored "sport" appeared. This small female was carefully tended. Eventually progeny became mixed in with hundreds of standard small rainbows. The characteristic, however, asserted itself as the fingerlings grew, and a number of "goldens" turned up. These were developed into a continuing strain. They are not albinos. They are yellow-gold, with pink swaths down the sides, handsome and unusual indeed. The first stocking was made during West Virginia's "Centennial," thus the name. They are now in many of the state's trout waters, and a few were also given to the state of New Jersey, which has since stocked them.

Brown Trout

Salmo trutta

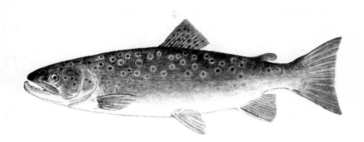

The brown, or Loch Leven, trout is not a native of the North American continent. Many years ago it was imported. Some of the fish came from Germany and were therefore called German browns, a name still often heard. Some came from England. Others came from elsewhere on the continent and were known simply as European browns. Still others came from stock native in Loch Leven, Scotland. These were planted chiefly in the West.

To this day, in many areas of the West, native anglers argue that their trout are not browns, but Loch Leven trout, and that the two differ vastly. The truth is, varying imported strains of brown and Loch Leven and European trout have been so thoroughly mixed by hatchery people that there is no pure strain. Originally they were all brown trout of one strain or another. They still are. The one area of brown trout lore, however, upon which all trout fishermen agree is that when these trout came to America something besides a new fish was imported—namely, a tremendous frustration of those who would catch them.

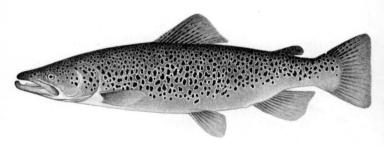

Loch Leven Trout

The brown is considered everywhere the most exasperatingly shy and wary and whimsical of all our trout species. Experts who have been able to cope with trout of all kinds have hurled their rods to the bank in utter despair over browns that just simply could not be caught. And yet, for all this the brown is an authentic enigma. This fish can be so stupid on occasion when in deep lake water, that it will chew away on practically anything let down to it on a hand line and act about as clever in avoiding capture as a bullhead. In another lake within casting distance, there may lurk huge browns that every angler in the region has given up as uncatchable. Because of these whimsies, the brown is a most intriguing and popular species.

It is also widely spread across the country. In almost every state where there are trout, brown trout are now either stocked annually or have become established and self-sustaining in lakes and streams. For some years, and in some places still today, the brown's reputation as a spawn and fry eater made it anathema. It is doubtful that the brown is as serious a menace in this respect as its detrators would have had one believe. It monopolizes certain waters simply because it can tolerate marginal or submarginal conditions of habitat in many instances better than other trout. The others would have disappeared regardless. In numerous waters where the brookie and the rainbow have difficulty, browns have saved trout fishing.

The coloring of brown trout differs widely in different waters. In general it is a brownish to olive-brown fish, dark above, shading to lighter on the belly. There are black spots on the back and rather large and distinct brick-red spots intermingled with black spots on its sides. These are often encircled by pale rings. The dorsal fin is also spotted, and the fleshy adipose fin is large and commonly tinged with orange. In some western mountain waters where the rocky bottoms are pale, browns are light colored, some even canary yellow. The number of spots varies greatly from strain to strain and location to location.

Along the northern Great Lakes there are areas where brown trout have for many years "gone to sea," so to speak, in the big lakes. They inhabit shoreside waters, and come into streams during late summer in preparation for spawning, since browns are fall spawners. These fish for years have been called "salmon" or "sebagos" or any of a variety of names. Commercial fishermen long claimed them as a legitimate catch, and were sure they were some species of salmon. There were, of course, no salmon in the region. These trout, usually very large, lose their red spots completely and bear numerous X-marks similar to landlocked salmon. They are simply lake-run browns.

In 1966 Wisconsin launched an annual experimental

Sea-Run Brown Trout

stocking of brown trout in Lake Michigan, along the rocky shores of the Door County Peninsula. Browns in such water are not inclined to roam as are rainbows. It was hoped the fish would thrive and form a spawning population, or at least do well enough so a replenishable population might be maintained by continued stocking. It was known that browns as they grow older and larger are inclined to cling to comparatively shallow shoreline waters. Thus it was hoped the mature trout would remain accessible.

Within a couple of years and on into the '70s phenomenal results were obtained. On the rich diet of alewives that had erupted in Lake Michigan (*see* SILVER SALMON) the trout grew swiftly and so deep and broad that they were literally out of proportion. Some fin-clipped fish of 3 pounds in April had become 6-pounders by July. During fall spawning runs, swarms of enormous browns congregated inshore. Fishermen during various months commonly took browns of 10 to 15 pounds. The region became a mecca for avid brown-trout anglers. Fish are caught both with fly and spinning tackle.

Also during the 1970s much the same phenomenon has occurred along Michigan's Lake Michigan shore. For trouters who will meticulously research opportunities, sensational fishing for big browns, even in shallow water by wading anglers, is available along the eastern Lake Michigan shoreline. Both fly fishing and spinning are productive.

In certain areas of coastal New England, brown trout have found their way into saltwater. When these fish, locally called "salters," return to the streams, they are silvery and unspotted except for a few X-marks. They are strong and excellent fish, and here and there anglers make a hobby of seeking them out.

Because the brown trout feeds a great deal on the surface, it has become popular with fly fishermen. Once hooked, it does not habitually leap, as does the rainbow, but it may leap on occasion. Indeed, in certain streams browns that have grown up in swift, shallow water leap as brilliantly as rainbows. Basically, however, the brown is a slashing, bulldog fighter. A heavy, stocky fish, it may run in size anywhere from a few inches to 30 pounds or more. In most good brown trout streams, fish of 2 to 5 pounds are considered excellent specimens. In lakes it may grow to 10 or 15, and in most streams there are a few tremendous brown trout—fish of 12 to 15 pounds (even in small streams)—whose existence few anglers even suspect.

This is because old, large brown trout feed much at night. The whole tribe are nocturnal feeders to a great degree, but large specimens often forsake daytime feeding almost entirely. The various methods used to catch other trout, and the various flies and lures, are all adapted to browns. But the dry-fly angler must understand that the brown often sucks down a surface insect very gently, leaving a boil but not showing its snout. Commonly very large browns begin suddenly taking tiny food, such as lesser winged ants, and it is impossible to tell by the size of the boil the proportions of the fish unless one is exceedingly expert at it.

The problem in dry flying for browns is that long, fine leaders must be used in most instances, and when a big brown takes, the angler is handicapped by his gossamer strand. A riffle on the surface will help, and indeed may sometimes be responsible for a limit of browns. They often surface feed during gentle rain showers, too, and at such times the dappled water surface helps to camouflage the leader. Browns will take bait and spinning lures just as will other trout. The main difference between fishing for mature brown trout and other trout is that while other trout may be difficult, browns are invariably more so.

Because of this, and the brown's nocturnal habits, dedicated brown trout anglers are generally nighttime fishermen, whenever that is legal. For some strange reason, large, wise old browns will strike lures with abandon at night that they would scoff at in daylight. Bass plugs, wobblers, huge streamers, large dry flies, and bass bugs all take browns at night.

This is tricky fishing. One must know the stream or lake well, and the most successful anglers listen first for their quarry. It is similar in some respects to hunting. One sits by a pool and locates a large brown that is feeding. Perhaps the angler may not even try him that night, but will come prepared the next evening. A position is taken where one may cast without fouling, even in darkness. The traditional method nowadays is to fish downstream, even with the large dry flies. The cast is made down and across, then the fly is slowly crept back over the pool surface, so it leaves a wake. The same procedure is followed with a large streamer or bucktail, or a plug.

Cast after cast is made. Often a large trout will not strike until scores of casts have been made. Then it will smash the lure. Playing a big one at night is a thrill like nothing else. Browns hooked at night have snapped 10-pound-test leaders in places where not even a 2-pound trout was suspected by daytime anglers.

When toward evening and at dusk a stream comes alive with browns taking small food, and they cannot be coaxed with imitations, if often works to use a large fly. An outsize White Miller, for example, cast time after time near rising trout, has on hundreds of occasions finally riled the fish enough to make them take.

In certain areas there are particular hatches on specific streams that send big brown trout into a frenzy of feeding. Many of these famous hatches (some are known as "caddis" hatches but are actually hatches of large mayflies) occur during June. In fact, June is a top month for brown trout fishing. Numerous anglers plan all year long to be sure to hit the proper stream at the proper time for one of these well-known hatches. At such times browns abandon wariness, and many are caught fairly easily, but invariably at dusk or after.

As a very general rule of thumb, brown trout are most likely to be found in places brook trout would favor. In fact, throughout the East the brown was stocked in many a stream from which the native brookie or speckled trout had vanished as civilization crowded it. And in such streams the astute angler will look for fish in lies fairly identical to those where brookies might be expected. In other words, the brown is not the trout of swift runs the rainbow likes. Conversely, of course, it must fit itself to available habitat. In many western waters browns do well in rough, swift water because they have no choice.

Fall is as good a time as spring to fish for browns. But because they are fall spawners many states close the season early enough to make sure spawn-heavy fish are not taken. Because it is a difficult fish, much misinformation has always been bandied about regarding browns. Numerous writers have claimed them as poor table fish. This is nonsense. There are brook trout and rainbow trout and all other kinds of fish not fit to eat, or mildly unpalatable, when taken from certain waters. Likewise for the brown. In most instances it is excellent.

Because it can tolerate a fair amount of pollution, and uncomfortably warm waters, the brown is in many ways a savior of trout fishing over vast areas. Because it is so wary, it faces fishing pressures confidently. Where it has been well established in western streams by stocking, seldom is restocking necessary. Many a frustrated angler has said grudgingly that "there will always be brown trout." If for no other reason, this imported species is an extremely important addition to our waters and our fishing future.

Brook Trout

Salvelinus fontinalis

Originally the brook trout was native only to the eastern third of the continent, from southern Canada, Minnesota, and Maine south to the mountain streams of Georgia. The Upper Peninsula of Michigan was its home, but contrary to what a great many modern anglers believe, the Lower Peninsula, where later the brookie became famous, was not, except possibly in a very few north-flowing streams that emptied into the Straits of Mackinac.

Because the brookie was an eastern species, it was the first of our trouts to receive the praise of anglers. Because it was always exceedingly willing, abundant, beautiful, and delicious, that praise was heaped upon it until the "speck" or speckled trout became our best-loved native species. To this day many an aged New Englander when he speaks of fish simply takes it for granted that the hearer will know he means the brook trout.

Unfortunately, the brook trout was not fitted by nature to withstand the pressures of civilization. It is a fish of

153

wild woodlands, where waters are extremely cold. As soon as the forests were cut, and pollution began, brook trout began to wane. In addition, they are far more gullible than other trout. Perhaps "vicious" is a better word, for the brookie is a savage feeder and possibly for that reason not very selective. Thus, it is taken with comparative ease. It is not a very prolific fish. Today brookies are gone from hundreds of streams where once they swarmed. Rainbows or browns have replaced them. In fact, over great sections of New England and the Great Lakes region good brook trout fishing has all but disappeared. Put and take stocking keeps brook trout in some waters. True native fish in most places are a rarity, and one of 10 inches a good one.

On the better side, there are still scores of lakes and streams in Maine, in Quebec, in Ontario where superb brook trout fishing can be had. And for many years the brookie has been stocked westward, where it has done well clear to the Pacific, especially in mountain lakes and streams. In the West and Northwest it grows more swiftly as a rule than in the East, particularly in waters where freshwater shrimp are abundant. Today almost every state where trout will live has at least some brook trout.

A few western lakes have sensational fishing for large brook trout. Overall, however, the brook trout has not been a popular or very successful western introduction. It seems to do best in small streams of the high-country West, and in the myriad beaver ponds along them. These streams and ponds do not draw many anglers, and the brook trout, which seldom attain large size in them, soon overpopulate. Most brookies high in the Rockies, on both slopes, average from 5 to 10 inches in length.

Arctic Char

In a number of states, this situation has led fisheries management people to set high limits on brook trout, hoping to appeal to fishermen who will utilize the resource. Limits as high as fifty per day have been offered, and in some instances a bonus limit of eight to ten brook trout may be taken in addition to a limit of other trout. Some regulations stipulate that the bonus brook trout limit must be of trout no more than 8 inches long, but the regular limit, which also can be of brook trout if one desires, may contain larger trout. The idea of course is to encourage catching overabundant small trout.

An interesting sidelight on this situation is the fact that in an age when catch-and-release is in vogue among trout fishermen, here are trout that should not be released, but utilized. Visiting anglers in the West, who like wild, uncrowded mountain waters, and love to eat trout, might focus on small-water brookies and glean both extra sport and delectable eating while assisting trout management. Curiously, New Mexico has recently had a similar bonus limit on brown trout, which many native anglers shun because they're more difficult to catch than rainbows.

In a few areas along the New England coast, and on

Blueback Trout

north as far as Labrador, brook trout go out into saltwater and return. These fish, called (like browns in the same region) salters, become extremely silvery and strong, and are generally of large size. A comparable fish is the coaster of the Great Lakes area, mainly of southern Lake Superior and northern Lake Huron. Coasters are large brook trout that live along the shores of the northern Great Lakes and around the islands offshore. These, too, are silvery, strong, and usually large. They are ordinarily taken by trolling.

In Maine, which furnishes some of the best brook trout fishing in the United States, the fish is known as "square-tail." The term usually refers to a large specimen. This brings up a matter that could prove most confusing to tyro anglers. Probably every fishing book, scientific and otherwise, has described the brook trout as differing from some of the other trouts by having a tail squared, not forked or indented, along the rear edge. The plain truth is, thousands of young brook trout have a rather deep indentation here, and some good-sized brookies have at least a suggestion of it. Large old brook trout usually have square tails.

Sunapee Trout

Brook trout are dark on the back, with vermicular markings. The sides typically are spotted with bright red dots each surrounded by a halo of pale blue. In some strains, especially hatchery strains, the spots may be few, or many, yellow, or totally lacking. The leading edge of the lower fins and the lower edge of the tail have a white border backed by black, and then generally with a touch of orange or yellow. The belly in male brook trout previous to and during spawning time (they are fall spawners) is either tinged with red or yellow, or else it is gaudy crimson.

As has been noted in the chapter on rainbow trout, the brook trout is actually a char. There are several other closely related species. The most important, the **Arctic char,** or Arctic trout—sometimes called alpine trout—*Salvelinus alpinus,* has a solid-colored dark back, pinkish spots on the sides, and a forked tail. Males are dazzling in summer and fall, flaming red below. This fish grows very large, well past 20 pounds. It is a resident of the Far North, from Labrador to the Hudson Bay area to Alaska.

It is a fish of great importance in some portions of its

Quebec Red Trout

range to Eskimos, as food both for humans and dogs. Although it is outside the range of the majority of U.S. anglers, opening up of fly-fishing camps in Arctic char country has in recent seasons acquainted many fishermen with it. In certain places, such as stretches of the Tree River, authorities are already disturbed about fishing pressure. This large and stunningly handsome fish will undoubtedly be more and more popular as new areas are opened where it is abundant. But regulations will become more and more restrictive, to keep it from declining.

The **blueback trout,** *Salvelinus oquassa,* is a slender species that appears to be a more southerly delegate from the Arctic char range. The back is bluish and without the wormlike markings of the typical brook trout. The belly, as in the brookie, becomes red during spawning. It is a rather small species, known chiefly from the Rangeley Lake area of Maine. Many years ago this char was common and a favorite food source for settlers. Now it is difficult to find.

The **Sunapee trout,** *Salvelinus aureolus,* is another

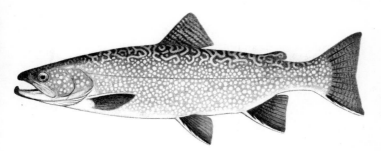

Splake

relative of the Arctic char that lives within our borders. Originally it was known only from a few lakes in Maine, New Hampshire, and Vermont. It was stocked in other New England waters, but has seldom proved successful. Sunapee Lake, New Hampshire, was its most famous home, with Sunapee golden trout, as they were commonly called, running as large as 10 or 12 pounds. This is a trout of deep water, rather similar in habits to the lake trout. In fact, hybrids with lake trout have been known. And the lake trout so thoroughly took over Sunapee Lake and other waters where the Sunapee trout lived that they were all but wiped out.

Efforts to save the species from extinction have been successful so far, with a hatchery established purposely to propagate it and at least one carefully managed colony of Sunapee goldens currently established at Tewksbury Pond, near Grafton, not far from Sunapee Lake. A few other small populations of these trout remain obscurely in Maine, but their position is precarious. However, carefully controlled fishing for the managed population does allow enthusiasts at least acquaintance with this handsome fish.

The usual method of fishing for this trout is trolling. Sunapee trout live anywhere from 25 to 100 feet down. Jigging on or near bottom also is productive. So is still-fishing deep with minnows.

The Sunapee trout is a beautiful char. It should by no means be confused with the golden trout of the high-country West (*see* material on this species under RAINBOW TROUT). The Sunapee golden has a dark back but without the markings common to brook trout. The sides are spotted, but the color differs widely from specimen to specimen. Some have pinkish-white spots, others yellow or red. Previous to and during spawning, the sides of the belly are golden or orange. Lower fins as in the brookie have a white leading edge, and generally these fins are colorful yellowish to deep orange.

The **Quebec red,** or red trout, *Salvelinus marstoni*, is a char restricted in range to a few lakes, and the streams emptying into them, in Quebec. It is less bulky than the brook trout, longer, more slender, and with a definitely forked tail. The spawning males have crimson bellies, from which the name is taken. While the brook trout seldom leaps when hooked, the Quebec red is often a leaper much like the rainbow.

The **Aurora trout,** *Salvelinus timagamiensis*, is still another form of char. It has so far been found only in a couple of lakes of northeastern Ontario. However, it is known well enough to be mentioned prominently in the Ontario fishing laws. It is a char of moderate size, similar in some respects to the brookie, but lacking the red spots on the sides.

Other species, as has been noted in the chapter on rainbow trout, have been named here and there. It may be doubtful, however, that they or even several of the ones mentioned here, should be given full species status. Quite possibly some of these fish are merely races of the brook trout or Arctic char that became isolated many thousands of years ago.

A fish that has reached a place of importance within the past few seasons, and which may become far more famous in the future, is the so-called **splake.** Hatcheries discovered long ago that the lake trout and the brook trout hybridized. From such crosses the "speckled trout-lake trout" mixture materialized into the splake. This hybrid has been much tried in the wild lately, is proving hardy and an extremely good sport fish. It has been stocked rather widely in Canada and in a few areas in the United States.

Brook trout are generally found in the quieter portions of their habitat: under cutbanks, in deep holes, under a log or log jam, in tangled brush, near a protective rock. Because they require colder water than other trout, small creeks and spring-fed tributaries harbor many brookies. Such fish are usually small, from 5 to 8 inches. A few larger trout may be found in holes. In the larger streams, brook trout will seek the same type of cover, but may be much larger, to 10 to 15 inches. Even in many a virgin Canadian lake, however, brook trout of a foot are the rule. They grow larger, of course. The large lakes of Maine, and such lakes as the famed Nipigon in Ontario, certain western U.S. and north-Canadian waters furnish brookies of 4 to 5 pounds with fair regularity, and fish on up to 6, 8, and more on occasion. Wherever they are found, brook trout are cover fish, fish of the slower currents, invariably found in shady, secluded places.

Fishing methods do not differ greatly from those used for any trout. On the whole, brook trout feed very little at night after full dark, and they feed on bottom more than some of the others. Smaller brook trout take dry flies avidly, and all of them feed on the surface to a great extent for several weeks in early summer or late spring, when surface temperatures are cool. June is an excellent dry-fly month. Afterward, in lakes, they move into deep water and are caught by trolling, stillfishing, or casting deep-running metal lures. Spinner and worm makes a good rig in any water. Ordinarily slow trolling does best, or, in a stream letting the spinning rig waft down into a deep hole or beneath a log.

Minnow fishing for large brook trout is deadly, and a method rather generally overlooked. Live minnows let down into holes work wonders. Leeches are another much overlooked (and very tough and lasting) bait. So are small crawfish or their tails.

The wet fly and the streamer and bucktail have long been recognized as among the best lures for brookies. The so-called "squirrel-tail" is very effective, fished just under the surface, or half-sunk, leaving a wake. Much has been made in popular writing over the fact that brook trout allegedly like gaudy, bright-colored flies better than do other trout, and better than they like drab flies. This is nonsense. Brook trout are simply less selective. When they take bright flies they will also take drab ones. They are just hungry.

Large brook trout are very commonly susceptible to trolled or cast spoons and any of the family of flasher-type lures. Colors may be bronze or silver, or red and white, or frog finish. Fished deep, and slowly, sometimes these artificials are most successful. In New England trolling in the big lakes with large streamers or wet flies accounts for many large brook trout.

Very rarely does a brook trout leap when on the hook. But it is a rugged, dogged fighter, and will try every way possible to snag the leader on brush or logs and break it. It will be a sad day for sport fishing in the United States if the native brookie ever passes completely from the scene in the face of the push of civilization. Future anglers should learn to respect this beautiful species and the wealth of fishing history behind it, and to conserve it carefully so that it may be here in its wild state for many generations to come.

Dolly Varden Trout

Salvelinus malma

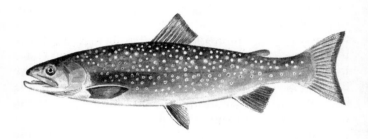

This beautifully marked trout of the char group (*see* BROOK TROUT) was allegedly named for a Dickens character, or her dress, many years ago. It is sometimes spoken of as the western form of the brook trout. That is hardly true. The Dolly Varden is the most abundant western, or west slope, representative of the chars, and the brook trout likewise for the East.

This species has been variously called western char, bull trout, salmon trout, red-spotted trout, and Dolly. It has not always, in all places, been admired. In fact, in Alaska where it is the most abundant of the trouts there was for some time a bounty on it because the Dolly Varden was supposedly so destructive of salmon spawn and young. The bounty did little good, but it does indicate the low rating the fish had. Even today in many parts of the West this trout for some reason is not very popular. Possibly this is because it is not as strong a fighter as the other native species, the rainbow and cutthroat.

Dolly Varden range is from Oregon to Alaska, and in

portions of Idaho and Montana. British Columbia has this trout in abundance and here there seems not always to be the stigma that is sometimes found elsewhere.

The color differs somewhat from the brook trout, with which it might possibly be confused in western areas where the eastern brook trout has been introduced. The back of the brook trout is marbled in pattern, that of the Dolly Varden rather plain, or at best only mottled. The Dolly often has light spots along the upper sides and back, and it is generally more slender than a typical brook trout. The red or yellow side spots are in evidence, however, and so are the white-bordered lower fins typical of the chars. Where possible it runs out into saltwater, and becomes very silvery in color. There appear also to be many subspecies, or perhaps only races, of the Dolly Varden, differing slightly in color. This is especially true in the Far North, where forms of the Arctic char and Dolly Varden are difficult to separate.

Although there are waters where the Dolly Varden grows only to the modest size of 8 to 18 inches, this trout is more likely to be a large one. Specimens from 3 to 10 pounds are not uncommon, and those of 20 are far from rare. In lakes, where the Dolly is perhaps more at home than in streams it grows large and fat. It is extremely voracious, feeding with abandon on the young and the spawn of its close relatives if these happen to be handy.

It is a fall spawner, like the brook trout. In some places the fish run out of lakes into tributary streams as early as June and July, staying in the streams through until spawning. On streams where such runs occur there is especially good summer fishing because of the concentration of the trout.

The Dolly Varden is not a high-quality fly fisherman's fish. The smaller ones, particularly those living in streams, and especially those in small headwaters where habitat dictates that they feed to an appreciable degree on insects, take flies readily. In some cases larger fish may be taken on streamers. By and large, however, the Dolly Varden is likely to be a bottom feeder more like its relative the lake trout, most gullible in the presence of stillfished bait, or a trolled bait or spinner, or spinner and bait combination, or metal lures of the wobbler and flasher class. There are no special methods applicable only to the Dolly Varden. In most instances lures fished for other trout will take this species in the same waters. Rainbow and cutthroat anglers often catch Dollys.

When they occur in streams, they are likely to be lying in positions similar to those selected by brook trout: near logs, rocks, and such cover, or on the bottoms of the deep holes. Lake fish will skulk along low reefs and the drop-offs. Predominantly the species will be low in the water rather than on the surface.

Although the Dolly Varden has been discriminated against to a surprising degree over much of its home range, there is utterly no legitimate reason for this. On the other side of the picture, there are numerous anglers scattered throughout Dolly Varden range who are avid "bull trout" fishermen, as they call themselves. They select a deep hole with a swift run above it on a stream such as Montana's Flathead, use a large red-and-white spoon or a gaudy, specially designed plug, make hundreds of casts and finally hang a large bull. Most of this fishing takes place during the summer run. The big bull trout apparently feed little during this run, but for some reason will whimsically smash a lure. Often the lure may pass a trout time after time and be ignored. Then on the next cast the strike will come.

In certain portions of Dolly Varden range, native fishermen shoot ground squirrels, which they locally call "gophers," and use the skinned legs for bait, drifting this odd bait into deep holes beneath logs or rocks in a large stream. This appears to substantiate the claim that the Dolly Varden will "eat anything." However, numerous other species might do likewise, if the same items were tried on them. A large Dolly Varden is a tough battler, staying deep and stubbornly balking until completely worn down.

This trout has been cast also as a poor table fish. Nothing could be farther from truth. Its flesh may be white, or pink, or red-orange. Large fish, steaked and broiled, are difficult to distinguish in taste from salmon. The Dolly Varden's reputation as a spawn eater evolved from the fact that it interfered to some extent with commercial salmon fishing while not bringing a price like salmon. Other trout are equally as avid eaters of spawn. The Dolly Varden's poor reputation as a sport fish undoubtedly grew from the fact that it lived in rainbow territory, but did not leap and fight as flashy a battle. Unjust reputations once acquired have a way of clinging. Those pinned on the Dolly Varden are outmoded and should be dropped.

Lake Trout

Salvelinus namaycush

The lake trout is the largest of our trouts. Some scientists have listed it in a different genus, *Cristivomer*. It was long an important commercial species in the Great Lakes, mainly Michigan and Superior. It is also commercially important in some of the largest Canadian lakes. It drastically declined in its former Great Lakes waters because of inroads by the sea lamprey. Now the lamprey appears controlled, and the lake trout reestablished. Although the lake trout is a most delectable species on the table, it has never rated especially high as a game fish. This is not so much that it lacks fighting ability, but because of its favorite habitat, which is ordinarily in very deep water.

Lake trout are fish of large, cold lakes of the North, clear lakes where waters are deep and the shores are of rock and gravel. They are colloquially known by a variety of names: in New England "togue"; in a few areas, "landlocked salmon," an extremely poor name because of confusion with the landlocked form of the Atlantic salmon;

as "gray trout" and "salmon trout" in various parts of Canada; as "Mackinaw," "Great Lakes," and "forktail" trout in the upper Great Lakes region. The color of this trout is a fairly uniform dark gray with pale irregular spots all over the body and head. The flesh in some specimens is white, in others distinctly pink, and in still others varying shades of yellow. This has led some anglers to use different names for the same fish.

The range of this trout is throughout northern North America. But its distribution is regionally spotty, some areas having many lakes with trout in them, while others have none. The size of the lake, its depth, and the quality of water appear to make a very decided difference in the size of the fish. Probably this is influenced by feeding possibilities for the trout. In some lakes the lake trout seldom exceed 3 to 5 pounds, in others they go to a maximum of 15 or 20. In Lake Superior lake trout up to 100 pounds have been netted. Specimens of 50 and 60 pounds have been taken by hook and line in several Canadian lakes. Seldom does this fish do really well in lakes having depths of less than 100 feet, and never is it successful in waters where the temperature rises in the depths past 65 degrees F. A temperature of 45 is roughly the favorite of this species.

New England, the Finger Lakes area in New York State, numerous lakes all over Ontario, and parts of Eastern Canada, others on across the northern Prairie Provinces and on to Alaska, a number of Washington and Oregon Lakes—these are the principal lake trout waters. There are also some in Michigan, Wisconsin, Minnesota, Wyoming, Montana, and several other states. Undoubtedly the most popular areas currently are Ontario, Manitoba, and Saskatchewan. Thousands of sportsmen make annual trips to these areas nowadays specifically for large lake trout.

In almost all lake trout waters these fish feed upon smaller fishes such as smelt and ciscoes. This of course gives the cue to baits and lures. However, lake trout are not too particular, and are in the scavenger class to some extent. They will take cut fish and sometimes even partially decomposed fish as well as live ones. They have been caught on bacon rind and all sorts of offtrail baits. However, live or frozen smelts (*and minnows*), or cut bait, are standard in most areas. Lures are usually selected from the family of metal spoons and wobblers. A medium-sized spinner with a hunk of sucker meat hung on the treble hooks works well.

The most common method of taking lake trout is by deep trolling, accomplished in years past chiefly by use of metal line and a stiff rod, now widely replaced by employing the modern downrigger. A saltwater boat rod and reel or saltwater spinning rod is the outfit popularly chosen. During the summer, trolling is done at depths up to 100 feet or more. A large wobbling spoon or a minnow is the lure. When trolling with smelt or minnows the tyro should pay close attention to how the native or experienced lake trout angler puts them on the hook. One excellent method involves a rig with a pin that holds the bait straight and firmly in position. In many areas where this fishing is popular these hooks and pins can be purchased in tackle shops or at fishing camps. Unless the bait is properly held, the fish sometimes refuse to strike. In Canada it is most helpful to hire a guide who knows the water and methods well.

The only drawback to metal-line fishing in deep water for lake trout is that the fish cannot fight too well at such depths, especially having to drag so much heavy line. Downrigger trolling, with its line-release device, cures that problem. A great many lake trout are caught by still-fishermen. In the eastern United States and Canada baiting of holes has been popular, where legal, for years. More and more restrictions against it occur presently. Cut or chopped fish is used, and the baited hook is dangled on or near bottom, sometimes 100 feet down, where the fish have congregated.

Happily for the angler who wants his sport more active, there are two periods of the year when the lake trout becomes quite a different fish. The first occurs just after the ice breaks up in spring. The time will differ in different latitudes, and even in different lakes close together, because of variations in water temperatures due to depth. But in general it will be from about mid-May to mid-June. During this time—sometimes, or in some lakes, for only a few days to two weeks—the lake trout will be on or very near the surface, inshore around the rocks, or out over shallow rocky reefs.

Because they are near surface, a hooked fish will now fight a totally different battle, and cannot be inhibited by pressure changes due to being hauled up from the depths. Some lakers will even leap at this time. They are hungry now and will hit almost anything, from cut bait or live minnows on bottom in 10 or 15 feet of water to cast spoons and plugs running only a few feet under, and even to streamer flies and bucktails fished with a fly rod.

In certain lakes of the Far North, because water temperatures in the shallows never get much above that most desired by lake trout, it has been discovered that trout can be caught by spincasting and other shallow-water methods all summer. More and more such lakes are discovered as the Far North is opened to fly-in fishing. Numerous lakes in northern Canada now offer this fishing.

However, the other regular period in waters farther south when lake trout can be taken inshore occurs in fall. The fish spawn in most waters just about the time the ice closes in, which on the average will be about November. Prior to this they will have begun coming into shallow water. Some may spawn deep, even at 100 feet. But in many a lake the fish will be available about October on or near the surface.

Both the spring and fall periods are exceedingly tricky to hit. The best way is to have some local person notify the angler when to make a dash to the chosen fishing ground. A number of fishing camps in Ontario and elsewhere advertise surface fishing for lake trout. By writing such a place one can get a very good idea of dates most likely to be peak times, and reserve accordingly.

Light tackle makes for great sport with these surface fish. It should not be too light. It should be matched to the average size of fish taken from the particular body of water. On the average, a bass or salmon-weight fly rod, a medium-action spinning rod or a light saltwater spinning rod, a moderate-action plug rod will all suffice. There are no complicated fishing techniques. If the fish are there they will not be especially selective or wary.

Lake trout are popular with ice fishermen, too. They are likely to stay very deep. Whitefish fishermen often catch both whitefish and lake trout. (*See* WHITEFISH for ice fishing methods described there.) Live smelt are a top bait for winter lake trout fishing. One must first locate the deep holes where lake trout congregate. Good oxygen conditions are likely to dictate these spots, and trial and error, plus a contour map of the lake bottom, are the tools the angler uses. A live minnow 6 inches or more in length allowed to swim around just off bottom is a killing bait. A threeway swivel with the sinker on bottom and the bait on a dropper makes a good rig.

Jigging for lake trout is also very successful. This is actually the identical method to that used for taking yellow perch and walleyes in winter by the so-called "Russian hook." A fluttering spoon is let down on bottom and then lifted with quick jerks 6 inches to a foot or more, and allowed to settle back. Motion is varied so it settles fast, or slow. It attracts the fish, which strikes at it. Practice allows the angler to strike his fish on the upsweep, the easiest way to hook them.

The lake trout has been undersold as a sporting species by many an angler who has never had one on light tackle in shallow water. As more and more anglers have tried this fishing, the lake trout has gained stature. It will undoubtedly gain more.

Grayling

Thymallus arcticus

The grayling, once abundant in several areas of the United States, chiefly Michigan and Montana, is today totally extinct in the former and only modestly available in the latter. Only a comparative few of today's fishermen have ever caught, or seen, a grayling. Yet an aura of romance seems to surround this handsome fish.

This is not to say that grayling are rare. Happily, they are still abundant in numerous north-Canadian waters, from northern Saskatchewan on westward and north throughout the Northwest Territory. They are also common in certain waters of Alaska. The American Fisheries Society now considers the Arctic and Montana fish as one species.

One reason for the grayling's romantic appeal is that today, for the best of this fishing, one must travel by plane or packhorse, or backpack, into remote regions. Also contributing are the eye-popping beauty of the grayling, and the fact that it is a fly fisherman's dream.

Grayling are closely allied to the trouts and the whitefishes. Originally there were three species, or at least races or subspecies—the extinct Michigan grayling, the Montana grayling (*Thymallus signifer tricolor*, in some references *Thymallus montanus*), and the Arctic grayling. In the 1800s, streams such as Michigan's Manistee were so filled with grayling that anglers able to make the then grueling trip into the frontier forest country commonly caught three at a time on a cast of three flies. Cutting of the forests, log jams that decimated spawning areas, the stocking of trout, and other influences swiftly destroyed the Michigan grayling. The last native fish were collected in a desperate attempt at saving the race by an expedition to the Otter River of the Upper Peninsula in 1932. Later, stocking of fish from Montana was tried a number of times with no marked success.

The Montana grayling was thought until recently to be going the way of the Michigan grayling. But today there is substantial hope for its continued existence. It has been able to survive natively and by stocking in numerous small lakes in the general Wyoming-Montana area, and it has been stocked in Arizona, Colorado, Utah, Washington, Idaho, California, and Oregon. In the high and isolated timberline lakes and streams, the grayling does well—but often too well. It overpopulates and becomes stunted, because so few fishermen fish for it. Many do not recognize it, and most go for trout in the same lakes, which are generally fewer and larger.

However, good grayling fishing for fair-sized specimens of this Montana fish still exist in a number of waters, for example Montana's Big Hole River, with few anglers aware of it. There are small lakes, too, where grayling of maximum size—about 1 1/2 to 2 pounds for the

Montana variety—still can be found. Fisheries departments in each of the Rockies states can furnish detailed
information to anglers seeking a grayling experience regarding location of waters that contain them. Much im-
proper information has been disseminated about this
fish. It is not actually on the verge of extinction. It has
simply failed to gather popularity among modern fishermen because they do not know it well enough. It has
never been abundant while this generation of anglers
was forming.

Another drawback has been the fact that usually where
it is found it is small. And another disadvantage has been
the impossibility in past years of raising grayling in hatcheries. That last problem has now been solved, and there
is no reason why, with proper management, grayling fishing in the United States should not become something
for all interested anglers to experience. The range is certain to be small, but the fish population under enlightened management can be worthwhile, if the will and the
demand are evident.

Those who may wish to enjoy grayling fishing as it
once was in parts of the country must now journey to
the Far North for the locally abundant Arctic species.
This fish averages from 1 to 4 pounds, is dark blue to
gray on the back, with overtones of shining bronze. The
sides are purplish-gray and bear a few dark spots forward. The scales are quite large, the mouth small and
without strong teeth. The high, broad dorsal fin is the
striking identification tag, as in all grayling. It is usually
gray to purplish, with row after row of blue dots, sometimes individually circled in red, and with the edge of
the fin often scalloped in red. All of these colors are set

off well in the grayling's habitat, which is the fastest, clearest, coldest water. It will not tolerate pollution or stagnation. As mentioned, it does occur in some crystal-pure lakes.

It is interesting to note that the scientific name *Thymallus* refers to wild thyme. When freshly taken from the water, the smell of a grayling is reminiscent of this pleasant odor. The species name used in older references, *signifer*, or "bearer of the standard," refers to the beautiful dorsal fin.

Food of the grayling, as the small mouth, weak teeth, and cold-water habitat suggest, is made up almost entirely of small insects and aquatic larvae. The fish are found over gravel, rock, or sand bottoms, and of course get many nymphs in such places, or catch them as they drift into the deeper pools where most of the fish congregate.

Grayling have a habit of occasionally taking a dry fly by leaping out of the water and seizing it on the way down. Once hooked, they usually streak off on a run, then make a few shallow surface leaps, finally go down and circle or run again. Then as suddenly as the struggle began, it is over. In all fairness, a grayling is mildly disappointing as a fighter, when compared to the trouts. It has so many other exciting attributes, however, that the lack of determined spirit when hooked is not important. One fine quality is that a grayling often will continue to strike at a fly after the angler has missed it several times. Another is that the fish has a most delicious flavor.

The grayling will occasionally hit small spoons and plugs and it will take bait, such as salmon eggs. But there is no reason to fish it with anything except flies. Wet or dry flies may be used, usually small, from No. 10 to No. 14, even sometimes down to No. 16 or smaller.

Standard trout fishing tackle is used. Fine leaders, though not always necessary, are a help in the clear waters inhabited by most grayling. Sometimes these fish can be as exasperating and selective as trout, but usually they are easy to induce. The swirl made by a grayling is very dainty and light, except during periods when they are wildly on the feed. When they are sucking down a dry fly quietly they are difficult to hook. They are likely to expel the fly before the angler knows they've taken it.

Since food in Arctic grayling waters is limited, and small, while the fish are very active, they need to keep feeding almost around the clock in order to make a living. This is a great help to a fisherman. Most of the time he can fish at any hour and still have action. In instances where the fish aren't rising, or refuse the surface fly, small nymphs allowed to tumble loosely through the pools will usually catch fish.

When a grayling is taken from a certain lake or stream, the angler knows what size all the rest of them are likely to be. In any given location, fish caught seem to run almost identical in size. When they are small, and a selection of grayling waters is available, an angler who wants larger fish should move on to try another. This beautiful fish is one with which every fly fisherman especially should have experience at least once. The memory of the action, and the taste of the fish, which should be cooked immediately since they do not keep well, will be difficult to forget.

Rocky Mountain Whitefish

Prosopium williamsoni

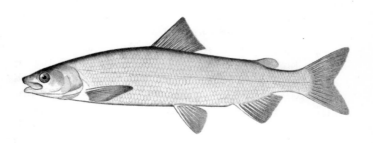

Unfortunately, the majority of anglers are unfamiliar with the Rocky Mountain (or Montana) whitefish, and even in the rather restricted waters where it is abundant many trout fishermen scorn it out of ignorance of its sporting and eating qualities. This is the only whitefish native to swift, high waters. It lives in the cold, fast streams and the clear, deep lakes of the mountain West, from Colorado, Wyoming, Utah, Montana, Idaho, to Oregon, Washington, and British Columbia.

This fish feeds much like a trout, and is similarly shaped, but rounder and with a sharper nose. Unlike the trouts, it is prominently scaled. Because it has a modestly high dorsal fin it is occasionally confused with the grayling. It has a small, toothless mouth, the adipose fin of the trout tribe, and is olive on the back and pearly silvery to golden down the sides. The average size is 11 to 14 inches, and a pound in weight, with exceptional specimens going to 20-odd inches and 4 pounds.

When surface feeding in summer, the Rocky Mountain whitefish barely dimples the surface. Its food is almost entirely insect, year-round. It is extremely selective. Small dry flies of No. 16 up to as large as No. 12, in patterns to match whatever insects are present on the surface, are usually successful, but must be fished daintily. Rises begin to show most often toward evening, just as in trout fishing. From then on until dark fishing is at its best.

When hooked there is no leap, as with the trout commonly found in the same waters. The whitefish may roll on the surface, but most of the battle is a dogged underwater fight, and a very substantial one. But because this species exists in waters most famous for trout, which have long held the spotlight, it has had little attention and publicity. It should get more.

As a matter of fact, it does get quite a lot of local attention in winter, when trout fishing is either closed or slack. After fall spawning these whitefish gather in groups in the deeper pools of streams. In these holes and deep runs, sometimes in very large schools, the fish remain until ice-out. But they continue feeding as actively as in summer. They are predominantly bottom feeders, and now their food is essentially nymphs.

The accepted tackle for this fishing is a long cane pole. It allows an angler to reach over the edge of thin ice, and to swing the fish back onto safe ice. The line (with leader) is measured so it will match the length of the pole (up to 15 feet), and the short leader is light nylon. A hook no larger than No. 12 is attached. Sometimes several hooks are used. A fairly heavy sinker is necessary, and a bobber. The bobber is placed to keep the bait, a stonefly nymph, just off bottom and still allow it to drift through a pool. The angler swings out his rig at the head of the pool. The sinker plunges the bait deep, where the fish lie. The fisherman follows the drift of his bait. When the bobber plunges, he raises his fish.

Generally the stonefly nymphs have to be gathered by the angler from beneath stones in riffles. Some anglers work in pairs, one holding a minnow seine in the current, the other kicking loose stones beneath which the nymphs hide. They float free, and being unable to swim, get caught in the net. Some winter anglers have found that when fishing is slow they can arouse whitefish schools lying inactive on pool bottoms by going upstream, wading into the riffle, and kicking over rocks and muddying the current. Nymphs float down the roiled current, the fish begin to take them, then the bait is floated through. Other baits such as maggots work fairly well, but nymphs seem by all odds to be best.

When spring comes, the whitefish in streams (which is the most sporting place to catch them) move back to riffles again. Some are then taken on bait tumbled along bottom. Later they begin rising for insects, and this is probably the most difficult fishing. Some experienced anglers think consistent taking of Rocky Mountain whitefish, which seldom move from their feeding position to take a fly nor often come back after a missed strike, is far more difficult even than taking brown trout.

There are many good waters in the areas mentioned. A few good examples are the Snake, Green, and Wind rivers in Wyoming, portions of the Madison and the Gallatin, the Bitterroot and Flathead in Montana, the Payette and Snake in Idaho, and Oregon's Deschutes. Often a stretch of stream containing mountain whitefish will have them in extreme abundance. Sometimes when a good hatch is on literally hundreds can be seen rising.

These fish are excellent fare when smoked. They are also delicious when boned and fried. This is done by slitting along the ribs with a thin fillet knife, then working the entire skeleton free and stripping it out.

Mountain whitefish do not appear to decline in the face of either fishing pressure or changes in their home waters, as do the trouts and the grayling. They are a great potential for excellent sport and deserve the attention of all fishermen who live or visit in their range.

Whitefish (Lake, or Common)

Coregonus clupeaformis

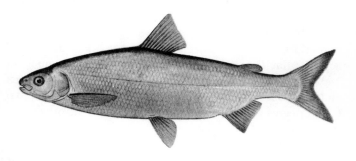

The whitefishes have long been known as extremely delectable commercial fish, but have never made themselves very substantial names as sport species. They inhabit a scattering of large, deep, clear, cold lakes from New England throughout the Great Lakes area, and north into Canada. They are probably most abundant in the Great Lakes themselves. Much of the time they stay in deep water, anywhere from 60 to 100 feet, and in Lake Superior, for example, they may hang out near bottom at several hundred feet down. Thus, they are not very accessible to the average angler.

In addition, they are weak biters and have tender mouths. These attributes, especially at great depths, make them hard to hook and to land. Fishing for whitefish has therefore always been a specialist's game. At rare times and places, however, whitefish may be taken on surface flies, or in shallow water on bait, and at such times and places they are very good sport, indeed.

Like the ciscoes, their close relatives, they are related

183

to the trouts. They have the fleshy adipose fin of the trouts and salmons, but unlike these small-scaled fishes, whitefishes have rather large scales weakly attached. There is a great deal of confusion about identification of the whitefish tribe. Numerous subspecies have been named from time to time. Most of these are named from a particular lake, and it is probable that in almost all instances they are not deserving of species or subspecies status. Probably they are only isolated races of the two type species, even though some, through hundreds of years of isolation, may have evolved minor specific characteristics.

The whitefishes are also commonly confused with their close relatives the ciscoes. The easiest ways for the layman to distinguish between the two groups with fair accuracy are as follows. Whitefish are pronouncedly ovate in cross section, much more so than are ciscoes or "lake herring." They are "heavy in the shoulders," too, large specimens appearing almost humpbacked. The whitefish has a projecting snout, so that the mouth opening appears, as ichthyologists say, to be very nearly "subterminal," while in most ciscoes the lower jaw projects well beyond the upper. Most ciscoes are bluish or greenish on the back. Whitefishes are silvery fish with bronze-shaded backs.

Discounting all the questionable subspecies, there are two well-known whitefishes: the common, Great Lakes, or Labrador whitefish; the **Menominee,** or round whitefish, occasionally called pilotfish. Of these, the Menominee frequents the shallower water and may quite regularly be taken near shore. Its scientific name: *Prosopium cylindraceum.*

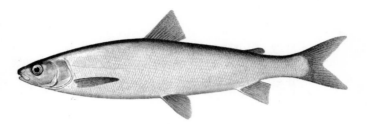

Menominee

There could be more sport fishing for whitefish if anglers would first ascertain which specific waters near them contain these fish, then go to the trouble to learn from natives of the area just how and where in those waters to turn the trick. For example, in Lake Medora, a beautiful cold lake far up on the Keweenaw Peninsula of northern Michigan, there is a whitefish called the Medora whitefish. During the mayfly season, about June, these fish feed on the surface and can be caught on dry flies. They are excellent fighters and leapers. One must be there at precisely the right time, or miss the fun for another year. There are many other lakes where a similar phenomenon takes place each year, but most of this fishing is still to be pioneered, even in our days of high-pressure fishing.

In Ontario there are certain streams flowing into the Great Lakes, and into other large Canadian lakes, up which whitefish move during spring and early summer. This is not a spawning run. Whitefish are fall spawners. Some few years ago, on one Canadian stream a waterfall used to stop the upstream migration and one could take large whitefish about June on dry flies. Dams have now ruined that spot.

Along the Lake Superior shore are numerous streams around whose mouths whitefish, especially the smaller Menominees (which average 1 to 4 pounds as against anything up to 20 for the common whitefish), congregate about May and again about September or October. At the mouth of the Two-Hearted River, for example, in Upper Peninsula Michigan north of Newberry, these whitefish have for years been caught by bait fishermen who cast out with small sinker, small hook, and small piece of worm. The bait is allowed to lie on bottom. At times the fishing is extremely fast. The fish must be handled gingerly because of their weak, toothless, tender mouths.

Such are examples of possibilities with whitefish. Some are caught by summer stillfishermen, in Minnesota, Wisconsin, New York, New England, and Canada. Finding the proper spot is, for a beginner, strictly hit and miss. It will be in deep water, certainly. Most anglers chop up fish, or use dough balls, or some such bait, and bait a place on bottom to attract the fish. Various ingenious devices are used for getting the bait down, such as the "baiting cone" popular in places in New England. This is a metal cylinder with a trip-catch bottom and holes in the sides. It is filled with the chum and let down, then a jerk on the line unlatches the bottom and spills out the bait. Sometimes the fishing is not done until the next day or night. Whitefish often bite well at night.

Actually there is probably more fishing for whitefish through the ice than by any other method. Holes are baited—if baiting is legal in the state—and white grubs, small minnows, or cut fish used to bait the hook. Most anglers expert at this specialized game prefer a hook with a broad bend and plenty of flange. These seem to hook the delicately nibbling fish better. The bait is dangled right on bottom or barely above.

It takes practice to know when to set the hook. Nibbles and the real take are almost identical. Even a large whitefish of 10 or more pounds still barely nibbles the bait. One good method used by eastern whitefish experts is a narrow, thin piece of spring steel attached to the shanty side above the fishing hole, or to the side of the boat in summer. The line is affixed to that. No bobber is used. The slightest nibble will register on the limber steel, and the fisherman then sets the hook.

On the whole, whitefish seem nowhere to be as plentiful as they once were. They are wonderful eating, especially when broiled or smoked. And serious anglers who will bother to pioneer new whitefishing grounds, particularly far north, will be well rewarded in sport, especially at those times when these fish come up out of the depths to feed on the surface or in the shallows. As more and more fishing camps open in the North, anglers are discovering a number of places where water temperature around the year is such that whitefish can be taken on or near surface much of the season. Visitors will be well advised to try this fishing wherever it is available.

Cisco
Coregonus artedii

Many people in the Great Lakes Region, where the cisco
is most plentiful, don't know what it is, even though they
may have been eating it for years. This is because they
have always known it by the wrong name, calling it "herring," or "lake herring." The cisco is not a herring, nor
does it belong to the herring family. The herrings are
almost entirely saltwater fishes belonging to the family
Clupeidae, which includes the shads. The cisco belongs
to the whitefish family, Coregonidae, a group of freshwater fishes.

One of the quickest and easiest ways to distinguish
between these two families is that ciscoes and whitefishes, silvery fishes that look, superficially at least, quite
a bit like the herrings, all have an adipose fin—that small
fleshy appendage on the back near the tail—and true
herrings and shads do not. This adipose fin tends to
prove that ciscoes and whitefish are closely related to
the trouts and salmons, which also have it.

There are a number of ciscoes—the common, or lake,
cisco (or "herring"), the bluefin, the Lake Erie cisco, the

Tullibee, the shortjaw chub, the Great Lakes bloater, and many others. Thirty-odd species and subspecies are known in Michigan alone, most of them native to only a single lake or chain of lakes. All look and act much alike. Some may be hybrids, or merely races. The family is confusing to professional ichthyologists, and all species and subspecies have so far not been entirely confirmed. The American Fisheries Society, in fact, recognizes less than a dozen.

Ciscoes are fish of large, usually deep, clear lakes where the water is cold. They are scattered over portions of New England and New York State and into Canada, their center of concentration being throughout the Great Lakes, and on west and north into Saskatchewan. The small species weigh only a few ounces, while the common ciscoe averages perhaps a pound, with large specimens going to 2 pounds or more.

A few ciscoes are caught by ice fishermen, usually in deep water, and on small pieces of cut fish or tiny minnows. This sport is very scattered and unreliable, however. A few are caught on hook and line by stillfishermen, usually when these anglers are after other species in waters where ciscoes may live. But the main reason for including the cisco here as a sport fish is that under proper and very specific conditions, the cisco is a fly-taking customer that ranks among the most dynamic and amazing of all come-lately species in the sport angler's world.

Ever since the country was young, the cisco has been a very important food fish throughout the Great Lakes Region. For many years this fish was the backbone of the commercial fishing in the Great Lakes, until the serious decline of recent times in all Great Lakes fishing. No one ever gave it a thought as a sport fish. Then, here and there, it began to be known that occasionally on certain small inland lakes "herring" would rise, in spring and early summer, to take insects from the surface. Simultaneously, along the Great Lakes, it was discovered that huge schools of "herring" came into comparatively shallow water near shore in early summer, and that by drawing a white button on a hook through the water the fish could be induced to strike.

Old hands knew how to catch the cisco at these times by stillfishing for them, usually with cane pole and very small minnow. But it remained for flyfishing enthusiasts to discover that apparently what brought the swarms of cisco shoreward were the fabulous mayfly (fish fly, willow fly) hatches occurring along Great Lakes shores, and on other lakes, usually during June. Here and there someone tried laying down a brown fly that mimicked the big mayfly, and found that "herring" would snap it up.

More startling, perhaps, was the fact that once hooked, these fish leaped and cavorted and raced away in swift runs in a headlong sequence altogether as brilliant as the battle of a trout. To make the proposition even more sporting, the cisco's mouth is weak and soft. The hook easily tears free. Because of their stubborn battle, three are lost for every one landed.

Until recently when so many difficulties such as pollution, invasions of lampreys and then alewives beset the Great Lakes, thousands of fishermen descended on hot spots for "herring" fishing each spring. Perhaps the greatest play given the sport occurred, and still does to some extent, in northern Michigan. It is certain that a search for other cisco waters where the fish are abundant could assure growth and continuance for this unusual flyfishing.

The fishing is done just before and at dawn, or else from about five or six until after dark. Unless one can fish from a causeway, or dock, a boat is necessary. One must first establish that the big hatches are in progress. They will begin in May and June. Depending upon the season, the hatches may come and go quickly, within a week, or they may continue night after night for several weeks. Fishing is not necessarily best when the hatch is greatest. A very heavy hatch places so many millions of mayflies on the water that the chance of a cisco taking one's artificial is a long gamble. A light hatch often brings best results.

Any modest-sized dark or brownish dry fly works well. A few anglers have learned to take cisco on wet flies, when they are feeding on stonefly nymphs and others. But the dry mayfly pattern is most surefire and standard. No special technique is required. One simply gets on the water and waits for the hatch to start, and for the fish to begin showing with a boil here and there. The fly is then cast, on a fairly light leader, and allowed simply to lie on the surface. Occasionally it may be twitched slightly, but this is seldom necessary.

Setting the hook is quite a trick and cannot be accurately described. If many strikes are missed, it is a good idea to slow down the strike. If they are still missed, speed up the reaction. Once a fish is on, it pays to play it gingerly. Otherwise it is almost certain to be lost.

Some flies will take fish much better than others. It is a good idea to experiment, or to check on local flies being used successfully in any given area. Any dry-fly enthusiast who successfully tries the cisco is certain to be delighted. There is still much to be learned, undoubtedly, about this fishing that will improve it. Ciscoes are delicious, but should be eaten very fresh, since they are a rather soft-fleshed fish. This characteristic has one great advantage: the backbone and ribs can simply be pulled out, all in one sweep, leaving a fine boneless double-fillet.

Smelt

Osmerus mordax

The streamlined, silvery little smelt is a delicacy, a diminutive second cousin of the trouts. It cannot truly be
said to be a sport fish, if the general connotation of the
term is intended. Yet it furnishes lots of fun. Smelt are
seldom caught on sporting tackle. They are dipped up
by millions during their spring spawning runs in small
dip nets, and even caught in the hands. The male at this
season is rough with small tubercles, and almost literally
sticks to the fingers. They are fished through the ice in
winter, usually from shanties set over water at least 50
feet deep.

The smelt referred to here is of course the eastern
variety, which is the most important of the smelts. West-
coast smelts are mentioned at the end of this section, as
well as some Pacific species called smelts along the west
coast, but not actually true smelts.

Millions of years ago, the smelt was a northern-Atlantic
saltwater fish entirely, but an anadromous species, that
is, one that runs up coastal freshwater streams in spring
to spawn. As was bound to happen, some became landlocked here and there along the New England and Ca-

nadian coast. They were able to tolerate freshwater all year, and continued to spawn. Eventually, through various means, the smelt was fairly well distributed over portions of eastern Canada and New England, in addition to its coastal range from Labrador to New York.

Some years ago smelt were brought from New England and planted in Crystal Lake, Michigan, as food for stocked landlocked salmon. The salmon disappeared, but the smelt ran on out into Lake Michigan, and soon populated the major share of the Great Lakes and tributary waters in overwhelming numbers.

During April, generally, the spawning runs begin. Streams large and small are often literally black with smelt. A few travel by daylight. The heavy runs, however, are invariably at night. Hundreds of people line stream banks attending these runs. They try to work together, especially on small streams. Everyone makes a dip or two, then the stretch of water is rested a half hour to let more smelt come in, and allow those fish still present to settle down.

Ice fishing for smelt is extremely popular in such places as Michigan and New England. It is often done by using some contraption such as a large homemade line winder attached to a shanty wall, over the hole, so a bait fished deep may be brought up and let down in a hurry. Minnows an inch long on very small hooks are the standard bait. The smelt is a voracious minnow feeder and is not shy. A fairly heavy sinker at the end of the line, with several dropper hooks spaced above it, is the rig. The best fishing is usually near bottom, in 20 to 75 feet of water. Near the mouths of northeastern coastal rivers the fishing is of course at less depth.

Whitebait Smelt

A rubber band tied to the line, once it is at proper depth, then tied again a couple of inches lower, leaving a bit of slack between ties, lets the angler know when he has a bite. The rubber stretches and he jerks the line to set his hook, then spins the big "reel." Most anglers fish several lines. A twist of line around a nail when proper depth is reached allows the sinker always to find the same depth.

Deep, clear lake waters, and big New England coastal rivers, are smelt habitat. Some streams emptying into such lake waters have good spring runs, others have none. Local people always know which is best. Smelt bite in winter both day and night, but invariably better at night. An ice-fishing rod can be used, and sometimes is, on open ice. But getting a long line up and down is not very convenient this way.

Smelt are never large fish. Ten inches is a large one. Those of 6 inches are excellent eating. Most people eat them bones and all.

There are several other smelt species. One enters streams along the mid-Atlantic and Gulf states. On the Pacific coast there are the **whitebait smelt** and the **night smelt,** both true members of the smelt family, Osmeridae.

Candlefish

These are taken in quantity commercially and sold both for human consumption and as bait. Sport fishermen take them in the surf with hand seines and dip nets. Another species, the surf smelt, is of less importance.

The **candlefish,** so named because it is so oily it was once dried and used by natives as a crude candle, ranges from northern California on north. It is also called eulachon. This is a true smelt. It is an anadromous species. It enters rivers in spring on spawning runs and is dipped up commercially and by sport fishermen of the Northwest much as are eastern smelts.

Another family of fishes, the **silversides** (Atherinidae), are called "smelts" along the Pacific. The so-called "jacksmelt" grows to fair size, as much as 12 to 20 inches, and is a good fighter on light tackle. In California it is an important commercial species, and has some favor with sport fishermen. A good many are caught incidentally by anglers after more desirable species. The **topsmelt,** somewhat smaller, is less important, but often found in schools of jacksmelt.

Best known of western silversides is of course the **grunnion,** long famous because of its spawning habits. This little fish, often dubbed a smelt, which it is not, comes onto the beach on certain tides to spawn. The fish come in on one wave, accomplish the spawning act while that wave recedes and another breaker forms. Waiting "anglers" rush in and seize the little fish in their hands. Oddly, years ago in California it was made illegal to take grunnion in any other manner from surf or beach. This little fish is delicious, and the source of much enjoyment, and therefore qualifies as a sporting species, even though it is never honored by hook and line.

Shad

Alosa sapidissima

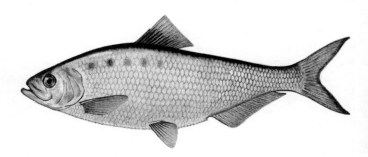

Whether or not the common coastal shad, American shad, or white shad, as it is variously called, should be placed here under the freshwater or later under the saltwater species is questionable. It is an anadromous species, that is, one that lives in saltwater but moves into freshwater coastal streams to spawn. Since it is only during this spawning run that shad are taken, both commercially and for sport, for all practical purposes it becomes a freshwater species.

Not so many years ago the status of the common coastal shad as a game fish might also have been questionable. Since the early days of America this fish has been a most important commercial species, with planked fresh-run shad and shad roe being east coast delicacies. About 1930 a Baltimore angler tied a black and white bucktail fly that, he discovered, running shad would occasionally hit. By 1940 some were being taken on various types of wet flies, and on small spinners and spoons. Today the sport is well established in a number of rivers from the St. Lawrence region to Florida's St. Johns. In early days shad were named for each river—Potomac shad, Susquehanna shad, etc.—but they were all the same species.

Some of the rivers that have become well known for their runs of shad attended by sport fishermen are the Connecticut, the Potomac, the Susquehanna, the Edisto of South Carolina, the Ogeechee of Georgia, and in Florida the St. Johns, which nowadays probably accounts for more shad caught on hook and line than any of the others. Since the shad ranges all along the east coast, undoubtedly there are many other good runs with sport fishing possibilities. Some in fact are known, but have yet to be developed.

Although the shad was not native to the Pacific, it was stocked there in the 1870s, a rather astonishing undertaking, and quite visionary for so long ago. Today it ranges the entire length of the coast, from southern California to Alaska. Sport fishing for shad is well known in certain Pacific coast streams—for example, the Russian River—and it nowadays attracts many anglers. There are good runs in Oregon and Washington. This is still an expanding sport. Salmon and trout of course get most of the attention, but as more and more fishing facilities are needed, it is probable that west-coast shad fishing will develop further.

The shad is a true herring, a fish both fairly long, and deep, with the body well compressed. It is mainly silvery, with the back greenish, and with a few indistinct spots along the shoulder section. In size it may go to 10 or 12 pounds, but averages 3 to 5, with the female usually larger than the male. Shads and true herring lack the adipose fin characteristic of the trouts and whitefishes. Also, the lateral line prominent on most fish is not discernible in shads and herring.

The strike and the battle of a shad are great surprises to anglers getting their initiation. Supposedly, shad do not eat after they enter freshwater on their spawning runs. Thus, they are not caught on bait. Just why they hit lures is not well understood. They are inclined to be moody and unreliable about it, but when one does take, it is with a slamming strike, and from there on the fight is a whirlwind affair, with the fish making smoking runs, and leaping time after time.

Not much is known of the ocean existence of shad, except that they migrate from offshore waters, apparently, into the coastal streams, and do not migrate up and down the coast. Possibly because of this, lures that catch shad in one river are sometimes worthless in another. Since they are tricky customers at best, procedure is to find out precisely which lures catch the most shad at any given location and to stick chiefly to those, while experimenting perhaps with others that may prove better. That is the way hot new lures have been pioneered.

Fly fishing and spinning are the two methods. Any spinning outfit is all right, but for fly fishermen a fairly powerful rod should be used, with a forward-taper line. The fish are likely to be skittish, and long casts necessary, at least long by fly-rod standards. The outfit recommended makes this distance possible.

Best fishing is in clear water. The lure is worked in the current, not in slack water. Shallow, swift runs are good places. The tail end of a strong-currented pool is a good daylight spot. In the evening the head of the pool will be

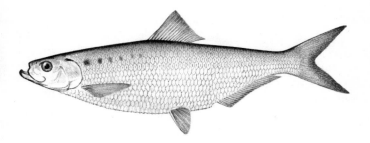

Hickory Shad

better, for the shad will now begin to move upstream. The water below a dam often has hordes of shad lying in it. In fly fishing, the lure is generally fished across the current, retrieved in sweeps of 12 to 18 inches. For beginners, the best way to learn pay-off technique is to watch successful and experienced shad anglers on any particular river. White flies with bodies silver-wound, take fish. So do orange and red flies. Anglers using small spoons (the 00 size is very popular in several areas) usually cast them upstream. The retrieve is not especially swift. Other small flasher lures work well, too. A spinning outfit is good for this work.

Shad begin to run about April on both coasts. This depends of course on weather, which affects water temperature. The river waters must be around 50 degrees before the shad will enter them, and must be roughly 5 degrees higher for spawning to take place. It is a good idea to keep close track of rising water temperatures in order to pinpoint the time of the run.

In addition to the big white shad, the **hickory shad,**

Alosa mediocris (in some books *Pomolobus mediocris*) another of the herrings, often runs into the same rivers to spawn. The hickories are smaller, seldom weighing over 2 to 2 1/2 pounds. This species looks rather similar to the white shad, but has longitudinal rows of faint dark dots on its sides. The hickory shad usually are first in the streams, preceding their larger cousins. They, too, will strike lures rather readily, and are excellent fighters and leapers. Except for roe, they are not considered as good on the table, however.

Sport fishing possibilities with shad are not by any means restricted to coastal areas, although very few anglers realize this. Almost totally overlooked by the sport fisherman is the **golden shad,** *Alosa chrysochloris* (or genus *Pomolobus* in some, as above), also called "river shad," "blue shad," and "skipjack." This fish is native to many large inland rivers of the Midsouth especially, such as the Ohio and Tennessee. It also ranges south to the Gulf, where it is anadromous. This fish is worthless as an eating fish, but it is one of the most dynamic fighters living in freshwater. Ordinarily it is used by local fishermen as bait for large catfish. Spring fishermen after crappies hold it in high disdain because it takes their minnows. For those interested in crystal-pure sport, however, this species, sometimes jokingly called "freshwater tarpon," or "Tennessee tarpon," is an excellent target.

As with the coastal shads, the only time to take this fish consistently is when it is concentrated during its spawning runs. Tennessee is an especially good place, because the species is abundant there, and because of the many big dams on large rivers. During April, as a rule, the run is at peak. These silvery fish with undershot jaw even look a bit reminiscent of tarpon, in miniature. They weigh from a pound to 3 pounds, and can be found by hundreds in the swift water below the big dams. One good example of a place to have fun with golden shad during the spawning run is the French Broad River in Tennessee, just below Douglas Dam.

They will strike many lures. One of the best is a small spinning-sized feathered jig with weighted head, in yellow or white. It is cast across the current, allowed to sweep around, and retrieved very slowly near bottom. This shad will also strike streamer flies, particularly in clear water, such as that in the Clinch River below Norris Dam in Tennessee. White is a good color.

Once hooked, the fish leaps time after time. Unless wanted for bait, it may as well be released. This fish should not be confused with the smaller, deeper-bodied gizzard shad with threadlike appendage on the dorsal fin that runs in great swarms in southern rivers of the Mississippi system at the same time. The gizzard shad is commonly and inadvertently snagged, but does not strike a lure. It is a forage fish for game species, and is far too strong and bony to eat.

Mooneye

Hiodon tergisus

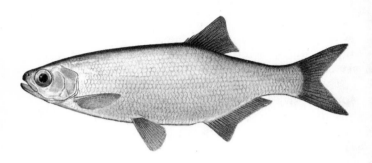

Some fishermen catch the mooneye occasionally without recognizing it, a few catch it and know it and are delighted, most aren't familiar with the species at all. This is not because it is a poor sport fish. Quite the contrary, this small, platinum-hued fish with a narrow, hard mouth and an enormous bright eye puts on a startling show reminiscent of a tarpon in miniature. Some references note the southern mooneye as a separate species, but there is reason to believe this fish may be identical.

The mooneye, sometimes called "toothed herring" or "white shad," is far from rare, and not especially restricted in range. But it occurs very erratically throughout the Great Lakes and the Mississippi Valley. In some of the Midsouth impoundments the mooneye is abundant, but even there few fishermen find it often, and since it is small (8 to 12 inches) and without table renown the average angler is not interested in making a search.

In general a search would do little good. Most of the time the mooneye swims the open water of the large lakes and rivers it inhabits, feeding fairly deep on tiny minnows and aquatic insects. During warm evenings, especially in spring, and occasionally on through summer and fall, schools of mooneyes work shoreward and feed avidly on the surface. In lakes like Kentucky Lake, for example, when the water is reasonably calm, in late April and throughout May and June mooneyes can be seen dimpling the surface from a hundred yards offshore right to the bank, from about five p.m. on into the night.

They are feeding on insects, often the so-called willow-fly hatch (mayflies), and at these times they will take dry flies readily. Even a very small bass or bluegill surface bug with cork body and rubber legs will intrigue them. Regulation trout flies in about No. 10 or No. 12 size, in grizzled gray or brown patterns, are best.

The swirls they make are not easily distinguishable from those of small panfish, but are actually lighter, more dainty. The strike is very quick, and usually an angler must spend some little time becoming proficient in hooking fish. A fine leader is generally a help. The fish are shy. When one is hooked, it literally explodes into action, hurling itself with abandon all over the surface, and not running down until utterly exhausted, when it can be released.

Fly fishing for mooneyes is a kind of purist sport, a fishing gem not often come upon but worth diligent sideline seeking by the angler who wishes to experience it all. For a fly fisherman, it is like a taste of exotic dessert. For best results, tackle of course should be as dainty as the fish.

The mooneye also readily takes bait, and in portions of its range, Missouri for example, is known as a "kid's

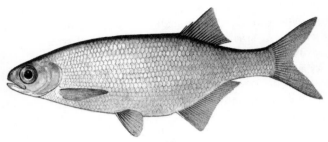

Goldeye

fish" because it is abundant and commonly caught on grasshoppers or worms. Incidentally, because of one colloquial name previously mentioned, "white shad," the fish is sometimes confused with the unrelated forage fish, the gizzard shad.

West of the mooneye's range is found its close relative, the **goldeye,** *Hiodon alosoides*. It is easily distinguished from the mooneye by the characteristic from which its name was taken. The large eye is a stunning canary yellow or gold. One other sure means of identification is the position of the dorsal fin. That of the mooneye has its leading edge a bit forward of a line drawn vertically down to the front of the anal fin. The goldeye's dorsal is placed farther back.

Although the goldeye, which often grows a bit larger than the mooneye, overlaps its range with its relative, it is most abundant in Manitoba. Saskatchewan, and in the Missouri system in Montana. The lower portions of the Yellowstone River, for example, swarm with goldeyes. The Missouri itself at Fort Benton has them by thousands. In Fort Peck Reservoir on the Missouri there has been a commercial fishery utilizing goldeyes for fertilizer. In some of the large Canadian lakes goldeyes have long been important commercially, but chiefly for human consumption, proving excellent when smoked.

Although it is predictable that the goldeye will never be utilized in the United States to any extent as a table fish, it might well bring enjoyment to hundreds of fishermen if they will but offer it the opportunity. It is almost totally neglected by sport fishermen, and indeed on its home grounds it is commonly despised by local fishermen as a superabundant nuisance. Yet it avidly strikes small spinning lures, takes both wet and dry flies, fights wildly with many leaps. For trout fishermen visiting the West at times when fishing is less than sensational, a pause along one of the big rivers of the Missouri system, for example, can offer very fast and exciting fishing for goldeyes.

They are most generally found in shallow stretches where modest riffles break over into deeper water. Here they feed in large concentrations on small minnows and insects, and can be caught one after another with no special technique other than continued casting. The goldeye is indeed a resource in sport fishing that should be developed.

Channel Catfish

Ictalurus punctatus

This fish (which some references list as *Ictalurus lacustris*) has many of the attributes of a true game fish, and has been caught on everything from worms and congealed chicken blood to bass plugs and trout flies. Regardless of how this catfish or any of the other species of the family may be caught, however, few noncatfishing anglers realize the tremendous importance, regionally, of the catfishes and bullheads as sport fish.

These somewhat sluggish, smooth-skinned fish with sensitive chin and snout barbels, or "whiskers," that assist them in finding their food belong to a family worldwide in distribution. There are probably a thousand species all told. On this continent there are some thirty-five varieties, most of them small, a few of medium size, and at least two that grow very large. The family is characterized by the spines, present in nearly all species, at the anterior edge of the pectoral and dorsal fins. These are extremely stiff and sharp, can inflict painful wounds, and in some species have a small venom gland at their base.

The channel catfish heads this section because it represents the family in the best style. It is unquestionably the trimmest, gamest, and most agile of the group, and by preference at least always gravitates to the cleanest water, and often to swift water—to the "channels." However, throughout their varying ranges numerous bullhead and catfish species overlap and are commonly caught together, on the same baits, by the same methods. Following are a few family characteristics, and then a listing of the more important American species, with a few facts about each.

Most of our catfishes are freshwater species. A few live in saltwater (*see* Part II). All have a large mouth, a distinct and fairly straight lateral line, and a fleshy adipose fin. Besides being naked of scales, their rib structure, or muscle structure along the ribs, shows through the skin to make them appear more naked than ever. The chin and snout barbels are completely harmless, folklore to the contrary, and are simply feelers. All species are predominantly but not exclusively nocturnal feeders, and will eat practically anything. The names "catfish" and "bullhead" are not interchangeable, but are firm divisions within the family. The catfish group of the freshwater catfish family (the Ictaluridae, previously Ameiuridae) is composed mostly of rather large species, the bullhead group under the same family contains smaller species.

Catfish and bullheads inhabit a great variety of waters, and are notable because they are capable of thriving in waters so warm and muddy that most other species are

Blue Catfish

excluded. Even rather severe pollution does not bother them a great deal. Everywhere east of the Rocky Mountains some member of the family is almost sure to be found. Original range did not include the west coast, but stocking has established several species there.

Because they are scavengers to a great degree, and can tolerate submarginal habitats, members of this family automatically took over throughout the centuries those water areas least suitable to the more highly developed game species. Thus catfish and bullheads have long been much sought in all of the larger, slower rivers, the silted streams, the sloughs, potholes, and muddy lakes. Throughout the northern plains states where winterkill has often been a severe handicap to other species, bullheads and catfish have long thrived, because the whole family is made up of fish exceedingly tenacious of life. The entire Mississippi drainage is a natural habitat for catfish. In this system grow most of the largest of our cats. In Iowa, the Dakotas, Kansas, Nebraska, the various catfishes have long been king. Stocking of farm ponds with bullheads is traditional procedure, for example, in North Dakota. Again, in the Deep South where heavy siltation clouds the large rivers, catfishing is the traditional fishing indulged in by the average fisherman. The same has long been true in certain sections of Oklahoma and Texas.

All members of the family are excellent table fish, have always been extremely important commercial as well as sport species. All are rather guileless, and thus rather easily caught. They are abundant, without whimsey in their tastes, and as has been noted, so widely distributed and able to fill so many otherwise barren waters, that their popularity, and a great variety of methods aimed at their capture, were certain to evolve. Four species are important.

The **blue catfish,** *Ictalurus furcatus*, lives in the larger rivers of the Mississippi system, averages 2 to 15 pounds, grows to 100 to 200 pounds. It has a deeply forked tail. Easiest and most accurate identification: the number of rays in the long, straight-edged anal fin. There are thirty to thirty-six. It is a valuable commercial species. An interesting sport fishery has evolved, with the blue cat as one of its main targets, below the big impoundment dams, especially throughout the South.

Here awesome-sized catfish are caught by anglers using saltwater tackles. Heavy weights are necessary to keep the bait (a whole "skipjack"—golden shad—or other bait fish, a hunk of meat or fish) down in the rough, mauling current below the dam, and this fishing can be dangerous when water is suddenly let down from above. The big cats come into the tailraces to gorge on chum from small fish that have gone through the turbines and been chopped to bits. This is highly specialized fishing and requires on-the-scene education by experienced anglers before it is attempted by the tyro.

Yellow Catfish

The **yellow, or flathead, catfish,** *Pylodictis olivaris,* has a short anal fin with only twelve to fifteen rays and a rounded tail. It is also a large species, growing to 100 pounds or more but averaging 4 to 5. It is a fish mainly of large rivers from the Dakotas and Nebraska and the Lakes States southward to the Gulf, with most of the catch coming from the western and southern portion of its range. It is important commercially and highly prized by anglers as a table fish.

The **white catfish,** *Ictalurus catus,* is a modest-sized species (2 to 5 pounds) of the east coast, but with some taken westward as far as Texas. It has also been stocked on the Pacific coast. The tail is moderately forked, there are twenty to twenty-three rays in the anal fin, and no body spots, as in the channel cat which it most resembles.

The **channel catfish,** *Ictalurus punctatus,* is a trim fish with a deeply forked tail and numerous dark speckles on its sides. However, these spots are sometimes lacking in large, older specimens. It has twenty-four to thirty rays in the anal fin. General color may be bluish to silvery, with overtones occasionally of pinkish along the sides. It is sometimes called "fiddler." Individuals average from a pound to 5 pounds, with occasional fish ranging up-

Brown Bullhead

ward to 20 and even above 50 pounds. Range is through-out the entire Great Lakes Region and on south to the Gulf through the Mississippi system, thence westward into Texas. It has been stocked on the west coast and also on the Atlantic coast.

Even though the channel cat was originally present in many natural lakes, they were perhaps most at home in rivers large and small. With the coming of the hundreds of large impoundments throughout channel cat range, hundreds of thousands of acres of new habitat were opened up for them to colonize. Many southern im-poundments in particular now furnish superb channel cat fishing. In certain states where no limit is in force, anglers sometimes take, via trotline or more sporty meth-ods, several hundred during a single trip. Wherever found, in lake or stream, the channel cat prefers cleaner water — and in streams swifter — than any other catfish, often over sand or gravel or rock bottoms. These fish are active and good fighters, are known to hit plugs and spinners cast for bass, occasionally smack a bass bug, and have been caught now and then in streams on

Yellow Bullhead

nymph-type flies the same as are used for trout.

There are four species of bullheads considered worthwhile as sport fishes:

The **brown bullhead,** *Ictalurus nebulosus,* called the horned pout in New England, speckled bullhead on the west coast. The lower barbels are dark brown or black. This one likes fairly deep lake water, grows maximum to about 18 inches. It is widely distributed and perhaps our most important bullhead.

The **yellow bullhead,** *Ictalurus natalis,* is slightly smaller, ranges very broadly over much of the eastern two-thirds of the United States and has been stocked westward. Lower barbels are light colored. It is often found in clear, clean lakes and streams, but usually where there is ample submerged vegetation.

The **flat bullhead,** *Ictalurus platycephalus,* is a southeastern species chiefly of streams. The lower barbels are pale, as in the yellow bullhead. The dark blotch at base of dorsal is a good distinguishing characteristic. Color pattern differs locally. In Florida streams particularly this fish is heavily mottled with black. Twelve inches is about maximum.

Black Bullhead

The **black bullhead,** *Ictalurus melas,* is a rather small and very widely ranging species generally found in the muddier, most sluggish smaller streams, and in ponds. Lower barbels are dark. Color, black above, with belly golden to greenish, and with base of tail light.

Catfish and bullhead fishing is best from dusk on and generally early in the season. They are caught by still-fishing with all sorts of baits. Worms are a favorite. Frogs take large catfish in some southern rivers. Rancid cheese, dough-balls, liver, fish, chunks of meat or fish, chicken entrails, congealed chicken blood, and endless so-called "stink baits" whose formulas their inventors usually hold in great secrecy are all highly thought of. Handlining, set lines, trot lines are all favorite catfishing methods. Jugging for cats is perhaps the most unique method, and aside from the heavyrod sport fishing for large catfish below the impoundment dams, probably the most true sport.

This is accomplished by stoppering glass or plastic jugs or sealing pairs of empty quart oil cans together to make airtight containers, then attaching a baited line with sinker and tossing several such rigs overboard in a large river. The jugs are followed with a boat. When a catfish takes the bait, it jiggles the float or, if a large fish,

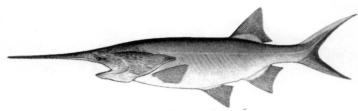

Paddlefish

takes it under. Even a large cat cannot hold the container down forever. The angler hurries to follow his dancing jug and haul in his prize.

In certain places catfish and bullheads will consistently strike small bass plugs. At times they even seem choosey about which plug. On the Myakka River in Florida, for example, a small red and white sinking plug has been known to take scores of large bullheads when cast across and brought slowly back along the bottom. On the whole, however, catfish and bullheads are still-fishermen's fish. Boys and bullheads have long gone together harmoniously and happily. Catfish and bullheads are not difficult to catch, yet the endeavor is not without its art. This art is of a most involved and interesting regional variety verging often on ritual. It behooves the interested angler, therefore, to acquaint himself with a native catfisherman and to try to worm out of him his secrets.

It is certainly true that bullheading and catfishing are homely pastimes. But they are well attended, they are basic, and traditional. They are also fun.

At this point we must discuss a fish quite commonly but improperly called the "spoonbill catfish." The only reason for placing it here with the catfishes is because of this error in identification made by so many fishermen who are acquainted with it. The so-called "spoonbill cat" is the **paddlefish,** *Polyodon spathula.* It is not a catfish, but is the single representative in our waters of its own ancient family. Oddly, its closest relative inhabits waters in China.

The paddlefish is a large, slate-gray, scaleless creature with a long, spatulate bill, small eyes, an enormous mouth, and huge, pliable, flapping gill covers. Although it looks like an authentic apparition, it is a mild creature, and feeds on plankton that is swept with water through mouth and gills. Paddlefish grow to large size. Specimens of between 100 and 200 pounds have been noted, but these larger ones are old records. The ones commonly taken today weigh from 30 to 70 pounds.

The paddlefish is present in scattered portions of the entire Mississippi system, from the upper Ohio to the Missouri in Montana. But today its population has dwindled until it is found most commonly in such places as below the big dams of the Missouri in the Dakotas, and at Lake of the Ozarks and the Osage River in Missouri. It was felt a few years ago that the paddlefish might be headed for extinction, as dams interfered with its spawning runs, and other influences narrowed its range. But Charles Purkett of the Missouri Conservation Department finally cracked the secrets of its spawning and of how to raise paddlefish from eggs in a hatchery, something scientists had been trying to do for a hundred years. Probably now the fish can be saved.

Whether or not paddlefish are true game fish is open to question. They are not taken on lures or baited hooks, but are snagged during their early-spring spawning runs.

Standard saltwater rods and reels are used, with heavy braided line. At the end is a large weight, with one or more large treble hooks used to snag the fish. A snagger drifts or runs his boat slowly through pools or areas known to be congregating places for the fish. He rhythmically jerks up and lets back, over and over, and by great gambler's luck now and then snags a fish. There is no way to tell where the snag hooks have attached. Needless to say, with fish this large and hooked just anywhere, some stubborn battles are entered.

Whether or not this is game fishing is a moot point. The endeavor has grown popular, particularly over the past few years, and rigid limits and restrictions and seasons are now in force. Paddlefish, incidentally, do not have a true bony skeleton but one of soft cartilage. The flesh is edible and some enthusiasts claim it as excellent.

Carp

Cyprinus carpio

Centuries ago the carp was introduced to Europe from China. Less than a century ago it was brought to the United States. Since that time it has found its way into waters over almost the entire continent. Undoubtedly we would have been much better off without it.

Carp are extremely prolific. They are bottom rooters, vegetarians. They not only monopolize living room in lakes where they live, but roil the waters incessantly by their constant rooting. They also in some cases almost totally destroy vegetation, thus harming habitat for game fishes. Carp are seined by millions, both for commercial sale and simply to help rid game-fish waters of them. They are poisoned by millions where feasible.

Nonetheless, sportsmen have found ways to utilize the carp. Bow-and-arrow enthusiasts now have organized carp shoots in many places, in the spring when the fish gather in shallows to spawn. During this time carp roll and leap repeatedly, splashing noisily. They may be stalked to close range by careful wading. Carp are also speared. And they are gigged in some places beneath the ice in winter, a highly specialized and regional undertaking. They are taken on set lines and also fished for here and there.

Oddly, the carp is perhaps the wariest of fishes. It is strong, amazingly swift, and puts up a tremendous battle when hooked, but hooking one is an art. A very few anglers have learned how to take carp on wet flies. The method does not get consistent results. Much depends on location. For example, in places in the northern Great

Lakes carp gather to feed on insects, take wet flies consistently. Where such a situation exists, the sport is sensational.

More commonly, carp are baited to a sand or gravel area over a period of days, by dumping cooked chopped vegetables, corn, or doughballs on it. Then extremely fine tackle is used—long, fine leader, small hook well concealed in a piece of the chum, perhaps a quill float—and the angler keeps himself well hidden. The fish are so wary that when they first discover the baited area they may swim round and round but not actually approach it for hours. Thus, taking carp on hook and line, especially in clear water, is unmistakable sport.

The carp probably will never be highly thought of in this country, as it is in some other parts of the world. "Sewer bass" is the contemptuous name often given to it, because carp will live in the most degrading of habitats. Although in many places carp live in clean water, and in some areas are seined, placed in clean ponds and fattened for market on grain, the average American angler is not a carp eater. As has been said, however, it cannot be denied that carp are real sport on light tackle, and require most delicate fishing. As a fascinating test of skill and a conservation measure if nothing else, more anglers might try their hand at it.

Carp belong to the minnow family, Cyprinidae. They are relatives of the goldfish. They grow large, anywhere from 2 to 50 or more pounds. There are three varieties present in U.S. waters: the common carp, a brownish to golden-hued, large-scaled fish with inferior, toothless mouth and two barbels on the snout; the mirror carp, which has only a few scattered scales; the leather carp,

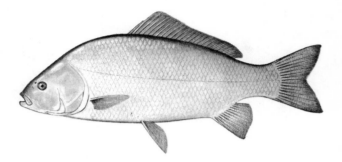

Buffalo

which is scaleless. The last two are not abundant.

During the early 1970s an exotic carp was brought to the United States for experimentation. It is the so-called grass carp, or white amur, native to the Amur River in Manchuria and Siberia. Although a member of the minnow family, as are the other carps, this variety grows at maximum upwards of 100 pounds, and is said to be a good sport fish. It is almost entirely a vegetation feeder. In some southern waters encroachment by aquatic vegetation is an extremely serious problem, especially because certain foreign varieties all but impossible to kill by presently known means have infiltrated, possibly brought in on ships, and transported lake to lake via sport fishing craft. The white amur is seen by some fisheries biologists as a "great white hope" for biological vegetation control.

There is, however, a go-slow attitude among most fisheries people. Texas decided against the fish and made it illegal to bring them into the state. Arkansas has actually done some stocking in lakes, but claims to have

Redhorse

the fish isolated, which is doubtful. Louisiana has experimented, attempting to develop a monosex strain that cannot launch a runaway population. Specimens have been found in the Mississippi system. This worries fisheries biologists, who fear it is already out of control.

The carp looks very much like another common American fish, the **buffalo,** or buffalofish, so called because of its humped back. The buffalo, of which there are numerous species, can be separated easily from the carp. Carp have a single heavy spine at the anterior edge of both dorsal and anal fin; buffalo do not.

Buffalofish belong to the sucker family, Catostomidae, and might best be described as suckers with carp shape. The minnow and sucker families are very closely related. Our buffalofish and suckers are extremely wide ranging, and of some importance to sports fishermen. There are over a hundred species all told, found in all manner of lakes and streams.

They are spring spawners, and it is during the spawning runs in streams, when suckers and buffalofish crowd by thousands, or when they move into the shallows of lakes to spawn, that angling activity in their behalf is at

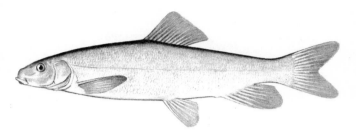

White Sucker

highest pitch. All of the larger species (from 1 to 5 pounds for suckers, larger maximum for buffalo) are taken on set lines, on trot lines, by spear, net, handline, snaghook, or "snatchhook" as it is sometimes called, and by regulation hook-and-line fishing.

The so-called **redhorse,** a large variety of sucker (there are numerous redhorse species), is extremely popular with anglers. In the Midsouth a sport has evolved not only of snagging these fish as they run in the rivers, but of snaring them with a wire noose. Enthusiasts operate from a boat, or even at times from stepladders placed in the current so they can see the passing fish. On one river a hatchery was even activated to make sure the sport would long endure.

Suckers all have tubelike sucking mouths. A worm or a doughball is the traditional bait, fished on bottom. Any tackle will do. Best places are stream mouths as runs begin, or deep holes farther upstream later, or sandy shallows of lakes. Numerous anglers find spring-run suckers and buffalo very tasty. Because all fish of this family are exceedingly bony, many sucker fishermen can or smoke their catch, which softens the bundles of "fagot" bones.

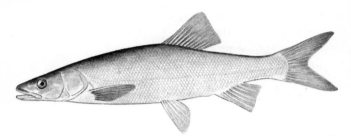

Squawfish

Trout and bass fishermen all too often sneer at the idea of sucker or buffalo or carp fishing. Nonetheless, the numerous species of these two large families have an astonishing number of fans. It cannot be denied, therefore, that they are sport fishes and have their rightful place in American fishing.

They are useful, too, on the sidelines of angling. Trout often follow spawning suckers, to eat their spawn. Locating suckers on the riffles and fishing behind them is common practice in some places.

Carp minnows make excellent bait, although many states prohibit their use for fear of spreading the species to waters where it would be undesirable. Small suckers are prime bait for lake trout, larger ones for muskellunge. Suckers are reared to some extent for hatchery use as food for young muskies.

One offshoot branch of the minnow family, the **squawfishes,** is composed of several species that grow to large size in the Far West and Northwest. They have large, toothless mouths, but not of the suctorial variety. They feed on insects and small fish, sometimes grow to four feet or more in length, and are occasionally taken on flies or spinning lures. At such times they battle well. But because they are believed to eat small game fish, they are not well regarded or especially sought by anglers.

In fact, trout fishermen in such states as Idaho, Montana, Utah, California often despise the squawfish. In certain lakes vast schools of them congregate, and these can be a nuisance when one is after trout. In many rivers squawfish—named thus because certain Indian tribes considered them excellent food—are extremely abundant. In the evening or during hatches they will readily strike flies, both wet and dry. There is no denying that the ensuing battles offer fast and exciting sport. It is doubtful, however, that any of the four species of squawfish, one of which, from California, is called the "Sacramento pike," will ever have any great esteem among sport fishermen. There are just too many more desirable species in their range.

Freshwater Drum

Aplodinotus grunniens

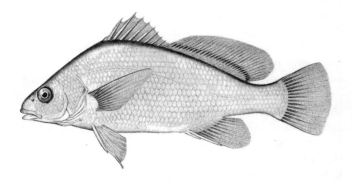

This is an interesting species, locally popular as a sport fish in a number of widely separated areas, from the southern Great Lakes to Texas. Since it is also abundant in those same places, it could serve to give far more sport than it does. It is a good fighter when taken on light tackle. It does not leap, of course, but its flat sides and sturdy build allow it to keep a rod bent very satisfactorily for some time.

The drum is a croaker, quite closely allied to the various croakers and drums of saltwater. It is commonly called a sheepshead, sometimes also gray bass. Gaspergou is a name used for it in the lower Mississippi region. White perch is another name one hears occasionally. The fish ranges from the Hudson Bay area clear to the Gulf of Mexico, following down the Mississippi Valley and eastward into New York State and the Great Lakes area. Of the big lakes, Erie is the concentration point, especially in the western half.

There is no reason to confuse this fish with any other. It is silvery gray, has fairly large, rough scales, and the lateral line runs out onto the tail. Some people confuse the freshwater drum with the white bass. If one knows both species there is no excuse for this.

Most average specimens weigh from 1 to 5 pounds. Those of 10 are not rare. Some much larger are taken, even to 50 or 60 pounds. There are indications that in pioneer days this fish commonly weighed up to a hundred pounds, and anciently perhaps double that.

It is a bottom feeder. The throat is equipped with paved teeth intended for grinding shells. The sheepshead feeds, as an adult, almost entirely upon mollusks, the various freshwater clams, mussels, and snails. Crawfish and some small forage fish are also favorite foods. Because of these feeding habits, the species is most likely to be found at modest depth, not far from shore or from silty or muddy reefs, and over a soft bottom. Large lakes and large, slow streams are the specific habitat.

In early summer—May or June—the drum commonly congregates below dams on big rivers, and may be taken from such locations in quantity. Whether these concentrations are spawning runs is questionable. This is not considered a migratory fish. It may be that new water coming into a river with spring or early-summer rains gives the drum an urge to move up into the current. When a river has been very low, for example, and spring rains come, occasionally drum by hundreds suddenly appear in pools at any point where a barrier stops them from further upstream movement. Some Texas rivers are good examples of this. The Nueces, after a dry spell and sudden rise due to heavy rain, offers fast fishing for drum at spots where obstructions stop them.

Under such conditions the drum becomes a rather good game fish. It will strike an artificial lure, such as a small spoon. This it will do occasionally anywhere throughout its range. But when hordes of drum are congregated, no doubt the competition for food makes each individual more eager to hit. By and large, however, the drum is caught by bait fishing. In impoundments or rivers where catfishing is done with hunks of shad, as many drum as catfish may be caught.

Old hands at drum fishing usually prefer crawfish as the standard bait. Soft craws appear more productive than hard ones, but the fish will take either. Worms are also effective, but the crawfish is probably best. There is no special technique required. Once a good location is found, the bait, without bobber, is simply tossed out and allowed to lie on bottom until the drum takes it. If the taker happens to be a large specimen, a substantial, dogged battle follows.

The drum was prized by Indians because of the otoliths, or ear bones, in its head. These ivory-like structures were supposed to bring good luck. To this day they are sometimes called "lucky stones" by the superstitious river-bottom dwellers in the Mississippi Valley. The drum is capable of making a grunting or purring sound. This sound is sometimes heard even above water, as the drum swims around. The fish also grunts when pulled out on the bank. Supposedly the sound is made by special muscles drawn across the air bladder. Whether the ear bone development is in any way tied up with the sounds the fish makes, scientists are not certain.

One interesting sidelight on the life history of the freshwater drum is that it may be used to raise its own food. Since it feeds constantly in mussel beds, it is a likely host for larval mussels. These—called "glochidia"—attach themselves to fish. The drum is one of the foremost transporters of them, thus planting many elsewhere, making new mussel beds on which it will feed later.

The table qualities of freshwater drum depend upon their size and the quality of the water from which they are caught. Extra-large drum are inclined to be tough and sometimes strong. Specimens from muddy water are often so-so eating. However, drum of small to modest size caught in clear water are usually excellent. The drum has gained a so-so reputation as an eating fish simply because so few anglers purposely fish for it, and try it. In southern Louisiana, for example, "gasper" is widely advertised in markets and is considered a top-quality table fish. Pan-sized drum from clear streams have sweet, pearly-white meat mildly reminiscent of the taste of walleye. All in all the freshwater drum deserves a better press than it has had to date.

Bowfin

Amia calva

Not many persons fish purposely for this ancient, tough, large-scaled, olive-colored species, the male of which has during breeding season a bright orange-and-black eye spot at the base of its tail. The bowfin, dogfish, mudfish, grindle, or scaled ling, as it is variously called, is often caught inadvertently, especially by anglers after largemouth bass in the South.

The bowfin lurks in the muddiest and weediest places of any of its warm-water habitats, and invariably where the water is still. It is awesomely powerful, swift when it needs to be, but ordinarily sluggish in actions. Its great mouth thickly studded with slashing teeth fits it for the role of savage killer that it thoroughly fulfills. It is a heavy, thick fish, with a long body. The tail is of the ancient, rounded type, and the dorsal fin runs almost the entire length of the body. This "mudfish" is ugly both in appearance and temperament, and its pasty flesh makes poor eating.

It is not, however, without several astonishing qualities. Bowfins rise to the surface to gulp air through the mouth. Their air bladders can actually breathe. These fish often bury themselves in mud and outwait and outwit a serious drought in this fashion, even when a pond dries up completely. But the most startling attribute of the bowfin is the quality of the battle it puts up when hooked.

It will strike bass plugs and spoons, and will take various baits such as shiners, various other minnows, and crawfish. Its strike is vicious, and the fight is likely to begin by a series of leaps as thrilling as those indulged in by any top game species. From there on it is a matter of slam-bang underwater action. Wearing out a big specimen is often a long, hard job. It pays to be cautious in releasing these fish. They habitually snap their jaws, and can do serious damage.

The range of the bowfin reaches from the Great Lakes to Texas, and eastward through Florida. It is also present in the St. Lawrence River and southward, west of the mountains, to Florida. An average bowfin will weigh from 2 to 5 pounds. Fish up to 12 pounds are not especially uncommon in the South, and some may go to 20.

to cruise about most actively toward evening. In Florida especially, where they are abundant, and active the year-round, they may be seen leaving a large wake in stagnant ponds or muddy, quiet bayous as the sun falls behind the timber. At such times a shiner cast and brought back before a hunting fish will usually elicit action. The bowfin will even take a larger streamer fly, but big specimens are difficult to handle in the cramped, weedy places they generally inhabit.

In the North and Midsouth, wherever mild cold weather strikes, the bowfin is inactive in winter. It is rather spottily distributed everywhere except in the South.

Burbot

Lota lota

Even the comparatively small number of anglers who intentionally fish for the burbot, freshwater ling, cusk, lawyer, eelpout, gudgeon, or mud blower, as it is variously known, will admit that it is a species of prime ugliness. This long, flattened, chin-whiskered fish (listed in some references as *Lota maculosa*) skulks on bottom hiding among stones by day, its mottled olive and black body blending perfectly with its surroundings. Its scaleless-appearing skin looks like the skin of an eel. Actually it has scales, but they are microscopic, embedded in the skin.

The burbot is a voracious feeder, especially at night, and when abundant is often quite destructive to other fish, gorging until its flexible stomach is tremendously distended. Occasionally burbots are caught in the lower reaches of trout streams, for this cold-water lurker ranges all across the northern United States and north into Alaska and Canada. It also lives deep in lakes and is quite abundant in places in slow streams. It is actually a codfish, its various slightly differing subspecies the only members of the cod family inhabiting freshwater.

Most fishermen would hotly deny that the burbot is

even remotely a game fish. It is neither alert nor especially agile, neither wise nor a dramatic fighter when hooked. In some waters, the burbot even smells bad when taken from the water, and there are numerous anglers who would prefer to starve rather than eat one. The fact still remains, as it does with most of our fish species, that in certain places the ugly burbot has a surprising number of enthusiastic fans.

Almost without exception, they are winter anglers, and most of them live in Wyoming, Montana, and eastern Washington, with a few in Minnesota, the Dakotas, and New England. The western ice fishermen in particular take some exceptionally large specimens, running occasionally to 30 or more pounds. This is lake fishing, and it is the big ones that fire the angler's enthusiasm.

Some anglers rig numerous hooks spaced along a line that is then threaded under the ice, using several holes to accomplish the trick. The outfit is so arranged that the fisherman can pull the entire line back to him. Chunks of fish, or such delicacies as bacon rind, are used for bait.

In Washington, small baitfish called "redsides," actually a member of the squawfish group, are first caught on small hooks baited with salmon spawn. The redsides are then used on large hooks as "ling" bait and fished deep. Fish of 10 to 20 pounds caught thus are not uncommon. In the Far North burbot of over 50 pounds measuring upwards of 5 feet long have been taken. The burbot will now and then strike a lure such as a spoon, and is taken incidentally by trollers after lake trout or other species in Canada and elsewhere.

Actually it is the looks of the burbot that has kept it uncommon in the kitchen. The flesh is by no means inedible, and small amounts occasionally even find their way nowadays into commercial markets. Burbot livers are exceedingly rich in A and D vitamins. Some years ago several processing plants were set up in Canada to turn the ugly, oft-spurned burbot into an asset of value.

Sturgeon

Scaphirhynchus platorynchus

Among the most ancient of fishes still reasonably common today are the sturgeons. They are also our largest freshwater species. There are at least half a dozen varieties in our waters. The white and the green sturgeons are both native to the Northwest. The common sturgeon lives along the Atlantic coast, the lake sturgeon in the Great Lakes and surrounding area. The shovelnose sturgeon (scientific name above) lives in Mississippi Valley waters. The shortnose sturgeon is a fish of the east coast. Several of these species—white, green, Atlantic, shortnose—spend part of their lives in saltwater and are anadromous, ascending coastal rivers to spawn.

Of all our species the white sturgeon grows largest and may attain a weight well over a ton. Sturgeon of 1500 and 1800 pounds have been caught in both the United States and Canada. The lake sturgeon once abundant in the Great Lakes but now at a low ebb usually weighs at maximum about 200 pounds. The shovelnose sturgeon is the smallest of the lot.

These are ordinarily bottom-feeding fish, sucking up their food in a mouth fashioned like a big, short tube. They grow slowly, may live to be over a hundred. Actually very little is known about their life histories. They do not have scales, but some of the species have quite a number of bony plates along their sides. Neither do they have skeletons of true bone, but rather of cartilage. All told they are very curious monsters, delicious to eat, and famous because of the caviar made from their roe.

As a game fish little has been heard of them. And yet, in certain areas they are the subject of great enthusiasm

White Sturgeon

among a scattering of anglers.

Two methods are employed to turn them into sport: spearing through the winter ice; fishing with hook and line at other times of year. The ice spearing over past years has been mostly in Wisconsin's Lake Winnebago, and in Michigan's Black, Mullet, and Burt lakes of the Lower Peninsula. Spearing is a patient man's game. Some experienced hands at it are confident sturgeon have regular runways in certain portions of any body of water where they live. A fishing shanty is set up over one such location. Its interior is darkened and the spearman, ready with a large spear with weighted head to which a rope is attached, watches hour after hour for the huge shadow to drift into the hole. Some spearmen use decoys of various kinds. These are not bait, but merely attractors. Some use colored blocks of wood, or ears of yellow corn. When the sturgeon appears, the spear is sent home.

Generally the thrust of the heavy spear, some of which weigh as much as 15 or more pounds, incapacitates the sturgeon. But not always, in which case a severe battle may follow before the big fish is hauled out.

Hook-and-line fishermen use set lines, where that is legal, and bait heavy hooks with scraps of meat or fish, doughballs, lampreys, or gobs of nightcrawlers. Others use rod and reel. This, of course, is where the true sport of sturgeon fishing comes in. A few areas in Wisconsin, and numerous ones in Ontario, have furnished good sturgeon fishing over the years. But it is most popular in a few rivers of the West and the Northwest.

During the early summer of 1956, the well-known outdoorsman Ted Trueblood did some pioneer experimenting in the Klamath River in California, fishing for sturgeon with both modest and heavy tackle. The first did no good whatever, and even a tough outfit with 45-pound-test line couldn't hold the larger fish hooked. But, though many anglers here and there had tangled with sturgeon previously, there is no question that Trueblood's Klamath experiments sparked a great deal of interest in this offtrail sport.

Since that time sport fishing for sturgeon has grown to some extent in certain western rivers, for example the Snake. Presently, in some stretches of that river, sturgeon may be caught and battled, but must be released. Heavy tackle is mandatory in the swift water. Rods 10 feet long, lines of as much as 135-pound test, 12/0 hooks and 12-ounce sinkers make up typical rigs. Baits of cut fish or fish entrails are commonly used.

These large sturgeon not only battle fiercely, but leap. This in itself is startling enough to kindle interest in the endeavor. There is nothing especially difficult about the technique of getting sturgeon to take a bait. The angler simply finds a place where sturgeon are present, casts out his bait, and waits for the sturgeon to pick it up. The difficulty, of course, is in holding and licking a great fish once it is hooked.

It is presumed that laws will be further tightened to

protect remaining sturgeon from overfishing. They cannot stand much pressure, but they are getting various kinds. Dams on western rivers interfere with spawning runs and cut down on natural movements, as well as destroying much stream habitat. In some waters pollution is a problem. In all, it is believed that poaching is a worse one. Nobody knows how many sturgeon are illegally caught. The future of these huge and ancient creatures appears precarious throughout their range.

Gar

Lepisosteus osseus

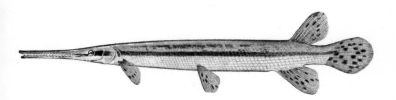

The gar with the scientific name listed above is the long-nose gar, or billfish, one of the three most common species found on this continent. The other two are: the **shortnose gar,** *Lepisosteus platostomus;* and the **alligator gar,** *Lepisosteus spatula.* Two other gar species are recognized: the spotted gar and the Florida gar.

The alligator gar is one of the largest freshwater fishes in the United States, exceeded in size only by the western sturgeons. Specimens well over 300 pounds have been taken, some of them 10 feet long. The longnose and short-nose gars are much smaller, 2 to 3 feet being average, with the longnose species the larger and sometimes measuring 4 and 5 feet. Both these fish, however, are almost cylindrical and not of great weight.

Gars are actually on the fringe of things as far as sport fishing is concerned. Most fishing literature, in fact, gives them no place whatever. Although they are edible, few people care about eating them. Gar roe is suspect as poisonous. The flint-hard ganoid scales are used to some extent in the manufacture of jewelry, and very occasional use is made of the exceedingly tough hides, but neither use is very important. Because their mouths are bone-hard, gars are not easy to hook; they are a great nuisance, especially in southern waters, to bait fishermen after bass and other game fish. They are exceedingly destructive of other fishes.

Nonetheless, regardless of all the counts against them, for hair-raising sport it is doubtful if any freshwater fish can compare with a big gar at the end of a line. The battle is wild and ferocious. The fish races away, leaps, tumbles, tail walks, and is very difficult to subdue. It is also difficult to kill. Gars are extremely tenacious of life, can live for hours out of water, and even when clubbed or shot sometimes keep fighting. The enormous alligator gar is the best performer. Quite a bit of interest has been centered in fishing for these brutes, by a few anglers out purely for the astonishing sport of it.

The gars range as a group from the Great Lakes on down the Mississippi. They are also in the St. Lawrence system, and are numerous in Florida and in eastern Texas. They like the warmer waters and bottoms of mud where there is much plant life. In lakes and slow rivers where they are abundant, gar often congregate in loose schools in the more stagnant bayous, but not always. They cruise the clearer portions, too. Wherever they are found, they are usually near the surface, and rolling noisily. Their gill structure is rather inadequate, but the air bladder is well supplied with blood vessels, and the fish are thus capable of gulping air, which they do regularly, taking part of their oxygen direct.

They will hit plugs and spoons, but seldom get hooked. Their bills are much too hard. They seize a minnow or other bait and carry it off, but again seldom get hooked, for the same reason. They must get the bait well down, which takes them a few seconds after the run is stopped, before a hook can be set, and even then it is likely to come free. For these reasons special methods of gar fishing have been invented.

For the smaller gars, with extended bills, a noose of thin, strong wire, such as piano wire, is made, and a minnow is dangled on a hook in the center. Some anglers run the minnow through with the wire, so it is strung on the loop. The idea is to get the gar to thrust his bill either through the loop, or to seize the wire while trying to get the minnow. A quick yank then snares him by the bill, and the fireworks begin. Bundles of nylon floss are sometimes used, with a bait. The floss entangles in the teeth of the gar and holds it as well as the hook.

Few anglers bother with this pastime, however. It is the alligator gar, entirely southern in range, that they go after. The lower White River of Arkansas, the Trinity River and the Rio Grande in Texas, the Atchafalaya in Louisiana are some of the better spots. The White has long been the most famous for the sport, from about mid-June on through until mid-September. Colder water from the big dams farther up, and work on the channel of the Arkansas, are thought now to be ruining alligator gar fishing there. Each expert has his own pet methods, but following is a general idea of how to go about catching one of these prehistoric monsters.

A favorite bait is the freshwater drum, which may be called "gaspergou" in the alligator gar country. These can usually be purchased from commercial fishermen. If not, other fish will do. The bait should be scaled. The gars appear to take it better that way. It is then cut into good-sized chunks, perhaps half-pound pieces, and hooked onto a gang hook. Trebles of 6/0 to 7/0 size or larger are used, with a steel leader of 4 to 6 feet, and swivels. From here on the tackle is standard saltwater gear: a heavy line, large-capacity reel, and a tough boat rod or saltwater casting rod.

A bobber is used, and as a rule is placed where line and leader meet. A cast is made and presently a gar picks up the bait to mouth it. The fish will then run with it. This run may be 50 or 75 yards, or less. The fish may circle several times. Finally it will stop and begin working at the bait. During the runs line must be taken in or let out gently, so not to disturb the monster. When the fish stops and begins swallowing the bait, the angler waits it out.

Often as not the bait is taken with no harm to the fish. If, however, hook and bait are swallowed, the fish will then begin to move off. The angler now gets the line snugged up gently and then strikes with all his might. If he has an alligator gar of 100 to 200 pounds or more, he may miss his lunch.

A pistol is standard equipment for alligator gar fans. No gar, large or small, should be taken into a boat unless it is "thoroughly" dead. Many appear to be dead, then come to life with a bang. Their teeth can very seriously wound an angler. Often a big alligator gar may be shot several times, right through the head, before giving up.

A curious characteristic of these enormous gars is that when they leap, which they commonly do, they often blow out air from the air bladder with such force that it sounds like a loud grunt. On the inhale there is a rasping gasp. With these dragon-like noises, the explosion of the leap, and the crash of the mighty fish back onto water again, alligator gar fishing has a full range of sound effects to go with the violent nature of the catch.

This is a highly specialized sport, and not many anglers will try it. But it is an experience never to be forgotten, and one trial has made enthusiasts out of a number of people. Some fly from distant areas each year to spend a few days killing big gars. Most fisheries management personnel wish they might be rid of gars. At least one state has had a law making it illegal to release any but the smallest gars without first slitting their bellies to make sure they will die.

part II

Saltwater Game Fish

Blue Shark

Prionace glauca

Whether or not sharks and their relatives, the skates and rays, are game species is an academic matter. Whenever a sportsman hooks one, and enjoys the ensuing battle, then certainly to him that species must be game. But when a deep-sea fisherman is desperately trying to catch a swordfish or other bluewater gamester, and instead hooks a shark, then the shark is a nuisance, and classed as trash. Regardless, the fact still remains that the sharks number among their many species several that are, in fighting qualities, among the world's great game fish.

A review of the sharks is likely to be confusing because there are so many species that appear at a casual glance so much alike, and the colloquial names used are so intermingled that they double the confusion. To compound even that, the scientists, as all too commonly occurs, cannot seem to agree about them. Consequently, if one depends on scientific names, three different current reference volumes may use three different names. And, species listed in one may not appear in others. For that reason scientific names, except with the chapter heading, have not been used here.

The mackerel shark group contains the Atlantic and Pacific **mako sharks,** both sometimes called "mackerel shark." The mako is found in many of the world's waters, and was first brought to attention as a game fish by Zane Grey. It may be anywhere up to a thousand pounds or more in weight and 10 to 12 feet long. It is a vicious shark, with tremendous staying powers. When hooked it usually leaps wildly and makes long, violent, unstoppable runs. It is a streamlined species, blue above, shading to silver

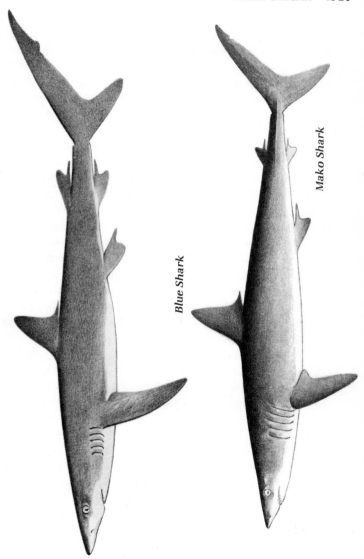

Blue Shark

Mako Shark

beneath, an inhabitant of warmer oceans, although it does range north on the Atlantic to Cape Cod. Makos are not abundant in our waters. Their greatest concentration seems to be near New Zealand. They are surface sharks, of open ocean areas, and because their general conformation is mildly similar to that of the swordfish, they are sometimes mistaken at a distance by big-game anglers for swordfish.

Sharks of course have large teeth. The size and shape of the teeth differ from species to species, and serves in many cases as a method of positive identification. The teeth of makos are very large and dangerous. They make landing a mako (and most other sharks) difficult, because it is all but impossible to keep them from slashing leaders, even heavy woven steel cable. They also have a habit of rolling up in line and leader as they fight. Thus, leaders for all large sharks are very long and heavy. The rough hide itself can sever line. Tackle for makos should be of the heaviest kind, such as that used for large marlin, swordfish and tuna. Reference to those fish in this book will give valuable tackle information.

The **porbeagle shark** ranges off northern Atlantic shores and most of our Pacific shore. It is quite generally confused with the mako, which it resembles. But it is usually more gray, or brownish, and the narrow, long, triangular teeth have cusps at the base. It is not as game as the mako.

The **thresher shark** is a species as large as the mako and unmistakable because of the greatly elongated upper lobe of the tail. Often this appendage is equal to or longer than the body of the shark. These sharks are as game as the mako, and make high leaps and long runs. Color is dark gray, brown, and bluish. The species is found along both our coasts. Both the mako and the thresher, as well as most other sharks of the open seas, are most often taken incidentally while anglers are trolling for other game fish. Few anglers fish specifically for these pelagic sharks. This has no relation to their game qualities. Most open-ocean big-game fishermen simply are after the bill fishes. This is rather expensive sport and therefore many anglers are perforce excluded.

The **white shark,** also called great white shark or man-eater, is also very game, and an extremely vicious, swift, powerful brute, one of the largest, at maximum, of life forms in the sea. At least one specimen almost 37 feet long has been taken, and those of 20 feet are fairly common. It is believed that still larger individuals roam warm seas. This shark is not abundant in our range, but is occasionally taken by big-game trollers.

The **tiger shark,** a large surface species of open water with dark vertical markings on the sides, is also a game shark, although nowhere in our range abundant. It is usually hooked on the surface, at night. Leopard, or cat, sharks are smaller, spotted, commonly caught along our Pacific coast. They are not especially game.

Two varieties of **black-tipped shark** (small and large) are good game species, mainly in the Gulf of Mexico, although they are also found occasionally along both our coasts. These sharks are gray above and have the fins tipped with black. They are not difficult to distinguish, therefore, from other sharks, but separating them from each other is a technical problem. These sharks may weigh anywhere from 15 or 20 to several hundred pounds. A common name for them is "spinner sharks,"

Tiger Shark

Hammerhead Shark

because of their habit of leaping straight up from the water, while traveling in schools, then making several spinning revolutions of their bodies while in a horizontal position.

The black-tipped sharks are not entirely species of open waters. They are often found around the surf line and near jetties, basins, and piers. They are purposely stillfished from such places, and are also trolled. Sometimes chumming is used to gather a school.

The **blue shark,** which appears here to head this section, is not an especially game shark, but it is typical of general shark outlines. It is a large species, with a reputation as a man-eater, although this is not wholly substantiated. It frequents both our coasts, and is rather common offshore in the Atlantic and, in summer, in inshore waters of New England. Quite a number are taken by sport fishermen, because these slender and somewhat sluggish sharks are scavengers that are easily induced.

The **hammerhead** is a shark species unmistakable because of its peculiar head formation, with the eyes set far out at the sides of hammerhead-like protrusions. A good many of these sharks are caught, both small ones of only a few pounds and large ones. Hammerheads may grow to 15 feet and 1500 pounds, and are considered dangerous sharks. They frequent both inshore and offshore waters, and often travel in schools. They are migratory and are found along both coasts. A good many, especially small ones, are caught by stillfishing from piers and bridges. Others are taken trolling.

There are a great many other kinds of sharks—the lemon shark, bull, bonnethead, Atlantic sharpnose, Pacific angel, and a host of others common and rare—but the ones listed above are representative of the most game species. Scads of sharks are caught incidentally by anglers after other fish, and go unidentified. Many fishermen consider them nuisances. However, shark fishing for any species that comes along is an exciting hobby pursued by a number of anglers all along U.S. Atlantic and Pacific shores and offshore, and throughout the Gulf.

Lately in fact there has been an accelerated interest in shark fishing. Some of it stemmed from the famous movie *Jaws*, but well before that specialist shark fishermen were spending every fishing moment trying for sharks of varied sizes, along both coasts but perhaps most avidly and with greatest dedication in the Gulf of Mexico. Many of them dote on fishing from or near oil rigs in the Gulf. There has even evolved a scattering of fly fishermen who go after sharks, especially in Florida waters, when the fish are feeding over shallow flats. Curiously, they find that presentation of the fly—usually some bright, large streamer concoction—is difficult, because of the fact that sharks have poor eyesight. The fly cannot be presented in front of the fish and drawn across. It won't be seen. It must be cast to the side of the fish's head and moved along past the eye. All told, sharks of all kinds have moved up in the angling world over the past decade or more.

The open-water sharks may sometimes be caught on trolled jigs, but are usually taken with bait, either whole fish or strip-cut. Stillfishermen take inshore sharks by using very large and often specially made hooks, baited with whole fish or large chunks of fish. Tackle must be matched, of course, to what one proposes to catch. By and large, all shark fishing may be said to require heavy tackle. The smaller species and young sharks can of course be handled on a variety of light tackle. But seldom can one be certain he is going to catch a small shark.

Sharks are nowadays quite valuable commercially and are netted, harpooned, taken on trot lines with steel chains for leaders, and on hook and line. Shark livers are used for making vitamins, some shark species are highly edible and are marketed, and shark skin, which is rough and exceedingly durable, is made into leather. Trash sharks are ground into fish meal and some are made into fertilizer.

Over the past few years shark teeth, and shark jaws, have become so valuable as decorative and "tourist" items that some conservationists are alarmed for fear the shark population will be decimated. Although the market in this country for shark as a food fish has so far been small, attempts are being made here and there to encourage Americans to eat it. Some party-boat skippers urge clients to keep and eat some of the smaller sharks— 2 to 5 feet long—that are commonly caught. Among the sharks, certain varieties are much better food fish than others. Texas has been testing shark meat in public "tastings" and trying to establish a market for it so that commercial fishermen can better utilize the large shark resources of the Gulf.

Sharks, though classed as fish, have cartilaginous skeletons, rather than skeletons of bone. They are without scales, although as noted the skin has many small rough projections, like saw teeth. A few species of sharks lay odd, horny eggs, but most give birth to their young, having held the eggs inside the body. Apparently sharks have a highly developed sense of smell, but poor eyesight.

Close relatives of the sharks, and worth mention here, are the skates and rays. The **sawfish,** with its long, spatulate, spike-studded snout which is in demand as a tro-

Largetooth Sawfish

phy, is actually a species of ray. Sawfish grow to large size (several hundred pounds) in warm waters of Florida and the Gulf of Mexico. They often are found in river mouths, and even some distance up large coastal rivers. They are a nuisance to anglers, although occasionally someone will stillfish for them, or harpoon them, for sport. They fight a hard battle, mostly because they are large and therefore strong.

The **manta ray,** or devilfish, famed in tall tales, is the largest of the butterfly-shaped rays, grows to a ton or more, and may be 20-odd feet across. It is occasionally harpooned for sport, and is an awesome adversary.

A great many species of skates and rays inhabit inshore waters, especially in southern localities on both coasts and the Gulf. The so-called "shovelnose shark" or "sand shark" commonly caught by surf anglers along the California coast (average size of those caught is from a foot to 5 feet) is actually the **guitarfish,** an elongated species of ray with the "wings" not as well developed as in some other species. Lately quite a sport has been developed by archers, who run a line from an arrow to a rod and reel. They then stand in the front of a small skiff and shoot rays. Once the arrow is in the ray, the archer puts down his bow and plays the ray on rod and reel. Fred Bear, the famed archer, has popularized this pastime to some degree by shooting leopard rays along the Florida Keys.

Anglers do occasionally hook various species of rays in numerous localities, and at times these rays put up a fairly good battle. However, it is doubtful that they should be included as hook-and-line game fish. They are for the most part troublemakers, because numerous spe-

Manta Ray

cies carry a stiff spine atop the whiplike tail and inflict painful, and in some cases poisoned, wounds on unwary persons wading at surf line. The wound most often occurs because the rays are stepped on as they lie flat on the sand, or all but buried in it. Some rays are capable also of giving an electric shock.

Over the past few years, as sport fishing has become more and more crowded and fishermen have therefore sought new horizons purely for action and not necessarily for food, shark fishing and fishing for large rays have both become more popular. The anglers pursuing these sports are a dedicated minority. They serve as pioneers of a sort who develop new endeavors which will eventually, perhaps, be pursued on a larger scale. In future years we may well need all of these species for recreational purposes, and since many of them are truly game they should receive more and more attention from heavy-tackle anglers looking for unusual thrills.

Swordfish

Xiphias gladius

The swordfish, broadbill, or perhaps most properly broadbill swordfish, makes a place for itself among the elite of the world's great game fish if by no other attributes than its size and violence of temperament. Not many anglers, comparatively, manage to beat a broadbill. Some have spent most of a fishing lifetime trying. It is a rather expensive, and altogether difficult, operation.

That is not to say that many swordfish aren't taken. They are not rare. Many are marketed annually by commercial fishermen who harpoon them or catch them on long, deep-set lines. Locating, luring, striking and landing a broadbill with sporting tackle is, however, exceedingly tricky.

The only other species with which the swordfish might be confused are the marlins and sailfish. It is not difficult to distinguish each. The bill of the swordfish is much longer than the others, and flat. Those of marlin and sail are cylindrical. Swordfish have no scales, nor pelvic fins. The others have both. The dorsal fin of the broadbill is reminiscent of that of a shark. It is sickle-like, in adult fish does not run on down the back with shorter spines. The forward dorsal of the marlin is broader, and the remainder of it running on toward the tail is easily seen. In addition, the color of the broadbill is brownish, of the others some bluish or greenish shade. The swordfish is also a much chunkier fish forward than the comparatively slender marlins.

Although swordfish are distributed throughout a great proportion of the world's seas, to have a chance at them in our waters one must be at a proper place, of which there are not too many, at a very carefully planned time. The broadbills appear off both our coasts, but in the Pacific are not especially abundant off California and are seldom seen farther up the coast. From San Pedro southward along the Mexican coast, and in some instances out around California's coastal islands, swordfish are taken. Fishing occasionally begins as early as May, improves through into the fall, with the best usually in September.

The best broadbill grounds are located on the Atlantic coast. Here, from Newfoundland on south these migratory fish range at varied seasons. During midsummer and to the end of August, waters off Nova Scotia's Cape Breton Island hold broadbills abundantly. The fishing is earlier off New York, beginning in June. On south, April and May are the months. Swords are often seen off Cuba, but they are not too commonly caught there. The chief Atlantic gathering places for swordfishermen are: Block Island, Rhode Island; Montauk, New York; and Cape Breton.

Not all swordfish are enormous, although even a small one is likely to have a fisherman thinking so before it is landed. Probably fish of 150 to 300 pounds may be called average. Quite a number in the 400 and 500 pound class are taken, some of over 700 and 800 are caught. Such fish are as much as 12 to 14 feet long. No one knows how large the maximum size is, but it is known to be at least 1000 pounds, and probably is more.

Swordfish are creatures of the open seas, deep-water monsters. They are known to feed very deep, but in fishing season they feed near the surface, and are fond of sunning on it. At such times a boat may approach quite closely.

The usual fishing procedure is first to go scouting swords. This in itself may prove a long, tedious, and possibly unsuccessful endeavor. They are not school fish. They are, in fact, ordinarily lone wanderers, or at most in pairs. It is nearly useless to troll in the hope of a chance strike, which seldom materializes. When the sickle-shaped fin of a swordfish is sighted on the surface, however, the fishing boat is brought about and circled so the bait may be trolled across before the fish. It may be necessary to make several smaller and smaller circles before the quarry sees it.

Baits differ with the area fished. Mackerel and squid are among the most popular ones. The rig is carefully set up. Either the backbone, or backbone and entrails both, are removed from a bait fish and a single or double hook sewed or lashed inside the bait. Some anglers use large, hookless, pluglike teaser lures to get the fish within striking distance, then put the bait over.

Like all billfish, the swordfish habitually feeds on schools of forage, lashing out with its bill to stun or kill its prey. It then makes a turn and seizes the inert food.

It does not always feed immediately, however. Sometimes the strike comes with a smash. Sometimes the angler must wait, after only a tap. In fact, there may be several such. But as soon as the first one is felt, slack line is instantly let out, so that the bait drops back and begins to sink, as if dead or injured. It may—or may not—be several minutes before the swordfish will actually take the bait.

If the angler strikes too soon, he ruins everything. Or if he strikes at a tap from the fish's bill, he may foul hook his prize. This occurs rather commonly. If the fish takes immediately, it may throw the hook instantly in a wild leap. When or if the monster finally seizes the bait it generally makes a torrid run. Line is swiftly paid out. It is doubtful that the fish could be stopped anyway. From 100 to 300 yards are given before the hooks are set. The mouth of a broadbill is not very tough for the size of the fish. Hooks can be torn out if the fish is improperly handled. This adds to the difficulty.

The battle is an awesome one, starting like an explosion the moment the hooks strike home. Broadbills occasionally leap all or part way out of the water. But they are fundamentally runners and deep fighters, and are not as spectacular leapers as the other billfish. They dive, only to surface with rocketlike swiftness, gaining slack into which they roll and against which they slash powerfully with the bill. When they sound, they must be pumped or planed up, by sheer muscle, or by backing the boat down upon them until slack is gained, reeling in, and repeating. Once up, the fish may shoot off across the surface for several hundred yards. Both the runs and the dives are practically impossible to stop. And a broadbill never quits, even at the gaff. This is a creature of tempestuous, explosive, and pugnacious spirit.

It is also an exceedingly suspicious, shy, and erratic customer. Experienced broadbill fishermen and boat captains claim each fish takes a bait with a different degree of caution and that each fights a totally different battle. It is a battle that is certain to last several hours, and may last from dawn until dark and still not be won by the angler.

The heaviest of tackle is needed in this game. Below would be a reasonable outfit. Some lighter ones are used, but only by experienced broadbill anglers. A rod with 26-ounce tip, reel 14/0, holding upwards of 800 or more yards of 39-thread linen, a cable-type stainless-steel leader 25 feet long with breaking strength near 500 pounds. Heavier lines and heavier rod tips are often used. Hooks are from 7/0 on up.

The beginner should be cautioned that the type of man behind the tackle is important, too. He must have strength and stamina. The whipping and landing of a broadbill swordfish is a feat requiring endurance and power. In no case should an attempt be made to bring aboard a swordfish not completely done in. Both sword and tail can be mortally dangerous.

Blue Marlin

Makaira nigricans

Of all the big-game fishes of offshore waters, the marlins are probably the most famous among the greatest number of anglers. They are very large, they are taken at the surface, and the violent display enacted after one is hooked has made them entirely deserving of the fame they have acquired. They are not much as food fishes, although smoked marlin is good. They are primarily a trophy fish. Of the several species, the blue marlin (in some references *Makaira nigricans ampla* or simply *N. ampla*) is, within our range, the largest. Blue marlin above 750 pounds have been caught on a number of occasions. Average specimens run from 200 to 500 pounds, and harpooned fish of over 1000 have been authenticated. Trophy anglers have long concentrated on the region of the Virgin Islands where twice during the 1960s the record was broken—by fish of 814 pounds in '64 and 845 in '68. However, some anglers had long suspected that substantial numbers of large blue marlin might be present off the U.S. coast along the Carolinas (see next page). The world of saltwater big-game fishing was astonished in mid-1974 when the world all-tackle record was utterly shattered, by a fish caught off North Carolina that weighed 1142 pounds.

In the swordfish section immediately preceding this section, distinguishing differences between marlin and swordfish are given. It is not at all difficult to distinguish between the marlins and their other close relative, the sailfish. The outstanding difference at once apparent is that sailfish have an extremely high dorsal fin, ragged at the upper edge but extending when opened like a high sail from just back of the head to midway above the anal fin. The marlins have only the fore portion of the dorsal high. It immediately dips down and runs very low along the back. There are other differences, of course, but this is all one needs for identification.

Although the blue marlin is our largest species, it is caught along our immediate coasts the least often. It is a fish of the Atlantic and the Gulf, ranging in our latitudes from the islands of the Caribbean north as far as offshore Long Island. There is also a Pacific blue marlin, which may or may not be identical. It is considered by some scientists as a distinct species. At the extreme northern end of the now known range of the Atlantic blue marlin, that species is caught only occasionally, usually in late summer. Farther south, off the Carolinas, blue marlin are caught in fair numbers in the Gulf Stream during July. Perhaps more are present there at proper seasons than are now suspected. Fishing conditions for them there are not easy, and not many anglers try the area for them. Some are taken off Florida during June and July, and occasionally in winter. The Gulf, offshore from Texas, furnishes an occasional blue marlin, again in summer. The best fishing area is around the Bahamas and off Cuba, Puerto Rico, and several other of the West Indies islands. May, June, and July find the most fish passing through. However, specific islands offer good opportunities during various months—March, April, September, and, in a few spots, on through the winter.

In the Pacific, below our ranges, or at least no closer than off southern Mexico, there is what has been called a **silver marlin,** about which scientists are still uncertain. Some say it is actually the black marlin. After a hundred years of study ichthyologists still disagree about several of the marlins. Some specimens called "black" or "silver" may have been Pacific blues.

Blue marlin are dark blue on the back, shading to silver below. There may be lighter bands or stripes running from the back down across the sides. Sometimes these appear only when the fish is excited or fighting the hook. The blue marlin can be separated from the only other certainly known species of marlin in our Atlantic and Gulf waters by noting the dorsal fin. The anterior lobe of the blue is almost like a sickle, the upper portion of it rather slender and sharp.

The **white marlin,** *Makaira albida,* the other Atlantic form, is a much smaller fish in average size, and has the anterior dorsal lobe broad, and very much rounded at the top. The dorsal fin of this species is also peppered with dark spots. In some references this fish is placed in another genus, as *Tetrapturus albudus.* The white marlin seldom weighs over 150 pounds, and averages from about 40 to 100. It ranges through the Gulf, eastward

White Marlin

to Cuban waters and throughout much of the West Indies, north as far as Cape Cod, and as a straggler even to Nova Scotia.

This is the marlin most often caught in the Atlantic. Like the blue, it is a species of warm waters; thus it is found at the northern portion of its range as a rule only in July and August. Off Ocean City, Maryland, is one concentration point where a number are usually taken each summer. The winter months, from first of the year to June, offer the best southern fishing, with March ordinarily the peak month in numerous sections. The general color of the white marlin is rather similar to that of the blue, but it is much brighter, and greenish blue. It usually has the paler bands running across the upper sides. It is a far more delicate appearing fish than the blue marlin.

In the Pacific the **black marlin,** *Makaira indica,* is somewhat below our ranges. There has been confusion about its proper scientific name. It is a fish of the Gulf of California and the coast of lower Mexico and South

Black Marlin

Striped Marlin

America. It is dark, and very large, possibly the largest of the marlins, and it is thought by some scientists to be the type species from which all others evolved. Incidentally, and unfortunately, the blue marlin of the Atlantic is sometimes called "black marlin," or "Cuban black marlin." This is a poor name, since the fish is not black, and the name only serves to confuse a situation already somewhat confused because research on these big fishes is such a slow and laborious process.

The **striped marlin,** *Makaira audax* (some references— *M. mitsukurii*), is the marlin of the Pacific within our immediate ranges, and is probably the best known of all the marlins and the one that has gathered the most fame in American waters. It comes north to about Point Conception, California. Most fishing is done from southern California ports such as San Diego. San Clemente Island and the Catalinas, and the Coronados are good areas. Farther south, Guaymas, Mexico, is famous for its striped marlin fishing. Late summer and on through September is generally the best time for striped marlin fishing off California, although some fish arrive as early as June, and some are taken on through even to the first of the year.

This marlin, like the blue, is a big fish, averaging anywhere from 100 to 400 pounds, and attaining a maximum of at least 750.

The marlins are all fishes of open offshore waters. They feed to a great extent on the surface, and can be spotted by anglers watching for them. All are leapers—that is, they often hurl themselves from the water as they cruise or feed. This habit is carried over into the battle they offer on the hook. All make sizzling and unstoppable runs, then hurl themselves from the water in breathtaking jumps. The big blue has a habit of "greyhounding" over the surface more than the others, and making shallower leaps. The white and striped marlins go end over end, thrashing their bodies as they skyrocket. All at times "walk on their tails" for many yards as they try desperately to free the hook. When marlin sound, they must be brought up quickly, if possible, or else one must try to keep them from sounding, because often they will go so deep they die, and then must be pumped up to the surface as dead weight.

All species feed on various other live fishes abundant in their range. Flying fish, mackerel, mullet, bonito, menhaden, dolphin, and squid are among their foods. All these, either whole or as cut strips, are used as bait, depending on the locality. Occasionally marlin can be induced to strike large feathered jigs, but they are so shy of artificials and take live bait so well, that few people care to fish them with anything else. Baits are often hooked through the lips. The traditional fishing method is trolling.

The experience and expertness of the boat captain is undoubtedly the most crucial factor in marlin fishing. In some ways marlin fishing resembles fishing for swordfish.

There is one most important difference. A marlin rushes in and strikes the bait with its bill, to stun it, just as the swordfish does. The angler then lets the bait back on a slack line, so that it will appear to the fish dead, or stunned. But whereas in sword fishing the reel is let onto free spool and a great amount of slack let back after the bill tap, in marlin fishing sometimes only a dip of the rod is enough. For while swordfish may take several minutes to return and pick up the bait, marlin usually wheel and rush to seize it immediately.

In general, the hooks are set as soon as the weight of the fish is felt. Some anglers, however, use the technique of stopping the boat the instant the fish hits the bait. Then as it picks it up, line is let free and the fish allowed to run with the bait in its mouth, sometimes for 200 or more yards. This run is usually very fast, and the fish may leap or break water at the end of it. At this moment the hooks are solidly rammed home. The shorter striking technique, however, seems to be the most popular one.

Heavy tackle is required, of course, for all large marlin. Thirty-ounce tips, 12/0 reels or larger, 600 or 700 yards of 39-thread or heavier, leaders of upwards of 500-pound test in lengths to 25 feet are common, and with hooks running from about 7/0 to 14/0. Many prefer the large hooks, especially for large fish. Pacific anglers use somewhat lighter outfits as a rule. For white marlin, much lighter tackle can be utilized than for the large species. Hooks are of course correspondingly smaller.

Marlin are not precisely school fish. Often they travel singly. Quite commonly a pair may be sighted, the tops of their tails thrusting from the water to give them away. And occasionally loose groups of marlin will be operating over a general area. When fishing them, some charter boats use a second bait, fairly close in, to help attract the fish. When marlin are sighted on the surface, and the bait presented to them, the sudden disappearance of a fish usually means it has spied the bait and submerged to rush it. If after the first tap and let-back, the strike does not materialize, an angler should reel swiftly for a moment, bringing the bait back to action again. Often this will elicit another rush.

Unfortunately, a great many marlin are hooked in shark waters, and sharks commonly attack them when they are on the hook. Many a beautiful specimen has been brought to boatside partially hacked to bits. Thus, it pays to use tackle heavy enough, where sharks are known to be present, so the fish can be fought down as swiftly as possible.

Atlantic Sailfish

Istiophorus albicans

The sailfish is the glamour queen of the larger saltwater game fish. On den and restaurant and office walls all over the country mounted sailfish catch the eye and add distinction, and the angler who has taken one can feel justly proud. Sails are beautiful fish. They are much smaller than the other billfishes, or spearfishes. The Atlantic variety (some references use the scientific name *I. americanus*) weighs from 25 to 100 pounds, averaging 30 to 50. The **Pacific sailfish,** *Istiophorus greyi*, a somewhat larger variety but colored identically except for somewhat duller tones, averages 60 to 100 pounds, with top weights reaching toward 200.

Some years ago sailfish were caught and killed in great numbers during the months when they were concentrated in our southern waters. Then various campaigns to save them from this useless decimation were begun. Buttons and honors of various sorts were offered to anglers for each sailfish released. Since the sailfish are not especially good food fish, although very tasty when smoked, there was little object in killing one unless a trophy was desired. Nowadays most of the charter-boat captains encourage clients to release sailfish.

Because the sail is a spectacular fighter, and present in large numbers off the east coast of Florida during the winter season, with all the publicity given to it over the past several decades it has become exceedingly popular. From the first of the year until the end of April or a bit later, sails are caught off Palm Beach and Miami, off Cuba and throughout the Bahamas. An occasional sail straggles on north, even as far as Cape Cod. But the concentration is much farther south. Winter visitors to the area can be fairly sure of catching a sail along the Gulf Stream or off the mouths of some of Florida's east-coast rivers. Sailfishing is not as expensive an undertaking as going after marlin, and so in some ways the sailfish is a kind of white-collar vacationer's marlin.

Although Florida and the West Indies get most of the sailfishing publicity, these fish are also common in the Gulf of Mexico, offshore from Alabama, Mississippi, and Texas. The concentration time there is generally in summer. Port Isabel and Port Aransas in Texas make good headquarters.

The battle of a sailfish is like that of a marlin only more so. It leaps grandly with its sail unfurled, somersaults, hurls itself out of the water time after time, and never ceases until utterly exhausted. The technique used to take sailfish is very similar to that used with the other billfishes. Strip-cut bait, from the belly of balao, bonito, etc., or a whole mullet or other small fish is used. Tackle is light, because of the modest weight of the fish. Some experts use the 3/6 outfit. This is too light for any newcomer. A 4/6 is much better for the beginner, and many use the standard 6/9. Hooks of 4/0 and 7/0 are usually employed, with wire leader of 8 feet or more in about No. 8.

The bait is trolled. A sail feeds like the marlin and swordfish, by smashing small live fish with its bill, then rushing to seize the stunned food. At the whack of the bill, line is instantly let back possibly 15 or 20 yards. Very soon the sail seizes the bait. The pause is ordinarily only a few seconds. When the seizing strike is felt, the hook is set.

Sailfish are somewhat more gregarious than are the marlins. They are commonly sighted in regular schools. Sometimes only the tail lobe can be seen above water as they cruise. And sometimes they are seen slashing dramatically into schools of forage. When they leap, which they often do casually, the great sail-like purple dorsal fin is unfurled. Sometimes they slice through the water after their food with the sail up and extending above the water. It is this sail, of course, that easily distinguishes the species from any of the other spearfishes.

In general coloration sailfish are rather similar to marlin. They are dark but striking blue above, silver below, and sometimes have lavender stripes running down from the back, but these are usually in the form of rows of dots. The purple dorsal fin may have dark blotches on it. When folded down, the huge dorsal drops neatly into a slot along the back, thus eliminating any possible water resistance. When swimming at high speeds, the fish of course keeps the sail down. Sailfish are awesomely swift.

The **Pacific sailfish** is much the same in habits and in appearance as the Atlantic variety, except that, as mentioned, it is larger, and less brilliant. Its range extends north about to Monterey, California. It is not as common within our ranges as the Atlantic species, but somewhat farther south it is exceedingly abundant. Charter boats may be hired out of San Diego and other southern California ports to go after sails, or one can go farther down, to Guaymas and southward, where the fishing is often sensational.

Off California and northern Mexico the best times will be from about May until midsummer, but farther south sailfishing remains good throughout the year. The 6/9 outfit makes a good rig for Pacific sails. Lighter tackle may be employed, of course, but too many inexpert anglers have, late years, attempted fishing with tackle far too wispy for the chore at hand. The best that can be said of the fetish in some quarters for extremes of tackle on the light side is that it is altogether as foolish as using tackle too heavy. It is a trick and a fad and cannot be recommended.

Because sailfish are fish of deep water, they are seldom caught very close to shore. Sometimes off Florida's east coast, however, they come in much closer than they do on the Gulf side. At the western side of the Gulf, off Texas, sails are caught at times within 3 or 4 miles of shore, but it is more common to find them as much as 25 miles or more out.

For those visitors to saltwater who do not own suitable tackle, it is possible to charter both tackle and boat. At the proper season, a day or two should suffice to catch a sailfish, and often a number of them can be hooked in that time. This makes the undertaking, especially if two or more anglers split up a charter, within the range of almost any vacationing fisherman. The experience is certainly worth every penny of the cost.

Tuna

Thunnus thynnus (Bluefin)

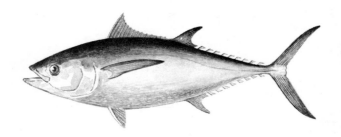

This species, in its maximum size, is one of our largest marine game fishes, and is considered in all sizes one of the best. There has long been a great deal of confusion among scientists as to the classification of the tunas. Whether or not there are several species or subspecies of bluefin tuna is at least questionable. For the purpose of anglers it is hardly necessary to worry about it.

The bluefin is found in both the Atlantic and Pacific. The maximum size in Atlantic waters is the larger of the two. Here it probably grows to 1500 pounds and more. Specimens of 700 and 800 are not at all unusual. The bluefin is occasionally called "albacore," a poor name because of possible confusion with the long-finned tuna, or true albacore, best known off California. Small bluefins, that is fish of 10 to 50 or even to 100 pounds, are usually called school tuna. Large bluefins, those upwards of 500 pounds or more, often are called "horse mackerel." This name probably originated through the inclusion in most scientific books of the tunas in the mackerel family. Tunas

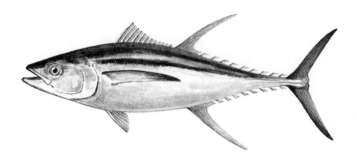

Yellowfin Tuna

and the various mackerels are indeed much alike structurally. The separation—for those scientists who use it—is in many ways one of scientific convenience.

The **yellowfin tuna,** *Thunnus albacares,* is the other main species of the group. It, too, is classified with the mackerels. All of these species with finlets running down the back and belly from dorsal and anal to tail—the tunas, mackerels, bonitos, albacore, wahoo—are closely related. In some books the yellowfin tuna has been split into several species, such as the California yellowfin tuna, *Thunnus macropterus,* or *Neothunnus macropterus* in some references, the Atlantic yellowfin tuna, using the scientific name *Thunnus albacares,* and the Allison tuna. This last one is a name given to yellowfins with exceptionally long anal and dorsal fins. However, it is thought by some scientists that these long fins may be simply a sign of older specimens. It is, in fact, doubted in many quarters if the yellowfins should be split up at all.

Yellowfin tuna are in general somewhat smaller than the bluefins, probably seldom if ever growing past 500 pounds, with the average less than 100. This is the important commercial tuna. It is also most abundant in the Pacific, and a great sport fish there. Yellowfins are most southerly in general range, found in the Gulf of Mexico and off the coast of California but seldom farther north. The yellowfin tuna are considered better food fish than the bluefins, although both are excellent.

The **blackfin tuna,** *Thunnus atlanticus*, is a much overlooked clan member, and a most delightful game fish for light- and medium-tackle fishing. It is a dark-colored tuna, and small compared to the others. Maximum weight is about 30 to 35 pounds, those of 20 are considered trophy size, and the average is from 5 to 10. Most books give the range of the blackfin as in the "western Atlantic," from Cape Cod south and throughout the West Indies. It is caught fairly often off Florida. The fact is, this small tuna also ranges clear across the Gulf to the Texas coast, where it is not at all rare. This fish has very little and often no yellow along its sides and on the fins. The finlets rearward of the dorsal and anal fins are dark, not partially yellow as in other tunas. The blackfin is a dynamic battler, its strength and tenacity out of all proportion to its size. It is also an utterly superb table fish, an authentic gourmet experience.

Because there has been so much confusion about identification of fish in the tuna-bonito-mackerel groupings, especially when specimens in the 10- to 60-pounds class are involved, it should be mentioned here that another species, the false albacore, sometimes gets called tuna. This one is popularly spoken of as "little tuna."

Because of its markings and general appearance it is placed in this book along with those other members of the family, the bonitos.

It is not especially difficult for the angler to differentiate between bluefin and yellowfin tuna. The latter usually has much more yellow in the fins, and has a yellow swath along the sides. It (the yellowfin) also has much longer pectoral fins; they reach to the rear as far as the second or soft portion of the dorsal fin. Both species have much dark-blue coloring and an iridescent sheen, with the backs very nearly black and the bellies varying shades of gray-silver.

The bluefin ranges in our waters from the West Indies, where a famous run draws big-game fishermen to Bimini in late spring, on north to Labrador. Over the water area from Wedgeport, Nova Scotia, to New York and New Jersey, the bluefins are abundant during the summer and on until about October. Much fishing is done for them out of ports along Nova Scotia, Maine, Massachusetts, and Rhode Island. In the Pacific the season may last from spring until well into the next winter, with the concentration—when the fish show up, which may be erratically—in the general Catalina area.

Although the yellowfin tuna is caught off Florida, in the Islands, and in the Gulf, and very occasionally farther north, it is mainly a Pacific game fish. It is most abundant off California, especially in the more southern ranges.

Tuna fishing cannot all be lumped into a single category. There are basically two varieties: fishing for mature tuna; fishing for small, or "school," tuna. This last is a bit of a misnomer, since all tuna run in schools. The first requires the stoutest of saltwater tackle, extremely heavy rods, enormous reels with hundreds of yards of line, and all the accoutrements that go with attempting to whip a fish that may outweigh the fisherman five or ten times over, a fish that is among the strongest pound for pound of all marine species. School tuna fishing, on the other hand, is quite often accomplished nowadays by the use of gear as light as saltwater spinning tackle.

All tuna, whether bluefins or yellowfins, large or small, fight alike. It is merely a matter of degree compared to size. A tuna hits with a smashing strike. When it feels the hook there comes a sizzling run completely unstoppable if the fish is large. Then the fish dives. It goes down, down, with frightening power. It may not stop until it is 300 to 400 yards beneath the surface. And then the long-drawn violent battle begins in earnest. It may last for hours. Of course the smaller specimens seldom go that deep, and can be done in more quickly. What is considered most important in fighting a tuna is never to let it have pause. This of course is as hard on the fisherman as on his quarry. Many a would-be tuna angler has changed his mind after the first hour fast to a big one. Further, the tackle ripped up by large tuna probably runs into scandalous figures.

Tuna feed on other fishes. They are inhabitants of big open water, where they take flying fish, mackerel, squid, and even dolphin. The Gulf Stream is a tuna highway. Kite fishing was originated here some years ago, so that a bait might imitate a flying fish, or at least be attractive to tuna because it was skipped over the water. This consists in flying kites to which the bait line is attached, with the bait running far behind and off to the side of the boat.

Outriggers are also used on tuna charter boats, much more in fact than the more complicated kite rig.

In some areas boats watch for schools of feeding tuna, then maneuver to troll a bait across in front of them. The bait is generally a herring or mackerel or any of the fishes upon which tuna feed, sewed carefully to the hook to make it look natural. In southern waters flying fish are a favorite bait. Trolling feathered jigs is also very popular and successful. Fishing the nets is another killing method. In waters where herring are netted, tuna boats work near where nets are being hauled. They chum with herring until tuna begin feeding with great surface boils. Sometimes these fish will then eagerly take a hook baited with a herring. If they will not, the angler cuts the herring open and sometimes coaxes the tuna in that manner.

Various methods of chumming are used, whether near the nets or in open water while trolling. Chunked herring or other fish may be dribbled over the side, and then a few whole fish slipped in when the tuna show. Or sometimes whole fish are used entirely. One trick is to strip off several coils of line from the reel and pile it carefully on deck. The bait is in place and ready. Now whole herring are dropped over the side and of course float back, sinking slowly. As tuna begin to "take," the one with the hook is slipped overboard. It drifts back on the loose line, taking the coils along, and the tuna smashes it.

Many precautions must be taken in all big-game fishing. The rough hide of a tuna scrubbing a line will quickly wear it in two. And thus a rather long (15-foot) wire leader of great strength must be used. Before fishing is started a number of yards of line is let over and thoroughly soaked, so that if a strike comes quickly the line will be flexible and handled easily. Line for all big-game fishing is doubled at the end, the last 15 feet or so, to give added strength. Swivels must work perfectly, and knots are avoided in attaching the line because they weaken the rig. A wrap-around-and-pass-through hitch is used instead.

Fishing for large tuna is an expensive and highly specialized sport. It requires a careful selection of tackle fitted to the method to be used. It requires ability in the skipper, and a proper choice of boat. In other words, this is not a casual undertaking, and for that reason only a general picture is given here.

Off California the smaller yellowfins as well as bluefins are often taken in some quantity by charter boats primarily in search of albacore. The same methods used for albacore (covered in another section) will be successful. Trolling is done rather swiftly, with a feathered jig or bait sometimes kept almost in the boat's wake. Chumming is routine. Fish in the 10- to 30-pound category are great sport on light tackle, either what has long been known as the 6/9 saltwater rig, or better still a saltwater spinning outfit with 10- to 20-pound-test monofil line. These smaller tuna are extremely popular with party-boat anglers, in the Atlantic as well as the Pacific, where several fishermen are working at a time. Large tuna of course are a one-rod-at-a-time proposition.

It is not always possible, obviously, to tell whether small or large tuna are going to take a bait. Generally, however, fish of more or less similar size travel together. In the last analysis, it all depends on how one wants to fish. For wonderful and economical sport, the smaller tunas are the target. For a challenge of the grim do-or-die sort where a man wants to prove whether he can or can't, the large fish give the greatest appeal. If a small specimen happens to take the bait fished for the monster, the job is just a minor annoyance to the fellow after bigger trophies. If the light-tackle man gets a bang from the big one, he simply (and swiftly) loses his line and starts over!

Albacore

Thunnus alalunga

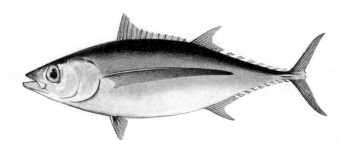

This fish has been switched about by scientists under such names as *Thunnus germo* and *Germo alalunga*, so be warned that references may differ, depending on their age and the whim of the time. It is a shame the albacore was not called by the common name long-finned tuna. That name fits it perfectly and identifies it.

When one eats tuna sandwiches, often as not they are albacore. This is the "chicken of the sea" that comes in cans, but which all anglers who have once had the experience much prefer to get straight out of the ocean at the end of a line. The albacore inhabits both coasts, but it is rare along the Atlantic coast. Occasional specimens are taken as far north as Massachusetts, and some are caught off Florida and throughout the islands, but this is primarily a Pacific species. It ranges up the entire U.S. Pacific coast, with good catches at times off Washington, but the albacore has made its fame as a dynamic sport fish off the coast of southern California.

It seldom if ever comes close to shore. This is a swift species of deep, wide-open waters where it feeds in large schools and ordinarily rather close to the surface on anchovies, flying fish, and all sorts of small, lively forage. Charter boats after albacore invariably wind up some miles offshore before hitting the schools. The Coronado Islands and the Catalina area are popular places. Farther north, boats find albacore as much as 30 or 40 miles off the Washington coast. Occasionally there is a season when the waters offshore from Vancouver Island are productive.

The albacore is a great traveler, an open-sea roamer that may turn up anywhere and conceivably at any time. Part of the challenge in fishing for them is the search that must precede the action. July and August are the months when boats out of San Pedro, San Diego, and points in between take their heaviest catches as a rule. But the albacore is most erratic, may show up one season in awesome numbers, and the next be missing entirely, or at best appear only in scattered and infrequent schools.

Albacore belong to the group of mackerel-like fishes. There is little reason for confusing them with any other species. The color is dark blue above, shading progressively lighter downward with an iridescent cast, to a silvery belly, with the fins usually bright yellow and bluish. The most outstanding characteristic is the striking length of the pectoral fins. These, when closed against the body, extend backward far past the dorsal. There are small finlets present along both back and belly, from dorsal to tail and from anal to tail. The long pectorals reach back to about the third dorsal finlet.

This is a middleweight, as saltwater gamesters go. Albacore average from 5 to 25 pounds, with occasional larger specimens. There are reports of rare 100 pounders. However, size is no criterion when an albacore strikes. It is used to living food that travels swiftly to escape. And it thus rushes headlong at a lure, which must be trolled swiftly, or at a bait anchovy, which must be lively, and it strikes viciously. Probably its speed is greatly responsible for the ripping strike. From there on, if the tackle holds, there is a smoking run, and perhaps several. The fish generally sounds and fights a dogged, deep battle, often having to be laboriously pumped up. It is not a leaper. But it is very strong, exceedingly tenacious, and difficult to whip.

Since albacore are extremely popular with southern California anglers, numerous charter boats make a regular business of searching for schools during the best months. The most common method is for a boat to take on several big tanks of live bait, such as anchovies, and then proceed to offshore waters known to be albacore habitat. Several anglers aboard begin trolling, with the boat held at possibly 6 knots. They may use a feathered jig (red and white commonly), a strip bait, or a live mackerel. When the typical albacore strike occurs, the bait tender starts heaving chum overboard. This is to attract and hold the school. The boat is stopped and the lines go over. It is a fast and wild melee from there on.

Sometimes gulls are sighted working on surfacing bait. When the boat draws near, the splashing boils made by feeding albacore may be seen. The boat pauses and the fishermen go to work, with the bait tender chumming if he deems it necessary. In all operations for albacore it takes a good boatman and chummer to know precisely how to work the fish. It also behooves all anglers aboard to follow instructions of the boat captain, for one mis-move may send the school down and ruin that phase of the fishing. A fish lost may frighten the whole school into streaking off as the scared one leaves.

Albacore addicts nowadays are using saltwater spinning tackle. They use about 250 yards of monofil line of 15- to 20-pound test. No swivel or steel leader is added. This is found much more effective than the old "tough-tackle" fishing, when a 6/9 outfit with corresponding terminal gear was considered the proper rig. The hook, of small size, usually no larger than No. 4 to 6, is tied directly to the line. A live anchovy is carefully put on, a long cast is made and the bait allowed to swim free. The striking fish may take 200 yards of line off the reel. Because salt-water spinning rods are long and whippy they probably do a better job of playing an albacore down than does heavier gear, and unquestionably the lighter terminal rig accounts for many more fish.

Surface-feeding albacore make tremendous white splashes as they boil into a bait school or into the chum. Sometimes when they are feeding lower, however, and not showing, a boat captain will suggest going down for them. Then sinkers of a couple of ounces are used on the spinning tackle, and stillfishing very deep is tried.

There is another species, the false albacore, which some anglers confuse with the true albacore. This is an Atlantic coast fish, a bonito. Lack of the long pectoral fins easily separates it. The albacore is probably the sportiest middle-weight of west-coast deep water, but like all good things may be difficult to locate. Feast or famine is the rule. When there is "feast," however, it extends in force right to the lucky angler's table.

Bonito

Sarda sarda

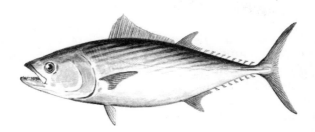

The common or Atlantic bonito and its cousins are excellent and most dashing game fish, but they have had several strikes against them for many years. Although considered inferior in eating qualities to the tuna, to which they are closely related, nonetheless a great many are canned and reach the market as "tuna," with qualifications on the label. Second, though the bonitos are beautiful fish, strikingly colored and marked, because they are of modest size, and relished by larger predaceous species as forage, they have long been considered one of the prime bait fish, either whole or strip cut. Somehow this has detracted from their role as game species in their own right. And third, science has managed to so muddle the entire group, possibly because of lack of facts to work with, and possibly because of too much hairsplitting, that the layman has very little chance of knowing precisely which bonito is which, or if it is a bonito.

To simplify the matter of classification and identification as much as possible, we might first place all the

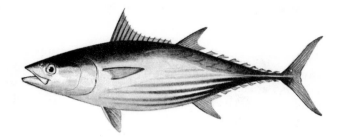

Oceanic Bonito

tunas and all the mackerels and all the bonitos together. They are all closely related. The American Fisheries Society officially classifies all of them together. But some scientists place the bonitos in the tuna family, some place them in the mackerel family, some assign a few to each, some lump all together, and some give a few of the bonitos families of their own. None of this is very important to an angler anyway. It is important, however, to know that the bonitos fall into two main groups.

One group consists of fish whose body is only partially scaled. In these the scales appear only in an area near the pectoral fins, and to some extent along the lateral line.

One of these which concerns us is the **oceanic bonito,** or skipjack (a name unfortunately much used for numerous fish), *Euthynnus pelamis*. This fish is strikingly colored blue and silver, with some reddish and yellow shadings, and with a pattern of darker lines usually showing along the rear portion of the back. Its distinguishing tag, however, is the pattern of four distinct longitudinal dark stripes running from pectoral fins to tail, below the lateral line, along lower sides and belly. It ranges along almost the entire length of both coasts, and in the Gulf of Mexico, but is predominantly a southern, warm-ocean fish.

The other member of the partially scaled group that falls within our latitudes has often and unhappily been called false albacore, *Euthynnus alletteratus*. That common name is also indiscriminately used for a larger fish, a large tuna. And, to make it worse, the fish of which we speak here is also called "little tuna," as well as "albacore," "bonito," and "frigate mackerel." The first one, little tuna, is now considered official, for this fish probably is a small species of tuna or at least closely related. Albacore and frigate mackerel are both exasperating misnomers, however, because each is of course another distinct species.

Nonetheless, this **little tuna** can be identified easily enough. It is shaped and colored quite a bit like the oceanic bonito, but it lacks the longitudinal dark stripes below the lateral line, and the lateral line is fairly straight, whereas that of the oceanic bonito has a sharp downward curve. Its range is in the Atlantic and the Gulf, and covers the same general area as that of the oceanic bonito there. Both of these species average anywhere up to about 20 pounds, but ordinarily the oceanic bonito averages larger, and may go to 40 pounds.

The second group of bonitos are fish whose bodies are entirely scaled. The **common** or **Atlantic bonito,** *Sarda sarda*, is a dark-blue and silver fish. It has dark bands running obliquely forward from the back to just below the lateral line. This distinguishes the species. It averages from 2 to 10 pounds, may grow a bit larger, and ranges the length of our Atlantic coast and occurs also in the Gulf of Mexico.

In the Pacific its counterpart, now called *Sarda chiliensis*, has had numerous scientific names, the most common of which is *Sarda lineolata*. It is almost identical in appearance to the Atlantic variety. For years variations were classified as different fish. They probably are not. This fish ranges up and down the coast, north at least to Washington, but is predominantly southern. It averages in size about like the common bonito, but is sometimes caught over 20 pounds. Some scientists believe that Atlantic and Pacific bonitos are only widely separated variations of a single species.

The **striped bonito,** or Mexican bonito, *Sarda orientalis* (some references *Sarda velox*), is a third member of the group having the entire body scaled. It is easily distinguished from the others by the fact that the dark stripes above the lateral line run horizontally, not obliquely. It is a rather small bonito, averaging only 1 or 2 pounds, but weighing a maximum of 6 or 7. This species is not well known, was once classified as several different species which are now thought all to be the same. It apparently ranges most of the Atlantic coast, again predominating southward, but in the Pacific it is found only below the border, and does not appear in U.S. waters.

The bonitos are school fish, and fish of offshore waters. Occasionally they wander close to shore when feeding. They are fabulously swift and very powerful. In general they are fish of the ocean surface, where they feed on smaller fishes and quite commonly on their relatives the mackerels. When hooked they are not leapers, but fight more like the tunas, which of course on one side of the family tree they are. They slash away after a smashing strike, making tremendously swift runs, and then they bore down and may stay deep until whipped.

Unfortunately for the sport involved, bonitos are often caught by trollers after larger game, and using heavy tackle. Fundamentally they are light-tackle fish. Nowadays more and more persons are spinning for them, with modest to heavy spinning tackle, when a school is located. They all strike artificial lures readily, from feathered and metal jigs to various plugs, wobblers, and spoons. A skiff kept near a school, with the anglers casting into it with such light tackle, is a set-up for high sport.

In southern waters bonitos are found from late winter to late fall. As they move northward, their stay in the colder latitudes is shorter. At the top of the range, summer months offer the best opportunities.

King Mackerel

Scomberomorus *cavalla*

This fine game and eating fish is never difficult to identify. The slender profile, the lack of spots or stripes on its iridescent blue-green and platinum body, the most individualistic tracing of the lateral line set it apart from other species. So does the name "king mackerel." The difficulty is, however, that this name is almost never used by anglers.

In Florida it is known simply as the kingfish, and in some other areas as cero or cavalla. Unfortunately, several other species are known by these names, too, so king mackerel—since it is the largest member of the Spanish mackerel group—is undoubtedly at least the best book name for it.

In American waters this is a fish of the Gulf and Atlantic. Although sometimes caught within reasonable distance of shore, the king is actually an open-water species. It is a school fish, the schools often numbering in thousands. It is a wanderer of the vast blue water, where it feeds mainly on smaller fishes.

Its slender, streamlined but muscular shape, and its

broad, deeply forked tail speak of speed. There are few ocean fish faster than king mackerel, and few that are stronger for their size. Happily, few others are more willing.

King mackerel range to the Carolinas and occasionally farther north. The best of the fishing is off the Carolinas and along southeastern coasts, especially off Florida and Texas. Florida natives and visiting anglers eagerly await the peak of the kingfish runs along both Atlantic and Gulf coasts. Some fish are taken all year, and some spurts of good fishing are likely at any time from November on through winter. March, however, is usually the peak month on the Atlantic side of Florida, and when the run is really on every boat that goes out usually comes back hull-down with fish.

The Gulf peak ordinarily comes a bit later. The Texas fishing begins in spring and runs on through the summer and into September. The Carolinas have good schools of migrating kings as a rule in spring and fall. Weather conditions may upset time tables anywhere in the range of this migratory gamester.

Possibly because it is a school fish of open water used to competing severely for food, the king mackerel is a vicious striker, hardly at all wary when a school is feeding. As long as the trolling lines are kept criss-crossing the school, anglers stay in business. Strip-cut baits are often used, and the king does have an annoying habit of cutting across behind this trolled bait, slashing off the end of it and keeping right on going. The troller who uses a nickel-finish spoon or a feathered jig doesn't have this difficulty. In fact, these artificial lures are in extremely common use for king mackerel. They work well, and save rebaiting time when a school is found on the prod.

Probably the average king mackerel taken by sports fishermen runs somewhere between 5 and 10 pounds. However, fish of 15 are common, and those of 20 to 25 certainly not uncommon. They go on up to 60 or 70 pounds, or even larger.

Off the Carolinas, king mackerel schools sometimes stay put along the outer edges of bays, chopping up schools of bait fish. Some anglers stillfish for them, using live bait. On the whole, however, the standard method everywhere is trolling. Commercial men use handlines, because of the speed with which these can be worked. But sports anglers use a saltwater trolling rod with a 4- to 6-ounce tip. In fact, the outfit long known as a "4/6"— 4-ounce tip and 6-thread line—is traditonal king mackerel gear, with a 6/9 outfit used for schools where fish run heavy. Reels should match—3/0 to 4/0. Monofil lines have of course almost entirely replaced braided lines.

Wire leaders of 6 to 10 feet are necessary. Kings have substantial teeth. Hooks should be rugged. Sizes of 6/0 and 8/0 are commonly considered proper for kings. Sometimes the fish will be near the surface and little if any weight is required. At other times a sinker is used to carry the lure deep enough to reach the feeding fish.

When a king mackerel hits, it does so with bomblike abandon. And the savage battle that follows—especially on reasonably light tackle—is just as explosive. It must be emphasized that the majority of king mackerel fight a below-surface battle, making sizzling deep runs. However, there is always the chance that one will go up. And when a king does leap, probably few other species could do a more spectacular job of it. Coming up from even rather shallow depth the fish shoots out of the water like a silvery arrow, creasing the air at fantastic speed and going on up as if intending to fly. A jump apex of 10 feet is not unusual. Leaps of 20 feet and more high have been reliably estimated. A leaping fish may heel over and come down like a precision diver, striking headfirst and disappearing with hardly a ripple on the surface.

Although high tides are favored for fishing king mackerel in specific areas, in most places tide makes little difference since the fish are taken quite a distance offshore anyway. The usual procedure is for several anglers to chip in and charter a fishing cruiser whose skipper knows where he is most likely to locate the schools. Fishing from a skiff is not recommended, because a small boat is not safe far out in open water.

As a general rule, king mackerel of a size school together. Thus, if a school is hit where the first several fish caught are small, one may find it advantageous to haul up and go looking for larger fish. Another interesting habit of kings is that they seem always to be traveling as if the Devil himself were on their tails. They never cruise easily or, apparently, laze about. They are restless, wild predators and quite deserving of the fine game-fish reputation they have built.

During the past few years much experimentation has been done with sportier fishing methods for this species. Particularly off the Texas coast, numerous fishermen have taken to using medium to light spinning gear, and also the standard baitcasting rigs used by freshwater bass fishermen. Such outfits turn kings into dynamic and hard-to-lick gamesters. Sometimes artificial lures are used. The boat locates a school of kings some miles offshore, cuts the motor and drifts, while the anglers cast. Far more successful and popular, however, is the now well-known method called "free shrimping."

Live shrimp are used. Sometimes no sinker is placed on the leader. But often a small weight such as is used in freshwater when bait fishing for bass is attached. This is just enough to take a shrimp quickly down into the schools of kings. The boat drifts, the hook is baited, and the wriggling, kicking shrimp cast overboard. The method is deadly, the big mackerel taking the bait solidly as it wafts down. Needless to say, the sport on such an outfit is classic.

Numerous boatmen have discovered that they can pinpoint with great accuracy where the schools of kings will hang out, simply by looking for drift streaks and places where currents clash. In the Gulf, for example, numerous whimsical and uncharted currents are constantly opposed. A charter skipper moves offshore, watching the green water. Suddenly it will change abruptly to a deep blue. On the surface a so-called "drift streak" will generally appear. This is formed by all sorts of small debris and forage that is trapped as one current butts up against another. Here the kings and numerous other species habitually feed. The schools will follow such current separation lines for miles because of the rich forage offered. This is the perfect line along which to employ the free shrimping method.

King mackerel are excellent when steaked and broiled, a fact long known in the East but oddly regarded with skepticism until recently by anglers of the western Gulf. They need to be iced as caught, and to be used in the kitchen soon afterward. They are at their best when cooked the same day caught, and when each steak is quickly seared on the outside on a hot fire. The fore portion of this fish may incline toward a fibrous quality. Steaks from the rear half are best.

Spanish Mackerel

Scomberomorus maculatus

The Spanish mackerel is considered by those who fish for it one of the finest game species on earth. There is little doubt that if this delicious, beautiful, streamlined species had the weight and size of a marlin it would outfight that fish tenfold.

Like all the mackerels, the Spanish mackerel is a school fish, and the schools may be very large. Occasionally, however, one may find a small school, or only a dozen or so running together, in some southern bay. It is very compressed in outline, an iridescent steel-blue to greenish above shading to shining, immaculate blue-silver below. The spots on the sides are mustard colored, or bronze.

There are records of Spanish mackerel that weighed as much as 20 and 25 pounds, but the average is much smaller. Some schools contain individuals of no more than a pound, others have fish of 2 to 4 or more pounds. These mackerels range as far north as New England, but they are never abundant, at least not for long, in any of the northern waters. They are warm-water fish, and are

299

most plentiful from the Carolinas southward, and especially about Florida and in the Gulf of Mexico.

Here great schools wander open waters, cruising near the surface and slashing into schools of forage fish. Spanish mackerel may be spotted occasionally as they leap from the water, and they may be noted churning the surface when into a school of bait. At such times gulls and terns and pelicans also dive upon the surface to gather in the small fish that the mackerel keep herded compactly. "Fishing the birds" in southern waters is an excellent way to locate mackerel schools.

The Spanish mackerel is not altogether a fish of the open seas. It is common in bays and channels, and near surf line, wherever in its wanderings it can come upon schools of small forage fish. In Florida waters, for example, during spring many Spanish mackerel are caught by stillfishermen using small bait fish which they call "glass" minnows. The anglers may fish from bridges that cross narrow bays, catching the fish as they cruise through.

This is an exceedingly swift, strong fish which is always very active. When hooked it is a brilliant fighter, making dashing runs, leaping high, hurling itself along the water, and fighting a wild battle. For that reason, and because of its modest size, the Spanish mackerel should be taken always on light tackle. It will strike a great variety of lures. Metal flashing spoons are among the best for it. Weighted feathered jigs also are deadly. The problem of fly fishing for Spanish mackerel is that they are used to pursuing their prey with great speed. They seldom pay close attention to a slowly fished bucktail or streamer, and to strip it in swiftly enough to attract them is difficult.

Spinning gear of freshwater weight is an excellent and most sporty rig for catching Spanish mackerel. They are most commonly taken by trolling. Here of course many anglers use tackle much too heavy. Again, the problem is that in saltwater one never knows how large a variety may strike. Nonetheless, one might better lose a bit of terminal gear occasionally, and have the fun of the mackerel.

It is necessary to use at least a foot or two of wire leader when fishing Spanish mackerel. Often when one is into a feeding school, fish will cut a line or a nylon leader as they snap at their prey. Some anglers believe the fish speed through the compact schools of forage with their scissors-like mouths open, and strike the line or leader unwittingly. Hooks should be of modest size, because the mouth of the fish is very narrow.

It is not possible to direct an angler to specific places, or types of places, where he is certain to find mackerel. As noted, they are impulsive wanderers, and they are where you find them. Certain southern bays do have a fairly predictable spring "run," however, and at such times one can usually clean up. Some seasons, regardless, the fish fail to appear. Off the Texas coast they appear about April and generally stay all summer.

Trolling is one of the best ways to locate fish. When one mackerel strikes there are almost sure to be more present. It is necessary then to keep in contact with the school, which may be traveling swiftly, or may be swimming round and round a school of forage. Great sport can be had by locating a school with trolling gear, then keeping a skiff or other craft on the edge of the wildly feeding host and casting into it with freshwater plug or spinning rods, or fly rods. Tide and surf rips at the ends of long channel jetties thrusting out into open Gulf waters are hot spots for Spanish mackerel. Here one may cast from the rocks, with a jig or spoon, and mop up.

In northern waters summer is the best time for mackerel. In portions of the Gulf, and up near the Carolina coast, late spring is the time. The schools are most active around Florida in early spring. When one is fishing open water offshore, tides have little effect on any kind of fishing. But inshore, in the bays, the channels, around the piers and bridges, and along the surf line, high tides are best for catching Spanish mackerel.

As is the case with many groups of saltwater fish, there is some confusion about species in the mackerel clan. There is a mackerel of the Pacific, ranging a short distance up the California coast but mainly a species of Baja California and Mexican and South American waters, called the Sierra mackerel. That is a name also used for the Spanish mackerel occasionally in the East. It is believed that these two are probably the same fish. There may be still other mackerel species of the same group, and quite similar in appearance, along southern California and southward, but they are rare. However, the matter is not well substantiated, and is not especially important to the casual angler. Whatever has been said of fishing for the Spanish mackerel of the east coast applies exactly to the Sierra.

Although these Spanish mackerels are perhaps the best sport fish of the smaller mackerels, several others are fine game fish, too. But again, before mentioning them in detail, it must be noted that a tremendous amount of confusion exists about their names. One in particular, the **painted mackerel,** *Scomberomorus regalis*, of the Atlantic, is called in some books the cero mackerel. This, in fact, has recently been offered from one influential source as *the* name by which it should go. However, the king mackerel (which is covered in the previous section) is quite commonly known, and has been for years, by this same name, cero. The Spanish mackerel is also occasionally called cero mackerel.

This painted mackerel (that name is used here to try to avoid some of the confusion, regardless of who is right or wrong) can easily be mistaken for the Spanish mackerel, but need not be. Sometimes they even associate with Spanish mackerel, in the same schools. The distinctive characters most easily and quickly recognized are these: The Spanish mackerel has the leading edge of the second, or soft, part of the dorsal fin set on the back slightly ahead of the positioning of the anterior edge of the anal fin below, while these two fins are positioned about even in a perpendicular plane on the painted species. The painted mackerel has spots somewhat more brown, and there are usually one or two fairly distinct longitudinal dark stripes running along the sides and crossing the down-slanting lateral line.

The painted mackerel is a fish comparable in size to the Spanish mackerel, with a range about the same. But it is not as common a species, except occasionally in the fall in the most southern portion of its range. Fishing methods are identical, except the painted mackerel does not appear to come close to shore as much as the Spanish mackerel.

For completeness a small mackerel called the **frigate mackerel,** *Auxis thazard*, should be included. It grows to about 12 to 15 inches, average, but occasionally to several pounds, ranges in large schools in the southern waters of both coasts. In the Pacific it is probably almost entirely below U.S. range, but does straggle northward up the Atlantic to Cape Cod. It is sometimes called a "skipjack" or "Mexico skipjack." It is a blue-green and silver fish, but often has dark oblique back markings very much like the common bonito. The striking characteristic is the great distance between the two portions of the dorsal fin. Only the forward portion of the body is scaled. Probably only rarely will sport fishermen happen upon this species.

There are at least three other mackerels that concern us, and these are the smallest of the group: the Atlantic (or common), the Pacific mackerel, and the chub mackerel. A great many of these three are caught, and they are very good sport on the lightest of tackle.

As with almost all fish, the **Atlantic mackerel,** *Scomber scombrus*, goes by a host of other names, but it is the mackerel of the wooden cask containing salted fillets, and the mackerel traditionally famed as broiled mackerel around Boston and other eastern cities. It travels in vast schools, wandering erratically, and usually staying close to the surface.

The fish is predominantly northern, traveling southward only to about North Carolina. It comes inshore in greatest numbers during the spring and summer, can be caught both inshore and off, around the reefs and bars and sometimes in the surf, by trolling, fly fishing, spinning, bait casting, and stillfishing. Since it seldom weighs more than a pound, or at best two, the lightest of tackle makes it the more interesting. It is a fine little scrapper.

Modest-sized flashing spoons and bright feathered jigs or bright flies do the best job of the artificials. Almost any bait will do, from shrimp and small crabs to minnows and pieces of fish.

The Atlantic mackerel is a striking dark blue above, with broad dark markings without regular pattern, and silvery below. A related species, the **chub mackerel,** *Scomber colias*, also a fish of huge schools and inhabiting roughly the same range, and often indeed intermingled in schools of Atlantic mackerel, is sometimes mistaken for the Atlantic variety. It is small, has an air bladder, which the common mackerel does not. The pattern of markings on the back, while similar, is much finer.

The **Pacific mackerel,** *Scomber japonicus* (*Pneumatophorus diego*, or *P. japonicus diego*, in outdated references) is the common mackerel of the Pacific coast. It looks rather similar to the Atlantic variety, at least it cannot be mistaken for anything else. Its habits are much the same, its size likewise, although occasionally its runs larger. Fishing techniques are the same. It will hit almost any active lure, and is a fine little sport fish, often caught from piers. Fall fishing is often as good as in summer.

Undoubtedly the future will see far more attention paid to these abundant, active little mackerels, especially since spin fishing and other light-tackle fishing in saltwater has become so popular and is still growing. It should be remembered that very often when larger and perhaps more desirable game fish do not strike, or cannot be located, species such as the common mackerels of both coasts can save the day and furnish fine sport. And of course all the mackerels are excellent food fish, with the Spanish varieties real delicacies.

Wahoo

Acanthocybium solanderi

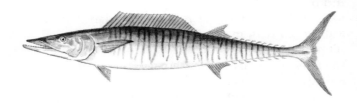

If the wahoo were as plentiful as the tarpon, and as accessible, it might well top the latter in popularity. This beautiful streamlined member of the mackerel tribe is unquestionably one of the world's most dynamic game fish. It is one of the swiftest fish on earth and would probably leave even the highly publicized bonefish foundering in its wake. It strikes with an awesome smash of the lure, while traveling at top speed. Without pause it streaks on, while the angler very likely is merely hanging on, slack-jawed, mesmerized by the sizzling of the line as it melts from his reel.

A hooked wahoo hurls itself out of the water in tremendous leaps. These may be 10 or 15 feet high. There are reports of wahoo leaping not only broadside over a fishing boat, but lengthwise. It may leap time after time, then suddenly sound, only to come up and race off in another smoking run. It is, all told, one of the wildest fighters of all, and it never quits until completely worn out.

The average wahoo will weigh anywhere from 6 to 25 pounds. They get much larger than that. Specimens of

30 to 50 pounds are not at all uncommon, and those of 100 and 125 and more have been caught. Fish of such substantial size and abilities would get more publicity if only the average angler did not have two main hurdles to overcome. Even at that, these hurdles make the wahoo an even more desirable trophy.

First of all, the wahoo is a lone wolf. Unlike the other highly gregarious mackerels, tunas, bonitos, and albacores, the wahoo goes its solitary way. Just because you catch one in a certain area is no reason to hope that you will quickly catch others. In addition, although this cannot be said to be a truly rare species, it is not very abundant. And because it is both scattered and scarce, catching one has a vast element of chance and requires persistent hunting.

The range of the wahoo in our hemisphere adds to the gamble of taking it. It is a tropical species. It may be found occasionally as far north as North Carolina, but in this range it is a straggler. A few wahoo are taken off peninsular Florida and off Texas, but mainly the species clings to the waters of the Keys and of Mexico, and is still more likely to be found farther out into the West Indies islands.

The Gulf Stream is prime wahoo territory. This is a fish living over deep water, often along the reef edges, where it may be found cruising the dropoffs. Now and then one is taken off west Florida, but by and large a try for wahoo is best made by headquartering at such places as Miami or Nassau and fishing out along the warm Gulf Stream.

The wahoo is beautiful and exotic in coloring as well as in shape. Above it is blue to blue green, shading progressively lighter downward into silvers and coppery browns, with a shining iridescence everywhere. Dark, uneven, rather wavy bars extend downward from the back. In specimens where these bars are broad, the fish may appear just the opposite, that is, to have yellowish bars on a dark background. When the fish is fighting, its markings are usually most distinct. Older specimens may have none at all, and in most they fade soon after the fish is landed.

There are few other species with which the wahoo might be confused. The king mackerel is about the only one. Actually the two do not look much alike, when comparison is possible. Superficially they do. The king has no stripes, of course. And it is very definitely a school fish. Quickest positive way to separate these two, however, is to count dorsal spines. The king mackerel will have fifteen, or sometimes one or two less or more. The wahoo will have twenty-five, give or take one or two.

The wahoo is called "queenfish" by many islanders in the Bahamas. "Peto" and "ocean barracuda" are other names. Nowadays however, with exchange of information much easier than it once was, and many anglers traveling far to fish, these other names are seldom heard. Queenfish is about the only one commonly in colloquial use.

Few anglers go hunting specifically for wahoo. Mainly they fish for something more abundant, but keep hoping for a wahoo trophy. The fish roam surface waters, where they feed on all kinds of smaller fishes, from flying fish to mackerel to mullet. The standard method of wahoo fishing—about the only way wahoo are ever caught—is by trolling. Charter boats ply the Gulf Stream and the outer reefs. A wahoo may be hung at any time of year, but ordinarily the best luck occurs from first of the year on through June.

Baits and lures used for other fish of the area catch wahoo: the usual feathered jigs, the spoons, the tin squids, whole mullets, or strip bait. Wahoo are often caught incidentally by boats after sails, dolphins, bonitos. Sails and wahoos feed in about the same manner, and regularly in the same places.

Anglers used to Gulf Stream or blue-water trolling for big fish will handle the wahoo capably with an outfit of medium saltwater weight. A healthy-sized reel is necessary, however, whether the tackle is heavy or light. A reel holding 400 yards or more of line testing 36 pounds is standard. Less experienced anglers should use heavier tackle, a stouter tip and line. A steel leader is always mandatory.

The wahoo, like all the mackerels, is a good eating fish. But those working on one with a trolling outfit for the first time are not likely to be thinking about eating. During the first few minutes of the fight, there is almost certain to be a question in the angler's mind as to who is running the show.

Cobia

Rachycentron canadum

This curious fish is similar to the mackerels in shape, and in many other physical attributes is reminiscent of that family. But in color it is brown above and cream below, with a dark swatch stretching lengthwise from the end of the snout to the tail, and with a less distinct stripe above and another below that line. In shape and general appearance, too, the cobia is somewhat like the suckerfish, or remora (on whose head there is a suction area by means of which it attaches itself to the sides or bellies of other, larger fish). In fact, small cobias are carelessly confused with remoras. There is no excuse for this except lack of even cursory observation.

Especially during recent years the cobia, also called crabeater because it feeds to a large extent on crabs, has become rather renowned as a game fish. It has picked up a number of other names along the way: ling, lemonfish, coalfish, and of all things snook, remora, black salmon, and black bonito. In addition the name cobia

has been garbled here and there, switched to cabio and
cobio.

What has endeared this fish to the hearts of those
anglers who have caught it is that it strikes with a vicious
blow, and then when hooked is very fast, strong, and
stubborn, putting up a rousing fight. The cobia in some
areas may average only 2 to 10 pounds, but in others,
especially off Mississippi and Texas, large fish are common. Those of 25 to 50 pounds in such locations are not
at all rare, and specimens of over 100 exist.

Cobia are found as stragglers well up toward New England, but their main range is from Chesapeake Bay, where
they are common during summer, on south and through
the Gulf of Mexico. Because they appear rather erratically,
and only spottily in real abundance at any specific place,
fishing them has been an incidental procedure in most
of their range for many years. Recently, however, a host
of cobia fans has sprung up in the upper Gulf area, along
the shoreline cities of Biloxi, Pascagoula, and others in
the region, from Alabama to Louisiana and Texas. Here,
about May, there are quite predictable runs of migrating
cobias of large size, fish from 30 to 80 pounds, and in
catchable abundance.

Although cobia are spoken of as offshore fish, actually
a good many are caught inshore in enclosed bays and
other quiet waters. They are fish that invariably are found
over rocks, or frequently near some kind of obstruction
or debris or floating object. The place where a power line
crosses a bay, with large poles and their concrete-shored
bases set into water, is a very likely spot to find cobia.
They will hang out near the poles. Bridges are another

good place to try. At Sarasota, Florida, for example, a few years ago cobia of good size were very commonly caught around pilings of the Siesta Key bridge.

In areas where rocks or pilings give shelter to one of their favorite foods, the crab, cobia will scrounge and linger. They also exhibit a strong penchant for proximity to almost any floating object. They delight in lazing near buoys or beneath floating debris even miles offshore. Old wrecks are favored hangouts. Off Mississippi, buoy fishing for cobia is a common method. The fish also come into coastal river mouths, frequent piers, jetties, wharves. Oil rigs in the Gulf of Mexico are hot spots for cobia. So are anchored or moving shrimp boats. Curiously, cobia often move in close to a sport-fishing boat trolling or drift-fishing offshore, and move along with it, almost rubbing against the side. They seem surprisingly unaware at times, and many are caught by dropping a bait over practically into the mouth of one lazing along beside a boat.

What makes cobia fishing something of a hunting trip is that they are not school fish, but fundamentally solitary wanderers. There may be two, or perhaps three or four, traveling loosely together, and often the cobia may attach itself to a school of fish of another species, and travel with it.

Ordinarily cobia are taken by stillfishing with bait, preferably live crabs. Chunks of fish sometimes get bites, and so do shrimp and small live fish. Trollers take cobia on standard saltwater trolling lures such as spoons, and on strip baits, but by and large stillfishing with bait probably accounts for the most fish. Tackle should be medium to sturdy. Large cobia are hard to handle, making unpredictable lunges and dives that strain tackle severely.

Because the fish are so scattered, it is not possible to say that they are active and accessible only at certain seasons. Some are taken throughout the year all along their ranges. But the fishing is more certain during the spring, summer, and early fall. When either bait fishing or trolling, anglers pick up most of the fish near bottom. This is not infallible. Some, near buoys, will take bait at various depths, almost on surface. But the tyro after cobia will have the best chance by placing his bait down and awaiting results.

Along the Gulf Coast, when the fish appear in spring, fishing is usually best just prior to a high tide or during the tide. Because it is a good fish as well as an excellent fighter it is regrettable that the species is also so casual in its appearances and that it appears to exist in such modest supply. Actually, the cobia is something of a mystery species. Not much is known about its life history.

Amberjack

Seriola dumerili

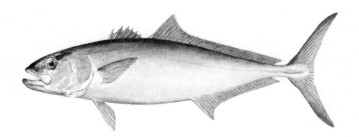

The amberjack is a fish chiefly of our southern Atlantic waters, but it ranges in scattered fashion also in the Gulf of Mexico clear to Texas, where it is fairly commonly caught as an incidental by red snapper fishermen fishing the deep offshore reefs and by anglers concentrating around deep-water oil rigs. It is a brutal, slashing battler of the reefs and the reef edges. This fish, presently called the greater amberjack as an official common name, has at least one relative—some references say two or three—in the Atlantic, but these are so similar that for our purposes no distinction is needed. They differ only technically from this type species. Some now outdated references use the scientific name *Seriola lalandi* for the greater amberjack.

Amberjacks are related on the one hand to the tunas and mackerels, and on the other, and more closely, to the pompanos and the jacks. The ancestral background on both sides has lent the amberjack a tough personality that has made it very popular with anglers. It is a fair food fish, not as good as the mackerels or pompanos, but better than the other jacks.

This is a heavy-bodied fish with a powerful, slender-lobed and deeply forked tail. Its general body conformation is at once somewhat reminiscent of the tunas. It is greenish or blue above, silver below, with some yellow in the fins. There is a most distinctive dark swath running up from the snout and continuing back of the eye. Although it ranges up from the Atlantic well toward New England, actually it is a fish of southern waters, predominantly in our range off Florida and throughout the islands, but with fair numbers appearing up to and including the coast of the Carolinas.

Although the amberjack cannot be termed a school fish in the strict sense, and is indeed often solitary, it does gather in scattered small groups, many of them over the reefs which are its favorite habitat. Here it prowls, preying on numerous smaller fish, and on crabs, shrimp, and practically anything it can seize.

It is by no means small. The average amberjack will weigh 12 to 15 pounds, and it is not at all uncommon to hook one of 25 to 50. Amberjack have been caught that weighed over 100. Because of its size and unusual strength, and its flat, heavy-bodied jack-like build, the fish is capable of runs that are startling both in speed and brute stubbornness. It is not a leaper. The first action after the slam-bang strike is a sizzling run, then usually a turn and a dive for deep water, where other fast runs occur. After this, or at any unpredictable time—depending on how far from safety the fish was hooked—it will make a determined try for the reef haven.

The single purpose of an amberjack at that point is to

either race into a hole among the rocks, or cut off the line by ripping it across sharp coral. Often it succeeds in doing precisely that. For this reason, rough tackle is used for amberjack fishing as a rule, that is, in comparison to the size of the fish. One must be able to turn or stop the fish before it can cut free, and this takes some doing. A fairly heavy rod is best, perhaps with a tip even of 10 to 12 ounces and line testing upwards of 60 pounds or more.

Hooks should be of good size, up to 10/0 or better, and steel leader must be used. Length of the leaders should be at least 6 feet, preferably more, whether baits or artificials are used. Amberjack fall hard for either. One may troll with strip bait, or drift with live mullet or other such bait. This last is an accepted method which seems to be especially effective. No weight is used. The bait simply drifts free. The fish are wary of taking it if there is a sinker attached. For lures, when trolling, any of the traditional spoons, plugs, and feathers are effective.

As with most of our fishes, unhappily there is some mild confusion regarding names. Anglers used to catching the fish sometimes speak of it simply as "jack." Others call it amberfish. The name great amberjack is not so bad, but "salmon" and "horse-eye bonito" seem on the preposterous side. There is as noted some confusion, too, about other species, and about other scientific names. There is a Pacific amberjack, *Seriola colburni*, but it is predominantly out of U.S. range. It is mainly abundant off southern Mexico and southward, and is quite similar in many ways to the amberjack here featured.

There is also the Pacific or California yellowtail, a very important close relative covered in the section following this one. It is locally called Pacific amberjack, and simply amberjack. That is not very confusing because a continent separates the two.

However, there is little danger that the average angler will be confused when he hooks an amberjack. He may get a chance to study the species closely. These fish have the odd habit of gathering round an unfortunate, possibly to see what is wrong. Like the dolphin, when one is hooked its buddies often follow almost to boatside, and if a lure is put over immediately while the hooked fish is left in the water, several may be taken.

An amberjack played down and brought alongside to be gaffed should be warily handled. Amberjack are notorious for finding new strength and exploding into furious action just at the moment the angler decides he has won and begins to relax.

In the northern portion of the range, the summer months are best for this fishing. In Florida waters, and adjacent regions, the fish apparently cruise all year, but most of them are caught during winter and spring, possibly because there is more fishing for them then. Tide does not make any great difference. Most anglers prefer to fish on a high tide because they are used to it inshore, but over the reefs the amberjack will strike or not, pretty much regardless of tide. They do not like a lure or bait to be trolled swiftly, as do the mackerels. They prefer a slower motion.

Sometimes amberjack can be successfully chummed. They will cruise and hunt at modest depths, say 20 to 30 feet, and by dropping out live or weakly moving bait fish over an area the hunting amberjack can be aroused and induced to draw near. Then the lure, or bait with hook in it, is cast out. When amberjack strike, they do so swiftly and very hard, but they do not always hook themselves because their mouths are tough. The angler should set the hook after only a brief run. Otherwise the fish will be heading for a hole in the reef to devour its prey, and it may be too close then for the fisherman to get it stopped in time.

Pacific Yellowtail

Seriola dorsalis

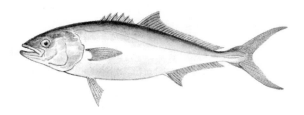

This is the amberjack (see previous section) of the Pacific coast, a beautiful fish of blue-green and silver with a broad yellow swath running from eye to tail along its sides. It is streamlined, tremendously swift and powerful, a school fish that gathers in great numbers and that brings together almost as many anglers during that annual time when it comes up from the south to swarm off southern California shores. It is probably the most publicized and popular of game fish in its size range and of its general category of all U.S. Pacific coast species.

The northern migration of the yellowtail early each spring, following up the warming Japanese current that comes fairly close to California's coast, has in great part sparked the kind of live-bait angling on party boats for which southern California is famous. Nowhere else along our coasts has this particular type of fishing been brought to such popularity, or been so thoroughly developed.

Anglers for hundreds of miles along the Pacific wait eagerly for the word that the yellowtail are showing up. The hordes have spent the winter much farther south, and by March or April they begin to appear off San Diego, the most famous of the yellowtail fishing ports. They congregate around the Coronado Islands, and later around Catalina, near the offshore kelp beds, near San Clemente, and on up to the Santa Barbaras. As they work up the coast, various ports become exceedingly active with anglers.

Because the yellowtail is a voracious species, a vicious striker on lively small fish, and because there is such a demand for it by anglers, the now-famed California party boats have long featured yellowtail fishing. One buys a ticket on most of these boats in the evening, goes aboard and to bed. The boat leaves during the night for the run, which may be of several hours, to the fishing grounds. Dawn and the hour or two after are usually the hot fishing periods. Each boat carries a large live-bait tank, and the better the condition and the quantity of bait, the more popular the boat. Also, since chumming with live sardines and anchovies is practiced, steady customers soon learn to patronize the boat that is most liberal with its chum.

Yellowtail weigh anywhere from 5 to 50 or more pounds. There is a record of over 100. The average hangs around 8 to 25. Light to medium tackle is used on the boats. Nowadays saltwater spinning gear is swiftly replacing a lot of older traditional tackle. On board a party boat, tackle too light is sometimes a nuisance, if the fish are running large. The rail may be lined with anglers all hung to fish, and it is advantageous at times to be able to wear a fish down quickly. Sturdy saltwater spin gear is of course perfectly capable of this.

On these boats each angler is furnished a sack for his fish. Workmen chum, assist in getting fish off hooks and in getting them aboard. The fees for all this, including berth aboard, are very economical because of the number of people carried. Food is available.

Occasionally a boat captain may see the swirls of feeding yellowtail while seeking the kelp beds around which they like to stay. But usually the beds, or other favorite areas, are first located and then chum is put over. Presently action is sighted, and the boat anchors. More chum is used until a school has gathered to take the live fish. Meanwhile anglers aboard are getting baited. The fish soon become shy of the hook, but spinning tackle has increased anglers' success in the sport. Lighter line and smaller hooks can be used. The bait fish is hooked so not to injure it, and no sinker, or only the lightest possible amount of weight, is used. The bait must swim free and naturally.

Like all amberjacks, the yellowtail does not leap. It makes powerful runs, then dives, and will try its best to get into the kelp, or to slice off the line on a rock. On these dives the fish must be held and turned if possible. Another trait of the family is that one of their kind struggling on a hook sometimes arouses the curiosity of others, which will follow it, darting around it as it labors. These excited fish are then quite gullible, and will strike if offered a bait. Occasionally quite a number can be taken by keeping one on the hook for a few minutes. However, a first fish lost is likely to upset things, in some unknown way making the others shy.

By September the yellowtail fishing in our waters is pretty well over. During the season they are of course taken in other ways than from party boats. Some anglers take them in the surf, where they have chased bait. Others find them in bays and inlets and coves, over inshore kelp beds, and rocks. They either stillfish as from the party boats or troll. Yellowtail will strike a wide variety of lures, from plugs and spoons to feathered jigs. Trolling is a most effective means of taking them, over kelp and near rocks.

Drift fishing, as for Florida amberjack, is a most effective method, too. The live bait is allowed to swim naturally and the boat eases along. Even the party boats sometimes drift, rather than anchoring. Sometimes yellowtail will take a drifted bait with a rush. But ordinarily, unless one is trolling, which forces the fish to hurry and strike hard, they simply seize the bait and run. Most anglers give some line before ramming the hook home.

When the fish fail to respond readily to chumming or are hard to locate, injured sardines or mackerel thrown out as a boat drifts will often bring yellowtail on the double. The injured fish splashing on the surface are quickly spotted by the predators. When one yellowtail rushes in, others follow.

There is little danger of confusing the Pacific yellowtail with any other species within its own habitat. However, all anglers should know that the fish spoken of in Florida and especially along the Keys as a "yellowtail" is something entirely different. This is a small and brilliantly colored member of the snapper family. It has a canary-yellow tail. The section of this book devoted to snappers will give details about it.

A trip after Pacific yellowtail, on a party boat or otherwise, is a must for the fisherman who wants the feel of the best southern west-coast saltwater angling. The early fishing is often the best: April (or even earlier) and May out of San Diego, a couple of weeks later between there and Los Angeles, May and early June off Los Angeles and on up toward Monterey. Eating this catch, incidentally, is as fine an experience as catching it.

Jack Crevalle

Caranx hippos

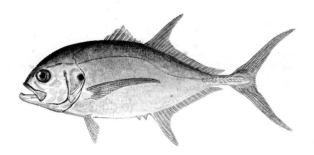

Depending on who hooks it, the jack, crevalle, common jack, jack crevalle, cavalla (and a host of other names) is either a wonderful sport fish, or an exasperating nuisance. It ranges throughout the warm waters of the Atlantic and the Gulf, most abundantly in the South, but goes north to Cape Cod. As a rule it travels in loose schools, viciously hacking to pieces schools of smaller fish, or boldly rampaging wherever it can find food. Usually it is a fish of inshore waters, the bays and channels, around islands or rocks, wherever abundant food fish live.

Especially about Florida and the Keys, and along all of the Gulf coast to Texas and Mexico these jacks are numerous. When a tide is running in or out, for example, under a bridge or through a channel, swarms of them will feed. Casting a plug or a feathered jig, one can catch jack after jack, with hardly a single empty cast. Down in the Everglades, in bayous and canals close to the Gulf, or farther down among the mangrove islands, thousands of jacks swarm. At times one can take a hundred in as many casts.

When an angler is fishing for something else, jacks thus become a nuisance. They will take bait as readily as they strike lures, too. They are not especially good as a food fish, in the estimation of most anglers, because they are very bloody and strong. However, if bled as soon as caught they are not bad, or when smoked. They appear in schools of 1-pounders, or fish twice or three times that large. At other times one will get into a school in which fish of 5 to 10 pounds are the rule. From here on this common jack goes upward to 35 pounds and probably more.

When hooked, a jack does not leap. It lays its flat, muscular side against the direction of the line and fights one of the most powerful and stubborn battles known in saltwater. Even small jacks are difficult to subdue. A large one of 10 to 20 pounds may take the better part of an hour, even on a rig of fairly good weight. It is for this reason, and their abundance in southern waters and their willingness to rush in and strike, that many anglers are annoyed by them. Nonetheless, the common jack is great sport as a pastime in its own right, even if one catches scores only to release them. To this day little has been done in the field of purposely fishing big jacks. For sheer power and stamina they will put more popular game fish to shame.

It doesn't make much difference what tackle you use for jack fishing. It all depends on where, and thus how large the fish are likely to run. Thousands are caught on freshwater plug rods and spinning rods from Florida to Texas from bridges, from shore, or from skiffs. Jacks strike streamers and bucktails very well, too, being exceedingly bold and not afraid to run in close to the angler to strike. Wearing out a large one on a fly rod, however, is quite a chore. For large jacks, of course, substantial tackle is needed. They will strike both surface and underwater lures, and take cut bait as well as live bait. They will strike both day and night. Shallow inshore waters as a rule contain the smaller jacks, and these will also form into the largest schools. The larger the jacks, the farther off-shore and the deeper they generally operate. Very large ones may be lone wanderers over rather deep places.

In color this fish is yellowish-green above, and yellow and silver on the sides and below. There is a dark spot fairly high up at the back edge of the gill cover, and there is a small patch of scales far back under the "chin," just ahead of the ventral fins. The rest of the breast is scaleless. The pectoral fins are quite long and mildly sickle-shaped. These points all help to separate the common jack crevalle from its relatives, which are many.

The jack family is a large one that also takes in the amberjack, the Pacific yellowtail, the pompanos, all of which are covered elsewhere in this book, the scads, and a number of other species. The jacks are relatives of the mackerels, but they have certain easily noted differences from the mackerel tribe. Most of them are deeper bodied and with front profile more blunt. Most of them have no finlets (or at best only one or two) following the dorsal and anal fin rearward, while the presence of several finlets is a characteristic instantly noted in the mackerels and bonitos. But perhaps the most notable distinguishing

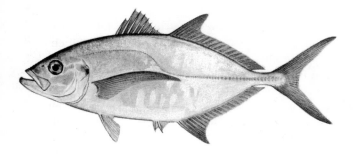

Blue Runner

characteristic of the jacks is that most of the species called by the "jack" name have the scales over the posterior portion of the lateral line developed into hard, enlarged bony scutes, that is, keeled projections. These appear to be a means of lending strength to the so-called caudal peduncle (tail section), which is very slender, yet must serve to sweep the deeply forked tail powerfully, because the jacks, being predators, must be swift.

The scads are small jacks, too numerous and unimportant as sport fishes to cover here. The **blue runner,** or **hard-tailed jack,** *Caranx crysos*, ranges about like the common jacks. It is smaller, seldom over 2 pounds, somewhat similar in outline except that the forehead is less steep. In color it is greenish and silver, lacking the yellow of the common jack. Best rough identification is to note the numerous scutes along the lateral line. These come forward so far that the sickle-like pectoral fins, when folded against the body, overlap them a short distance. This is not true of the common jack.

The blue runner is very abundant about Texas, Florida, and on north, running in schools and sometimes in the company of the common jack. It strikes well, is an excellent battler. It is particularly adaptable to fly tackle and small streamers, or to light spinning gear. In addition, although many anglers who have not tried them spurn them, thinking they will be strong and bloody, they are a delicious food fish when broiled whole in their skins. The skin will roll off like a shuck, and the flesh will vie with Spanish mackerel.

The **runner, bar jack,** or **skipjack,** *Caranx ruber,* has fewer scutes than the blue runner, has blue swaths along the back, and a head still less blunt. It is a small jack found sometimes in company with the blue runner, and sometimes cruising in schools of its own in open water. Like many other species of various families, it is often called a "skipjack," a meaningless name because of indiscriminate usage.

The **yellow jack,** *Caranx bartholomaei,* is a deeper fish than the common jack, with sloping forehead. It is a silvery-blue fish, with the fins yellow, seldom growing to more than 12 to 15 inches. It ranges over most of the range of the common jack, but is really abundant only in southern waters.

Out over the reefs, in fairly deep water, the **goggle-eye,** or **horse-eye jack,** *Caranx latus,* is fairly common. It grows large, matching common jacks in size. The large eye is very noticeable and helps identify this species.

In the Pacific there are several jacks, but most seldom get north into U.S. waters. The **green jack,** *Caranx caballus,* is occasional there; the **big-eye jack,** *Caranx marginatus,* is of Mexican waters; the **blue jack** or **blue crevalle,** *Caranx stellatus,* is caught by west-coast anglers in Lower California waters.

Rainbow Runner

The **Pacific jack mackerel,** or **California horse mackerel** (both names are commonly used), *Trachurus symmetricus,* is a long and more slender jack, green above, silver below, with a conspicuously large eye. It is caught rather commonly along the California coast, but usually not purposely. It is taken commercially and canned. This fish superficially resembles a mackerel.

Another species, *Alectis crinitus,* called the **Cuban jack,** or **African pompano** (*Hynnis cubensis* in older references) should be noted because of its rarity, which has made it a desirable trophy fish among anglers in southern Florida and throughout the Islands. It is an oddly shaped silver and pale blue fish with a blunt head and deep body that narrows swiftly toward the tail. Some mystery surrounds it. The young of many species, especially of marine fish, look radically different from the adults. The threadfish, or threadfin, a most peculiar fish only a few inches long, with a diamond-shaped body and long filaments trailing back from dorsal and anal fins, is now known to be the young of the Cuban jack. This species is probably closer to the pompanos than to the true jacks.

In the northern portion of the Florida Keys a few of these odd jacks are taken each winter, and occasionally at other times of the year. They hang out in exactly the same places as the amberjack. This trophy fish runs fairly large. Specimens above 30 pounds have been caught.

Possibly the most striking of the jacks is one which hardly looks like a member of the group. This is the **rainbow runner,** *Elagatis bipinnulatus.* It is a long fish, not deep like most of the jacks, but reminiscent in outline of the amberjack. It is beautifully colored. The upper parts are vivid blue, the lower portion and tail yellow. There are lighter blue stripes down the sides. It lacks the bony scutes toward the tail. It has a well-separated finlet above and below, just aft of the dorsal and anal. This positively distinguishes it from the amberjack. In size the rainbow runner usually is small, to possibly 15 inches, but it may weigh, maximum, 10 to 15 pounds and be 3 feet long. It is a fish of warm seas, but is caught occasionally northward. Gulf Stream trollers catch it off Florida's east coast, and it is also taken in the Gulf of Mexico.

There are several other species of jacks and their close relatives. Most important are the pompanos, immediately following. Others, such as the moonfish, lookdown, and leatherjacket will be found in the chapter on Saltwater Panfish, headed by the northern porgy. Although the numerous species of jacks and their relations may seem confusing at first, the fact is the majority of anglers will catch the common jack crevalle, or the blue runner, with only the odd one of the more obscure varieties turning up here and there. The fact that the jacks are such ripping fighters and are so abundant and willing makes them well worthwhile. The casual visitor to Florida, or any of the Gulf coast, especially the angler new to saltwater, can have fun with them almost without fail, whether or not other species perhaps more desirable give him a ready tumble.

Common Pompano

Trachinotus carolinus

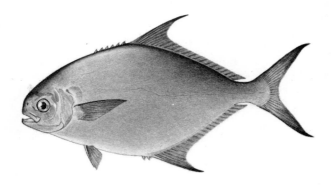

The history of this fish is most interesting in several ways, and so is the fish itself. For many years pompano has been a delicacy in fine seafood restaurants. But as short a time as forty years ago some authoritative books stated that it was impossible to take pompano with hook and line. Today the pompano is still just as great a delicacy (broiled pompano with chopped pecans sprinkled over it!), and still just as expensive a dish. But the fish is also now considered one of the finest and most intriguing of the smaller marine game fish.

The reason pompano has long been expensive is that, while not at all rare, the species is erratic in its movements, much affected by slight temperature changes, and travels about not in true schools but in small groups of perhaps three to a dozen. Thus the commercial catch, except in rare instance, has seldom been more than a few at a time from any one haul of an inshore net. Netmen rarely pin pompano down even to consistent places and times.

Oddly, since the advent of hook and line fishing for pompano, many times experts at "pomp" fishing do better than the commercial men. Some of them fish with bait. The so-called sand flea, a small beetle-like crustacean that burrows in wet surf-line sand, is one effective bait. Pompano feed in shallow water, close to shore, in inlets and channels, bays, in the surf, and they take most of their food, predominantly small crustaceans such as the sand flea, right from bottom. Some old hands claim pompano have an excellent sense of smell. They cast a sand flea out at an angle, reel it slowly back along bottom. Then they take a few steps down the beach and cast so that the second retrieve makes an X with the first. Now they cast to the intersection and let the bait lie. A pompano, they say, will follow one or the other of the trails right to the bait. It is a nice theory, but of somewhat doubtful value.

Because the pompano is swift and strong and a most beautiful silver and pale-blue fish with a golden iridescence, and because it requires specialized angling, a regular society caste of pompano anglers has evolved. On Florida bridges, for example, certain retired men who fish every day have given up all other fishing. They may take only one pompano in a day, or one in a week. But each lives for that day when a group goes wild and each specialist may land half a dozen.

Pompano are extremely shy. Part of this is because they feed in shallow water, rooting with their blunt snouts and underset, small mouths in sand and mud after their crustacean delicacies. No experienced angler will try to approach them closely, if the water is clear. This is one reason fishing from bridges has been successful for pompano. They do not so easily see anything to disturb them. When one strikes, it is with a fast and voracious chop, with no probing or nibbling involved. The trick of properly setting the hook, which must be instantaneous, is most difficult for the beginner to master.

Pompano are also whimsical about tides. Ordinarily high tides are best for them, whether one is fishing a stretch of surf known to be their feeding grounds, or from a bay bridge, or the mouth of a tidal river. River mouths are especially good places for pompano, and they sometimes go some distance up the stream with the tide.

Some of the first successful experiments with artificial lures for pompano involved a weighted jig, called the "dude" in Florida. This small feathered lure, with hook riding upturned and the eye on the side of the weighted head rather than at the end, was attached to a length of wire leader about 2 1/2 feet long. At the end of the leader a sinker was placed. It was an awkward rig to cast, but the pompano anglers used a very short, stiff bamboo casting rod. Many of these rods were only about 4 to 4 1/2 feet long overall. A standard black nylon plugging line was used on an oversize freshwater reel.

When the rig was cast, say from a bridge above the water, it sank quickly. When it touched bottom the fisherman might let it lie for a moment, then he picked up quickly and retrieved with a reel, jerk, reel, jerk, technique. This was varied in speed and length of rod jerk, keeping the jig close to bottom, but making it bounce along. The sinker ahead of it gave a peculiar pattern to

the motion. Some of the first pompano caught on artificials were taken thus. The jig may have appeared to be
a live shrimp swimming with its bouncing motion.

Today there are many refinements. Spinning rods are
much used. New lures are in vogue. Yellow was long the
favorite color, and still is with most pompano anglers. A
lure developed in Florida some years back utilizes a shell
from the beach as its body. It works very well. Small
spoons have also been developed that catch pompano.
Lines have become lighter, and dyed nylon monofil
leaders and lines, to make them as invisible as possible,
have come into wide use. Rather light tackle can be used,
because a pompano of 4 pounds is considered large. Fish
of a pound are about average, with quite a few going to
2 and 3. Maximum size is 5 to 7 pounds.

Although the pompano ranges north as far as Cape
Cod, it is not common there. Chesapeake Bay southward
is the main pompano ground, and they continue on
around the Gulf clear down the Texas coast. In fact, some
of the best pompano fishing is along the south Texas
area. Padre Island at Port Isabel often has pompano in
large numbers in its surf. Florida waters, especially the
southern ones, have long been favorite pompano grounds,
with both sides of the peninsula furnishing good fishing.
Bait fishing is of course still popular in many haunts of
pompano, especially with natives who have been bait
fishing in the surf for many years.

Oddly, bait fishing for pompano—and pompano fishing in general—appears to be far more successful along
the mid-Gulf and Texas coast than the Florida coasts.
Conceivably more of the fish congregate there, or their
feeding habits may be somewhat different. At any rate,

off Louisiana around near-shore oil rigs dozens of pompano are often taken during a single session, either using shrimp for bait or else by casting spoons and jigs. From Texas fishing piers such as the one at Port Aransas, it is routine in May, June, and on through summer for anglers using even dead shrimp for bait to take three or four good pompano in a morning or afternoon. Farther south, a great many are regularly caught, six or eight to the string, from certain stretches of Padre Island surf. Giving some substantiation to the theory that pompano may "run" in greater abundance here, a well-authenticated net haul from surf along St. Joseph Island, north of Port Aransas, Texas, during the spring of 1966 weighed in over 500 pounds of pompano at one pull.

Over most of the pompano's U.S. range, fishing begins to pick up shortly after the first of the year. By April it may be at peak. In some places it remains good right on through spring and summer. In others it appears to taper off.

This common pompano is not the only one. The pompanos are an offshoot of the jack family. Occasionally a poor observer has confused the delicious pompano with a far less edible jack. Catastrophe has struck when a tourist tyro, seeking bait on a bridge where many others were fishing, has sliced a chunk from the side of a prize pompano in the belief he was taking it from the body of a discarded and disdained jack. There is really no reason whatever for mixing up the pompanos and jacks. The deep body of the pompano, and its general outline and coloring, are entirely different.

Neither is there much reason to confuse adult pompanos of other species, although the young often are

similar and difficult to distinguish. The common pompano has twenty-five rays in the dorsal fin, twenty-two
in the anal. The **round pompano,** *Trachinotus falcatus,*
with a range about like the common variety, has fewer
rays in both those fins. It is much deeper bodied, almost
round. Both anal and dorsal have the forward lobes much
longer, so that they trail backward, the dorsal one reaching at least even with a line drawn vertically across the
base of the tail. The eye is much larger than that of the
common pompano. There are of course other more technical differences, but this should suffice to separate the
two. The round pompano is nowhere as abundant as the
other, never grows as large, maximum. Its habits are almost identical to its common relative.

The largest pompano of the lot is the famed **permit.**
But there is much confusion about its name, and at least
some about what it actually is. Many excellent standard
references, even recent ones, list the round pompano
under the name "permit." The great pompano, which
most references list as *Trachinotus goodei,* is the fish
most anglers call the permit. It averages from 10 to 20
pounds and weighs at maximum upwards of 50. There
has been some suspicion among certain scientists that
the round pompano—or even the common pompano—
may be at their average sizes only young or less than fully
grown great pompano, or permit. At any rate, though
fishermen and almost all references very emphatically
separate widely the round pompano (permit), *Trachinotus falcatus,* and the great pompano (permit), *Trachinotus goodei,* the American Fisheries Society in its latest
list uses only *T. falcatus* under the heading "permit," and
in its index of common names refers both great pompano

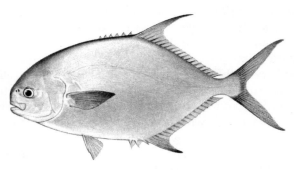

Permit

and round pompano to the same listing. Any angler can thus take his choice!

The extra-large pompano that most anglers call "permit" is at any rate one of the most desired trophies of the southern Atlantic areas. It ranges outside the surf, is probably most often caught in our ranges throughout the mangrove island areas of south Florida and the Keys, and over the reefs along the edges of the Gulf Stream. It feeds much like its smaller relatives, takes bait or lure with a quick, rough, smashing strike and fights a stubborn battle. Trollers account for quite a few permit, using either bait or lures such as spoons and feathers. Bait fishermen in most hot spots for permit use hermit crabs or live shrimp.

In the Pacific we have no pompanos strictly within our range. There are some farther south. But there is a species that must be noted here, because it is called the **California pompano.** It is not a pompano at all, but rather *Palometa simillima*, a member of the butterfish family. All easterners have undoubtedly seen butterfish, the small, iridescent silvery and gray-blue species common in the markets. The California species is quite a favorite of pier fishermen along the west coast.

The fish seldom grows to more than 10 inches, is green or blue above, silvery below, and most beautifully iridescent. It is quite reminiscent, in shape, of the pompanos. The body is extremely compressed. Anglers use very small hooks and tiny pieces of cut bait, and stillfish for it. When the fish are thickly gathered about a pier, some use snag hooks to catch them. This species is included here with the pompanos, rather than in the section on saltwater panfish, simply because it has acquired the pompano name.

Bluefish

Pomatomus saltatrix

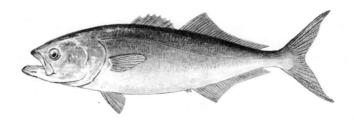

The bluefish is an uninhibited savage. Its slam-bang feeding sprees vie with any fish in the sea for pure voraciousness. It is a marine gamester that may be said to have just about everything.

It is a vicious striker. It will chop at practically anything that moves or looks as if it might. It is a brawling battler, considered by many seasoned marine anglers the hardest fighter per pound of all. It is unquestionably the toughest of those species caught from the surf. It is an utterly delicious table fish. When present, bluefish are usually extremely abundant, and just as willing. And, to top it all off, they appear and disappear suddenly and with some mystery, lending bluefishing a taste of uncertainty.

The average bluefish is not large—2 to 4 or 5 pounds. Occasionally schools of larger fish are encountered, running to 10 or even 15 pounds. Some may be larger, but nowadays rarely so, although old records indicate blues of up to 50 pounds. The bluefish is sometimes called "tailor" or "skipjack." The latter name is unfortunate, since it is so indiscriminately applied to dozens of other fish. The name "snapper blues" is commonly given to small bluefish of around a pound in weight.

The color of a bluefish matches the name. It is sparkling blue over the upper body, shading to blue-gray and gray-silver progressively. It is a beautiful species. Its appearance is almost as great a satisfaction as catching it.

Bluefish are erratic wanderers, covering vast territory in reasonably warm waters. They travel in tremendous schools, usually following schools of menhaden, their favorite prey. When a school of blues rushes into a school of forage fish the water is swiftly churned to a bloody froth in which chunks of fish, entrails, and crippled fish are left floating.

Ordinarily they are not surf fish, but a species whose true habitat is offshore. However, they habitually drive great schools of menhaden or other forage species into the surf, the better to slash them to pieces. Sometimes they drive schools of bait fish right onto the beach. This trait brings the blues within reach of surf anglers as well as boat fishermen.

Although bluefish schools follow the forage, and the warming temperatures from south to north during spring and summer, and back again in fall, they are unpredictable. Places where blues have been abundant and right on time year after year may one season be barren. It may be years before they reappear. Then, again inexplicably, the hosts arrive once more on schedule. In our waters this is an Atlantic species, ranging abundantly in season from Nova Scotia to Florida. New England, the Carolinas, and the east coast of Florida, as well as Florida Bay, are popular bluefishing locations.

The bluefish looks a bit like the jacks of southern coastal waters, and is thought by some scientists to be related to them, and by others to be more closely allied with the sea basses. But it has visible, though rather weak, small scales, is much longer and less deep than the jacks, and has most effective teeth, whereas the jacks do not. In fact, so efficient are the teeth of bluefish that care should be taken by the angler when removing a blue from the hook.

When a bluefish strikes it does so with murderous intent. Sometimes it hooks itself. If it does not, the fisherman must instantly react, or the fish may be gone and probably won't strike again. Once hooked, a blue speeds off, hurls itself into the air, rolls and slashes, dives, bulldogs, and in general puts up a wild battle. It is exceedingly powerful, and the fight is likely to last an astonishing length of time. Even small, or snapper, blues are startling fighters and stayers. These small blues, incidentally, often come into bays and rivers, commonly frequenting brackish water. Long Island Sound is periodically a mecca for snapper blue fishermen.

It is important to be at the right place at the right time, if one wants to catch bluefish. During the middle of the winter bluefish are caught off Florida's east coast. In the Gulf early spring on into summer is the time. During May and June bluefishing is famous along the Carolinas and Virginia. Mid and late summer, and early fall, find the fish off New Jersey, New York, and New England. For large bluefish one should go offshore into deeper waters.

Average blues will be found in the surf and within sight of shore. They often cruise near the surface, where they can apprehend and surround schools of bait fish, and get below them.

There is really no standard method of fishing for bluefish. They are caught by stillfishermen, trollers, surf casters, plug casters, spin fishermen, and even by fly fishermen. On the whole it may be said that the medium outfit is probably the best all-around one for stillfishing or trolling. Stout hooks from 3/0 to 7/0 should be used, except for snapper blues, which require a small hook. Because of the bluefish's teeth a wire leader is imperative. It need not be long. A foot is all right, size No. 7 to a bit larger.

Standard surf-casting outfits are also used for blues. Here, because the fish are so sporty, the two-handed saltwater spinning outfit is perfect. It is a good idea whatever outfit is used to have a fair-sized reel carrying plenty of line, at least 200 yards of it. For fly fishing, the saltwater fly rods now quite popular are called for, and a light steel leader is placed before the fly. The leader should be No. 2 or perhaps a bit heavier. In all categories, of course, the above rigs are merely suggestions. Bluefish, like all other species, can be taken on any outfit the angler happens to have, light or heavy, as long as he can handle them on it.

Cut bait is often used for surf fishing, strip mullet for trolling. So are menhaden, the soft shelled crab, and live shrimp. Blues are not choosey. Eel skins are a popular trolling bait, too, as are small eels. Many northern anglers, especially, chum for blues, using chopped menhaden or any oily fish.

Lures can be as varied as baits. Standard are the flashing wobbling spoons and feathered jigs. Plugs are also effective. For light-tackle spin fishermen, smaller copies of all these lures are perfect. Fly fishermen use streamers or bucktails. The double-wing (open and close when retrieved) streamers in yellow, red, white, and combinations of those colors are standard. Invariably, lures of all kinds are fished swiftly for blues because these are swift carnivores always prowling after frightened prey.

Dolphin

Coryphaena hippurus

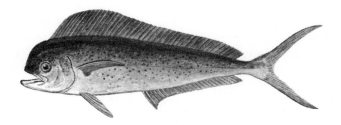

The dolphin is one of the most beautiful of the world's fishes. Attention is called to its blunt, near-vertical forehead, its long, high dorsal fin running from head to slender-lobed, deeply forked tail, its swiftly tapering, streamlined body bathed in a riot of brilliant colors. From purple and blue in the dorsal, to green and yellow shining iridescences over upper and lower halves of the body, here is a species that rivals the rainbow. To set off these swaths of gently merging colors, blue dots are scattered indiscriminately over much of the fish.

The dolphin is incredibly swift. It is a fish of the open seas, where it preys upon other fishes. One of its mainstays of diet is the flying fish. When in pursuit of this prey the dolphin leaps from the water to follow its sailing course. Quite often a dolphin will charge from many yards away at lightning speeds, leave the water, and come diving down from above upon either living food or a moving lure.

When hooked, dolphins are even more dynamic in action. They are exceptionally strong, and seem stronger because of their speed and agility. A hooked fish may first make a smoking run, then hurl itself into the air time after time. When led back exhausted, it may take new strength and suddenly become airborne once more in a wild display.

The dolphin does not average very large. A weight of 3 to 6 pounds would take in the majority of the ones caught. However, they grow much larger. Ten to 20 pounds is not unusual, and the record is over 60. The males are called "bulls." The head of the male, especially as the fish grows old, becomes startlingly steep, until in large specimens it is almost vertical in front. Such big old bulls are particularly prized as trophies.

Unfortunately, the cold-blooded dolphin with fins has been too often confused with the warm-blooded dolphin, which is a species of porpoise, a mammal. Both creatures appear to have the name solidly attached to them, but it is well to know that this confusion does exist.

The dolphin is a school fish ordinarily. Although some old bulls may run by themselves, as a rule when one dolphin is struck the angler can plan on a school of anywhere from three or four to several dozen being present. They have the curious habit of following a hooked member of the school. When that one is played in close to the boat, the others may often be seen darting and flashing alongside.

Because of this habit, a unique method of enhancing the sport long ago evolved. The first dolphin solidly hooked is played in as swiftly as possible, but is not brought aboard. It is left in the water within reasonable distance of the fishing craft, and immediately other rods are readied. If the fish has been hooked while trolling, the boat is stopped and light casting gear is pressed into all hands. Now lures are cast in the vicinity of the tethered dolphin. Others of the school usually strike instantly, and the action is on. On occasion an entire school can be taken thus, in a frantic melee of flurrying sport.

There are dolphins along both our coasts. In the Atlantic most of them are found hanging out in or near the Gulf Stream, which they follow from the Gulf on up to offshore North Carolina. Stragglers go farther north, but the Carolinas are about the limit of good dolphin fishing. And, though many are taken in both the eastern and western Gulf, the best fishing is usually off Florida's east coast. Erratically hot fishing is had along Louisiana and Texas. In the Pacific these fish range as far north as Oregon, but are considered for the most part tropical and semitropical, with greatest abundance in our western waters off southern California.

A peculiarity of the dolphin most helpful to the angler is the fact that even though it is a fish of the open ocean it seems to like floating debris around which to cavort, and under which to hide. When scanning the seas for likely fishing places, the experienced dolphin angler looks for patches of floating grass, or bits of driftwood or other flotsam. Sometimes a single bobbing chunk of driftwood will attract and hold in its vicinity a whole dolphin school.

The most common method of dolphin fishing, undoubtedly because of the pelagic habitat of the fish, is trolling. This activity covers the greatest amount of territory, and is thus most likely to find the fish. For trolling, it is not good practice, especially in the big waters where dolphin are found, to use foolishly light tackle. One may strike some large fish.

When a fish is struck while trolling, and the school is brought in close, then any kind of light tackle may be used. Freshwater plug-casting outfits, spinning outfits, saltwater casting rods of 5-foot length, and even the saltwater fly rod with streamer fly, all make for fast action and heady thrills.

Wire leaders are used for dolphin. When into schools of small ones, however, they are not always necessary. Many different kinds of lures work well, the most popular being feathered jigs and wobbling spoons. The fish will hit plugs, too. Bait is the usual way of taking them, however, at least while trolling. And this bait may be flying fish or simply cut strips of mullet. Other baits can be used, but these will usually bring best results. It is a good idea to have plenty of line on the reel. A big dolphin can peel it off at an astonishing rate when it takes the trolled bait.

These fish are a warm-water species. Therefore the fishing is best as a rule during the warm months. Florida dolphin hit over much of the first half of the year, and those in the Gulf and along the Carolinas usually better in summer. Likewise for the Pacific. Of course some dolphin are taken around the seasons. Since they are open-ocean fish, tides are not important influences on fishing.

One of the most remarkable characteristics of the dolphin is the phenomenon of color changes that takes place over the fish's body as it is dying. Wave after wave of color sweeps across it, becoming brighter, then dull, in an intricate and rainbow-hued pattern. Artists attempting to produce good likenesses of this fish have long had difficulty because of this curious trait.

Many lovers of sea food consider dolphin a delicacy. Others shun it. The flesh is inclined to be red, almost beeflike. Chilling it well enhances the flavor, which is really very good. In some fishing places, and some markets, the dolphin is colloquially called "dorado." To avoid confusion, anglers should know this name.

Tarpon
Megalops atlantica

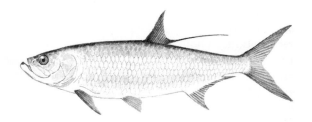

Certainly no angler needs to have the tarpon described
to him in very lengthy detail. This superb game fish of
inshore waters (previously with the scientific name *Tarpon atlanticus*) has undoubtedly had more publicity than
any other, and in many ways it deserves every accolade.
This is the leaper to end all arguments. A hooked tarpon
is in the air more than in the water. It is such a spectacular fighter, and fortunately so accessible to so many
anglers, that nowadays almost everyone who has visited
southern saltwater has fished for tarpon, and those who
haven't yet made the trek are planning toward the day.

The tarpon is not much as an eating fish. No one in
our range bothers to try, although some tropical islanders
do. It is a species related to the herrings, the shads, and
odd as it may seem, distantly to the little smelts and the
rugged salmons. It is exceedingly bony, and with soft,
oily flesh. Tarpon have very large scales. These, in fact,
are one of its identifying characteristics. Between the
branches of the lower jaw there is a bony plate, called

the "gular plate." This, too, helps to identify the tarpon. But perhaps the most noticeable feature is the long filament into which the last dorsal fin ray is extended. Some scientists believe this ray has a specific use. It is concave beneath, forming a kind of suction tube. When flipped either way it sticks to the side of the fish and secures the dorsal fin to right or left. In a leap, the direction of fall is controlled by the position of the dorsal.

Regardless of identifying characteristics, few anglers are in danger of confusing this strikingly iridescent silver fish with any other. Even very small tarpon are easily distinguishable. Although tarpon are known to come north in the Atlantic to the vicinity of New York, they are definitely a southern sports fish. Southern Florida and the Florida Keys, and the Gulf coast clear around to Texas and down the Mexican coasts, is the tarpon's main hangout. In fact, southern Florida, the south Texas coast, and the east Mexican coast are the famous havens for tarpon fishermen.

Tarpon are taken in a number of different ways. Plug fishing with regular freshwater bass tackle, or with something heavier, in the maze of mangrove islands and bayous of southern Florida, particularly around the Shark River region, became popular years ago. After spinning tackle was more and more developed and refined, it too came into similar use. For many years plug fishing was popular along the southern Texas and upper Mexican coast.

During and following World War Two, fly fishing with streamers, bucktails, and bass bugs along the roadside canals in the Florida Everglades and Big Cypress was launched and became extremely popular. At first the targets were the hordes of small tarpon, up to 10 pounds or so, that swarmed in these waters. Later the sport was carried on into the mangrove bordered bays, heavy fly-fishing tackle was developed, and methods refined. Over recent years hundreds of fly-fishing experts have worked on large tarpon, fish of anywhere up to 100 pounds or more.

The old standby method of tarpon fishing is with bait, usually a crab or a shrimp, or in some sections of Florida and Texas a pinfish, a small, common species of coastal waters. Either drifting or stillfishing is effective. For years, during a time when tarpon were exceedingly plentiful along the Texas coast, pier fishing, from piers thrusting into the Gulf, was extremely popular. Wherever this method is used, the bait is let down 6 or 8 feet below a large bobber. The angler allows the fish to run a short distance with the bait before setting the hook.

Thus, tackle for tarpon is whatever one may choose. For large tarpon, if one really wishes to land them, not just watch them jump, solid tackle is a requisite, at least for the average angler. A rod of about 12-ounce tip, with the rest of the rig to match, might be considered about standard. Wire leaders are used, and rather large hooks, up to 10/0. Bait fishing is a deadly method of tarpon fishing.

Plug casters operate in many ways and in varied localities. Some years ago it was discovered that large tarpon in the famed Panuco River near Tampico, Mexico (where records have been taken), were often found feeding right on bottom, or at least hanging near bottom.

Plugs allowed to sink and lie inert, or moved slowly along the bottom, were often picked up by the fish. In many other places, and at most times, surface plugs or shallow diving plugs take tarpon regularly. A tarpon is difficult to hook because of its hard, bony mouth. And it is difficult to keep on a hook. Often with light tackle an angler may consider himself fortunate if he hooks one out of ten strikes, and lands one out of ten hooked. They are masters at throwing the lure, or breaking off, as they leap.

Tarpon are school fish. This of course makes for rare sport with them, because usually where one is caught there are many more. Commonly they are traveling, and the angler must keep up with them. If he is, let's say, on the bank of a canal in the Everglades, fly fishing, he must wait for the next school to pass. Most of the time the greatest activity with tarpon will occur early and late in the day, at night, and on the high tides. However, the movement of tidal water back in the brackish bayous and lower stretches of coastal rivers, which are favorite hangouts of tarpon, will often set tarpon striking regardless of direction of the movement or time of day. Tarpon lying beneath mangroves are disturbed as the water changes, and they thus become aroused.

Many small tarpon, to about 20 pounds, commonly move into freshwater, and far up in the mildly brackish water of coastal canals and rivers. In fact, such places are among the most famous of tarpon fishing areas. In the smaller cuts and inlets and streams, one finds the smaller fish. But big tarpon are in the big canals and rivers, too, sometimes many miles inland. The fly fisherman usually selects the spots known for small fish, since there is little point in trying to subdue a 100-pound tarpon on such light gear, in such tight quarters.

Tarpon grow to 300 pounds and over. One rod-and-reel specimen from the Panuco River weighed 247 pounds. The average catch runs from 30 to 100 pounds, with fish of 50 or 60 most commonly hung.

Charter boats can be obtained in all good tarpon waters, and the fishing is invariably within sight of shore. In fact, wading and fishing for tarpon is popular in numerous places. Scores of anglers also simply use a seaworthy skiff. In using small craft, one should be very careful not to let a tarpon leap into the boat, or try to bring one aboard that is "green." Occasionally someone is injured by leaping tarpon. They are the wildest of wild fish, and during the battle seldom give the angler an instant of rest. Leap after leap is the rule.

The strike of a tarpon is one of the spectacular things about the species. It is probably the noisiest, most startling, and violent strike of any game fish, especially when the angler is in a position to hear and see it, that is, when using a surface lure or one running very shallow. Even very large tarpon will sometimes hit bass bugs twitched along under the mangroves, and small tarpon readily strike them. There is literally an explosion of water. Newcomers to the sport usually are so astonished they fail to strike. Needless to say, fly fishing for tarpon requires a rather strong rod, even for fish of 10 to 20 pounds, if one is to do anything at all with them.

There is much trolling for tarpon, as well as casting and stillfishing. It is commonly possible to locate schools by watching them greyhound along with their backs showing, or to sight their vicious forays among bait fish. Trollers use white and red lures rather often, as well as various spoons with or without strip-cut bait.

Although tarpon are caught to some extent around the year in portions of their range, concentrations along our Atlantic and Gulf coasts occur from about March on through the summer. The best fishing in Florida usually occurs during May and June. Along the Mexican coast concentrations occur much earlier. The Tampico area, for example, is often good all winter and most of the summer.

Tarpon fishing along the upper Gulf coast of Louisiana and Texas has declined drastically over several decades. At one time, for example, Port Aransas was nationally famed as a summer hot spot for tarpon. The old Tarpon Inn there, still standing even though so old it was rebuilt in 1924, was known nationwide as lodging for tarpon anglers. The lobby "wallpaper" was a solid mass of tarpon scales, with signatures of those who had caught the fish, many of them dating back three generations. The mouth of the Rio Grande, and surrounding Gulf water at the southern tip of Padre Island, was also famous tarpon water.

There are many theories as to why the tarpon "disappeared." At one time, farther south, Mexicans at coastal villages dynamited vast tarpon schools and used the fish for fertilizer. Some believe this launched the decline. Others suspect temperature changes and Gulf pollution. At any rate, currently few tarpon are caught along the western Gulf. Baby tarpon have been seen in warm canals along Texas, and some large fish are caught during the traditional late spring and summer period when the fishing was once superb. For example, on May 30, 1980 a fish was caught about 3 miles offshore from Port Aransas that was one of the largest caught in recent years, 148 1/2 pounds.

A fair number of fish are caught near the Mexican border and off South Padre Island each year. In fact, the current state record—a 210 pound fish— was taken there in 1973. The discovery of baby tarpon occasionally has given hope to tarpon enthusiasts of the western Gulf. But whether or not tarpon fishing there will ever be reestablished to its former proportions is questionable.

The beginner should understand that tarpon are fished purely for sport. It is unfortunate that in pier fishing tarpon must be gaffed with a long-handled gaff, and killed and wasted. Unless one wants a fish for mounting, all those landed should be released. There is no sound reason for keeping them otherwise. Both the beginner and the old hand will at that do well to get one of mounting size aboard. No fish on earth is harder to hook solidly, and keep hooked. The least bit of slack line during the battle and the fish is gone. It is a tremendously powerful creature.

Incidentally, plug and metal-lure fishermen new to tarpon fishing should watch closely when a fish is on and jumping, for often the thrown plug travels long distances at high speed. It is a good idea to be on the alert and ready to dodge. This is just one more proof that tarpon fishing, which was to a great degree responsible for the launching of marine big-game fishing many years ago, is among the most spectacular of all angling endeavors.

Bonefish

Albula vulpes

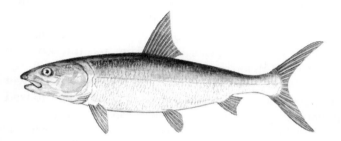

Of one fact in the history of its skyrocketing flight to fame the bonefish may be justly proud. It made the grade as one of the most elite of marine game fish without the slightest assistance from the kitchen. It is edible in a sense, although bony, but the crystal-pure sport it offers is what made it famous.

A relatively few years ago few anglers knew the bonefish. Today almost all at least know its reputation as a streak of lightning on the semitropical flats of the Florida Keys. Bonefish range north to Cape Cod, and on the Pacific coast well past Santa Monica. But they are only incidental in our hemisphere except on the famous bonefishing grounds along the Florida Keys, and around the Caribbean islands. Although most tourist-anglers to the Keys fish the bonefish flats during the winter, actually the fish are more abundant there in summer.

Bonefish are relatives of the tarpon. They have glistening bronze to bluish-green backs shading immediately to bright silver. Occasionally there are a few darker markings along the sides. Unobservant anglers confuse bonefish with ladyfish. A look at the mouth and nose of bonefish is all it takes to positively identify them. The bonefish is mildly sucker-like in form and the nose is a definite snout, for rooting.

That snout is the key to catching bonefish. These swift creatures move from deep water in upon the flats to feed in very shallow water, where they root in the soft, pale-colored bottom for varied crustaceans, and gobble up hermit and other crabs. When rooting, nose down, the tail breaks the surface. This characteristic disturbance, or the muddying of the water, gives away the presence of a bonefish from a great distance to an angler poling quietly over the flats, standing up in his skiff with his back to the sun, watching.

Thus, bonefishing is part hunting, part fishing. The prey is exceedingly wary. If a feeding bonefish is disturbed by the slightest sound, shadow, or sight of angler or boat, it is gone in a flash. Many bonefishermen wade, to keep the silhouette and the water disturbance down. Many, with or without guide to do the poling, anchor the boat and get out to make the stalk once the quarry is sighted. Sometimes single bonefish are seen. Sometimes several feed together. Quite often an expanse of flat may be alive with scattered fish from small groups. Lone fish are best to stalk, for there is no chance of disturbing one and having its flight send them all jetting off.

An angler fishing bait will spot his fish, then put himself in position where the fish will feed to him. He gingerly casts out the bait, lets it lie where the fish will come upon it. The most popular bait is a hermit crab. Next is a shrimp or a sand flea. A bonefish picks up such a bait very gently. This is one of the crucial moments. Line must be slack, so the fish detects no tension as it mouths the bait. Presently it will move off a few yards. The hook must then be set instantly, before the fish can drop the bait. When the hook goes home, the fish leaps from a "standing" start into high gear, commonly making a run of 100 to 300 yards at incredible speed. No light tackle—which is invariably used for this fine sport—is capable for stopping this first run of a fair-sized fish.

The purist bonefisherman, of which there are more and more nowadays, looks down his nose at bait. A few use plugs or feathered jigs. The real fanatics fish with streamer flies only. Red and white, red and yellow, brown, pink—those are among the most telling colors.

The stalk is made as in bait fishing. But now the fly must be cast across, and brought back with interesting motion to intersect the path of the feeding fish. Stealth, skill, and proper use of sunlight for maximum conceal-ment are necessary, in order to make the cast from a range where the fish may be reached, and still not frighten it.

The type of tackle is a matter of personal choice. The main consideration is to have a large-capacity reel, for the runs of bonefish are long, and often unstoppable on light to modest gear. Curiously, when bonefish are in water about 3 feet deep they can be caught more easily by using a bucktail jig—the standard type with lead head and upturned hook. Much fly-fishing gear has been de-veloped especially for bonefish fishing. The new light but powerful graphite and boron rods have refined the tackle somewhat. Forward-taper fly lines are best, and a substantial amount of backing line is mandatory, at least 150 yards. Leaders need to be strong and durable, yet as fine as practical.

Bonefish move inshore with the tide, purposely to get in over good feeding areas newly flooded with each tide. They are present all year along the Keys, but come in more abundantly in summer.

Bait fishermen usually, but not always, use an egg-shaped sinker and run the line through the end hole, so when the fish picks up the bait the line will run free. They also chum for bonefish, using chopped shellfish scattered over an area to lead the fish to the bait. There is, however, little point in bait fishing for this species. It is not an "eating" fish, but strictly a sport fish. Therefore one may as well get the most out of it in challenge and action. Fly fishing is far and away the best method for doing this.

The bonefish does not leap. It makes a first awesome run, then doubles back and does it all over time after time, finally circling the boat stubbornly until exhausted. Fish of 2 to 5 pounds are average. A 10-pounder is a very good fish. The maximum in our range is probably around 15, although larger ones may exist. There is little point in keeping one unless the angler wishes it mounted. Bonefish fight until so frazzled they will usually die when released unless they are held upright in the water, the angler grasping the tail, and swayed back and forth so water filters through the gills to revive them.

There are many odd items of bonefishing lore important to consistent success. For one thing, seldom do bonefish feed over the shallow flats when the water temperature falls much below 70 degrees. They stay in deeper water then. Also, some flats that look fine to the angler almost never have fish, while others always do. One must learn the quirk too, that bonefish coming in over the flats on a rising tide are not half as wary as they become when the tide starts to fall. Thus a fisherman must take tide conditions, as well as light conditions, into consideration. And whatever he does, when fly fishing he had best keep his slack line under control. If, as it races through the guides when a hooked bone runs, the line so much as catches lightly on anything, such is the power of the run that the leader will instantly be snapped.

Ladyfish

Elops saurus

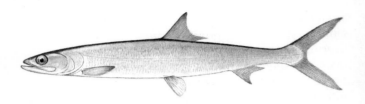

Long ago someone called this dynamic and explosive small relative of the tarpon the "ten-pounder," and that is the name by which many scientific books have long insisted it be known. This is perfectly foolish because the species almost never reaches the weight indicated by that impossible name, and besides, it is doubtful that sports fishermen ever use the name, or ever will. To confuse matters further, the bonefish is called by some natives the "ladyfish," and the ladyfish the "bonefish." However, today the bonefish is so well known to anglers and the ten-pounder so consistently called a ladyfish that eventually the confusion will disappear.

A second handicap forced upon the ladyfish stems from the fact that it is terribly bony and not of much account on the table. Therefore, thousands of meat fishermen fishing from bridges, causeways, and skiffs have for years despised and destroyed it because it voraciously takes baits and lures angled for edible species. The ladyfish is a perfectly wonderful light-tackle game fish, a most dramatic leaper, and though it is abundant the disrespect for it and the wanton killing of it to no purpose is a disgraceful fact of inshore fishing, particularly in the Southeast.

The ladyfish is not, however, without friends. Fishermen interested in sport first and their stomachs second have more and more highly touted the ladyfish late years. The incoming tides usually bring school after school of these swift, streamlined predators swarming into bays, lagoons, and tidal rivers. Here they cruise the dropoffs near channels, or patrol back and forth around bridges and the edges of weedbeds, avidly snapping up small fish, shrimp, squid, crabs, and crustaceans.

The ladyfish is long and silvery, with a green to bluish back, and usually a few scattered spots along the sides. Because of its large, bright eye, it is sometimes called "bigeye herring." Others call it a "skipjack," a name used for scores of other small marine species. When one fishes a channel through which a tide is running, ladyfish will strike furiously for a few minutes, then subside, only to begin again shortly, as school after school cruises by.

This is not an especially wary fish. It is nearly always willing. That, for many fishermen, makes it a problem and a nuisance. For example, when schools of ladyfish are present while one is casting or trolling for other species, they are eager to hit, given baits they're capable of seizing. They make sizzling runs and numerous spectacular leaps, and are unbelievably adept at throwing a hook. However, when one is using a certain type of wire leader, the leap of a hooked ladyfish will put a kink in it that can't be straightened out. This leads to much exasperation and muttering.

The dramatic battle, nonetheless, should be worth it. The fish fights out of all proportion to its size. Most ladyfish average from 1 to 3 pounds. Some go 6 or more, a few reach 10 or 12. A fish of 3 pounds is about 2 feet long. Occasionally poor observers confuse ladyfish with tarpon. There is little excuse for this. Even a cursory glance at either should immediately apprise the fisherman of the marked differences in shape and appearance.

This species ranges north to Cape Cod in the Atlantic, and is present in the Pacific below U.S. borders. But it is most abundant about Florida, both in the Gulf and along the east coast, and along the western Gulf coast. It strikes as well at night as in the daytime.

Many are taken by trollers after other species. Thousands are caught by bridge fishermen and skiff fishermen using boat rods or short, stiff saltwater casting rods and feathered jigs with lead-weighted heads. This exceedingly popular saltwater lure, in yellow or white, catches scores of different species, and is especially deadly on ladyfish. There is no need to use anything more sturdy than standard freshwater-bass casting tackle, rigged with nylon line of 12- to 15-pound test, a short wire leader with snap swivel. Such an outfit handles the feathered jigs well, and also diving plugs, which ladyfish will hit voraciously. Some terminal tackle may be lost, of course, if larger fish strike. But it is worthwhile for the high sport of hooking the ladyfish on light tackle.

Still more sporting is the spinning outfit, nowadays very popular for fishing of this sort. The outfit can be as light or heavy as the angler wishes, whatever he thinks he can handle successfully without too much tackle loss. Small diving plugs, nickel-finish spoons, and the feathered jigs with upturned hook, in spinning size and weight, are all good.

Specialists use fly-fishing tackle on schools of ladyfish. This is exciting sport. A large-capacity reel with plenty of backing behind a forward-taper line of good weight for long casts, a fairly stout leader, and a streamer fly make up the outfit. The trick is to fish the lure swiftly. All predaceous saltwater fish are used to cruising fast and slashing at top speed after moving prey. A fast-moving fly is therefore likely to be more attractive than one lazing along. Streamers in white or yellow, or combinations of these with red seem to be most attractive.

Ladyfish can be caught with bait, and are thus caught by hundreds as incidentals while fishing for other varieties. But there is little point in using bait purposely to catch them, since they so readily strike artificials and are caught only for the sport.

Spring, summer, and early fall bring the most ladyfish in from open water as they cruise northward out of the tropics. They can be taken all year around Florida and southern Texas.

Striped Bass

Roccus saxatilis

The striped bass is the great prize of the New England surf fisherman. It is a rough-battling hard striker, a delicious food fish, and grows to a size to satisfy any angler who must catch big fish to be happy. It probably grows, maximum, to well over 100 pounds. Fish over 70 have been taken on hook and line, and fish of 20 to 50 are not uncommon. Smaller ones—2 to 10—are abundant.

This is by no means a fish only of the New England coast. Southward it is found clear down the coast and along the Gulf. For the most part it is taken in its more southerly range during its spawning runs. Striped bass are anadromous fish, coming into coastal rivers and traveling many miles up them during the spring to spawn. In Gulf rivers of upper Florida such runs occur about March. Famous runs such as that on the Roanoke River come about mid-April. In Maine runs are about May.

Many years ago the striped bass, originally native only to the Atlantic, was stocked in the Pacific, and has now long been a most popular sport fish in the bay areas around San Francisco and in several other spots. Stripers are taken, for example, at the mouth of the Russian River in California. Farther north, Coos Bay, Oregon, with its many sloughs leading to the Coos River is a striper angler's paradise. The Columbia River also has striped bass, and so do the Umpqua and many other west-coast rivers. Undoubtedly many more would be caught in the surf of the upper west coast if more anglers learned to go after them. For the striped bass—or "rockfish" as it is known along the Carolina coast and southward—is strictly a coastal species and is never found more than a nominal distance offshore. Presently Texas is attempting to establish a coastal population in the Gulf, which will make spawning runs up coastal rivers.

It is just about impossible to list the baits and lures best for striped bass. They take a great variety, from cut bait or chunks of fish (popularly stillfished on deep, slow bends of the Coos River in Oregon), to small bullheads with the pectoral spines clipped (another famous Coos River stillfishing bait), to crabs, shrimps, clams, bloodworms, menhaden, and mullet, popular in the East. They are susceptible to chumming and are often gathered to the hook this way by surf anglers anywhere along the coast from Massachusetts to the Carolinas.

On east-coast rivers during the spring run, some anglers catch the smaller fish by stillfishing close to shore with minnows. Others use wobbling spoons with a pork-rind trailer, and troll with them. An odd method used by commercial and food fishermen during such runs is dipping up "rock" with a huge, long-handled bownet. The fisherman, drifting in his boat, watches for a "fight." This is a roiling of surface water by numerous males attempting to fertilize the eggs of a single female. The netman cranks up and races to the scene, slides the bownet beneath the commotion, and may pick off as many as a dozen or more at one sweep.

In certain Florida rivers experts at the game ease along until they come to what they call a "boil." This is where a bottom spring swirls up. The large stripers like to lie in such a place on an upstream migration. Using bait, or favorite plugs, anglers who know these waters have good luck. Plugs, jigs, spoons, eelskin rigs, and many others are popular for northern coastal surf fishing.

Rips and reefs near rocky headlands, or bays where a surf churns against the rocks and forms deep pockets, make excellent places for striper fishing on the upper Atlantic coast. Bays, inlets, and channels are all good spots, too. In many inshore areas of Chesapeake Bay the striper fishing is excellent during spring. Often the reedy salt flats where the tides sweep over marshes offer good sport. Wherever the food is plentiful, there the big stripers are likely to be found.

It is not difficult to distinguish the striped bass from other species. In fact, there are few if any fish within its habitats with which it is likely to be confused. In isolated cases it may be found in coastal streams with white bass, its freshwater counterpart. But the freshwater white bass is smaller and built quite differently. It is deeper, less elongated, more compressed. The striper has an undershot lower jaw, a long, heavy body along which run seven or eight horizontal dark stripes. The spiny and soft dorsal fins are separated. The color of typical stripers is silvery, with their dark stripes most evident, and with a gold to brassy shading in varying degree overlying all. Some of them also have a greenish cast.

Striped bass are not leapers. They hit with a smashing strike, and then put up a rough, slam-bang fight that is a tackle-strainer. They feed by night as well as by day, and many experts prefer to fish at night, often listening for the slosh of the big fellows as they splash through forage swirling in tidal rips and around the rocks. Discounting the spawning runs, even though stripers are present all year in most localities, they strike best during the warm months. Beginning about May all along the coast, and on through until well into the fall, fishing is usually good.

Some anglers have developed fly fishing for stripers, and take fair-sized fish this way. Most such fishing is done in the bays and sloughs, in quieter water where a bucktail or streamer, or a big popping bug, may be worked to best advantage. White streamers have been popular, with the Polar Bear and variations heading the list. Large flies tied in Florida especially as snook flies (streamers) work well, too. Fairly strong leaders and forward-taper lines are best for this fishing, and a powerful rod helps.

For surf fishing standard surf tackle is used by most striped-bass anglers, some even handling large specially developed plugs on these outfits. Lighter tackle is used for sporty trolling. The saltwater spinning rod is popular. This is a sound outfit, capable of wearing down many a big striper, whether one is using lures or bait. Regular freshwater plugging tackle is also often in evidence for smaller stripers.

Whether high or low tide is best depends a lot on what section of the coast one fishes. In most places the general rule is that a strong tide will be best, especially if it runs at break of day. The fish seem to feed especially well at dawn. On the other hand, ebbing tides often bring violent action, especially around the mouths of rivers. Doubtless this is because much food is swept down with the tide. By and large, a moving tide, which moves the food, arouses the fish to action. During the hot months, night fishing is often advantageous. The stripers feed more voraciously then.

Chumming is never amiss. It works well for trollers. The chum must be dribbled out so that it rides down the current and so that fish may follow it up toward the boat. Chumming while stillfishing or when casting from shore, using chunks of bait, or live shrimps or other bait, is a good idea, too. If the fish are actively feeding, of course no chum is necessary.

Because the striped bass is anadromous and apparently feels no discomfort either in mildly brackish or wholly freshwater, it has become the basis for one of the most important fisheries management stories of the century. In landlocked form the burly striped bass has been established almost from coast to coast and a good part of the way border to border as one of the most powerful and popular species of large freshwater lakes and streams, mainly impoundments. By 1980 every state across the southern half of the U.S. and a few above had a striped bass fishery in progress. Most states had established records of fish of at least 30 to 40 pounds, and several stood at 50 or 60.

The spark for the massive nationwide projects was struck in 1941, when striped bass became landlocked in the huge Santee-Cooper impoundments in South Carolina, Lakes Moultrie and Marion. Fish in the rivers at the time the dams were closed off and the lakes filled were trapped there. Shortly there was great excitement among fisheries biologists because striped bass of varying age classes were turning up in sport catches. This meant there had been successful spawning, and growth of young in landlocked form.

Striped bass spawning is a highly specialized sequence. The freshly deposited eggs are not adhesive, as those of some fish are, but float free in the stream where they are released. They require 30 to 70 hours to hatch, depending on water temperature. This means a float as a rule of somewhere from 40 to 100 miles. Apparently landlocked fish had gone right on with their spawning runs and were able to succeed in the tributary rivers. By 1957 anglers had taken almost 30,000 landlocked stripers from the two big South Carolina lakes.

Biologists realized stripers would be unable to spawn naturally in most settings. But in South Carolina hatchery projects had begun for establishing controlled populations in other lakes. By 1960 other states were eagerly asking for striper eggs or fingerlings. At first these were difficult to come by. But soon other states had learned hatchery culture techniques and were raising their own supplies of fry. Stripers were swiftly stocked in scores of impoundments across the nation. Very few rivers tributary to large impoundments were suitable for spawning. A small amount has occurred in Texas, Oklahoma, Arkansas, and regularly in the Colorado River bordering California and Arizona.

Populations on the whole, however, are built by gathering eggs and milt each spring from fish trapped as they attempt spawning runs. The striper was seen long ago as an excellent large "policeman" for reservoirs overrun with undesirable rough fish. They are large enough to forage on rough fish that are too big for the capabilities of native freshwater game fish. Because of lack of spawning, striper populations can be precisely controlled, cannot overrun a lake. Meanwhile, however, the landlocked striped bass has become such a fetish for sport fishermen that it has changed the inland angling picture presumably forevermore.

A whole new mass of fishing techniques has evolved for landlocked striped-bass fishing. The fish are caught numerously by fishing the tailraces below big dams. Additionally, anglers have discovered that often schools of stripers lie very deep in lake channels, to 50 or 60 feet or more, and can be located by depth sounders and caught by jigging slab-type spoons or similar lures. Bait fishing is also extremely productive. Baits differ from area to area, but consensus across much of the South is that a live sunfish of fair size is one of the most productive baits.

Occasionally striper schools chase shad on the surface, like white bass, and are caught on surface or near-surface lures. Most are caught deeper. Time of year for best fishing differs from lake to lake, and by latitude. In South Carolina and that general region, March on into summer is favored. Fall-winter is best from Nebraska to Texas. The

Colorado River, now famous for striper fishing, produces from March right on through August.

Striped bass are fine food fish as well as sensational gamesters. The surf anglers and fish stalkers of the beaches and rocky headlands of New England claim the striper as their most desirable trophy. Its temperament, to be sure, seems to fit the tide rips and roaring surf of those northern waters. But striped bass are now being stocked in the western Gulf in hopes of forming a population there. The striped bass seems to fit into myriad situations, and is undoubtedly on the freshwater scene to stay, in addition to continuing in its old saltwater haunts. Midwestern anglers have even caught stripers through the ice in winter.

Snook

Centropomus undecimalis

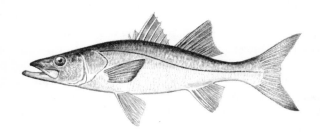

This jut-jawed inshore and tidal-water species is one of the finest and most popular of light-tackle game fish found in southern saltwater. The snook, or robalo, is sometimes spoken of as a marine pike, but its temperament is likely to be more like that of the mercurial muskie of freshwater. The snook strikes with a hair-raising smash, and on days when the fishing is "hot" nothing seems to make it wary, nor is it especially choosy about the lure offered. At other times, however, snook may be seen cruising or lazing about moodily, and for days at a time nothing will tempt them.

The snook is not easily confused with any other species, once it or its likeness has been seen. The undershot lower jaw, the long and fairly slender body with high-humped back sloping from the forward spiny dorsal to the dished snout give it a most individual shape. Perhaps the best key to positive snook identification, however, is the lateral line. That line is broad and dark, strikingly so against the silvery body, and it does not stop when it reaches the tail but continues on out almost to the apex of the fork. This is a most distinctive physical characteristic.

The size of the average snook is from 1 to 5 pounds. This weight range is by no means maximum. Fish of up to 10 pounds are not at all uncommon, specimens of 15 are caught fairly often, and they go from there on up to 30, 40, and even 50 pounds. Not only does the snook strike with a vicious lunge, but it battles the same way. It is not a high jumper, but does roll and lash furiously, and its runs in cramped spaces are powerful and sizzling.

Actually this is a tropical species, which puts our southern waters at the limits of its northern range. It is plentiful all along the Florida coasts, particularly so the farther south one goes. It ranges on throughout the Gulf, with special abundance again along the lower Gulf coasts. Once abundant along southern Texas, it has for unknown reasons become rather scarce there. Farther south, in Mexican waters, many snook are caught. Although there are snook in the Pacific, too, they do not range far enough north to come into our waters.

Happily for the angling majority, who fish close inshore, the snook is a species of sandy shores, and of flats, bays, the vicinity of bridges and pilings, and of brackish waters. Coastal rivers are prime snook habitat, the fish often moving inland in swarms when the tides run. Many of them live out their lives in tidal bayous, and such places as the brackish tidal canals along the Everglades highways. In places snook ascend streams until they are in water completely fresh. Other excellent snooking grounds are the channels formed between small mangrove islands along Florida's coasts, or inlets from Gulf to bay where tides run in a heavy-currented stream.

All such environments are to the liking of the snook because it is a most predaceous species. It feeds on small mullet, which it chases down in shallow water, and on crabs, shrimp, and almost anything that moves. Because it is not selective in feeding habits, the snook has long been popular not only with fishermen using spoons, plugs, and feathered jigs, but with fly fishermen as well.

Probably the best all-round flies for snook are certain streamers developed some years ago in Florida. These flies, all rather lightly dressed, are tied with pairs of long (2 to 3 inch) feathers placed back to back on opposite sides of the hook. Thus, when dry, the streamer feathers curve out sharply on either side of the hook. When wet, and worked slowly through the water, the outcurved feathers open and close with a swimming motion. Orange and gray, red and white, yellow and white are among the favorite color combinations. Such streamers are cast into places like the Everglades roadside canals, allowed to sink a bit, and then retrieved very slowly. A big snook may follow along for some distance, then strike with an awesome, spray-throwing smash.

The standard freshwater cork-bodied or hair-bodied bass popping bug is also a good fly-rodder's lure for snook. It should be fished exactly as one would fish it for freshwater black bass. Surface plugs are also good. Snook often bat such lures hard enough almost to knock the hooks off, either hooking themselves or sending the lure skyrocketing.

Most snook are taken in fairly shallow water, or at least

in water of no more than modest depth. Deep-running lures are therefore seldom as productive, when underwater artificials are used, as diving plugs or lures that run no more than a couple or 3 feet at maximum depth. Often feeding snook can be observed cruising along near surface, snapping up small fish.

Bait fishermen account for a great many snook. Most common bait used is a live shrimp. In creeks and rivers flowing into the Gulf, bait anglers often make a killing on snook as the tide comes in. They fish a live shrimp barely a foot below surface, using a bobber to hold it up. The fish come swarming into the stream, and may work many miles up it, feeding as they go. They seize the shrimp and take the bobber down in one sweep.

Tackle used for snook is of infinite variety. Plug fishermen usually operate with the same outfit one would use for freshwater bass or pike. Some use standard saltwater casting rods of 5 or 5 1/2 feet, with a reel of modest capacity, and a line of about 18-pound test. A great many stillfishermen using bait fall back on the ancient cane pole.

Trolling is also a popular method of taking snook. For this method a standard saltwater boat rod is often considered best, simply because it is stiff enough and heavy enough to make trolling easy. Spinning tackle is popular for snook fishing, both with two-handed surf tackle and with standard spin rods of fairly stiff action. The monofil line is a great help at times in fooling large snook in shallow, clear waters.

Because fly fishermen after snook often must work in rather cramped quarters in the bayous and canals—such as those in the 'Glades where this fishing first became popular—rather heavy fly rods are the rule. They need to be powerful in order to handle and subdue this wild-fighting fish at close quarter.

Whatever tackle is used, it is a good idea to tie on a short wire leader. The gill covers of a snook are very sharp. They cut a line readily when the fish rolls. Of course monofil is not easily sliced in this manner. Fly fishermen often fish with no wire leader, taking their chances. Handling snook after they are caught requires caution. The gill covers can slash hands severely.

Although incoming-tide fishing often seems to be particularly good, snook are caught on all tides, and they are also taken year-round. Peak snook fishing, however, usually occurs during spring and early summer. Just as with freshwater bass fishing, dawn and dusk as a rule produce the most activity. The appeal of the snook is not restricted entirely to the waterfront. It's an excellent food fish.

It is unfortunate that so desirable a game and food fish as the snook should be facing difficulties in U.S. waters. Around Florida they have declined to some extent, possibly due to overfishing, and the state has experimented with attempts to propagate them. Texas snook fishing, once extremely popular in the southernmost waters of the shoreline, has all but disappeared. There is some feeling that a comeback may occur. Skin divers often see snook in summer, some of large size, along a recently dredged land cut from bay to Gulf on Mustang Island, but catches are rare. No one seems certain why snook have become scarce in the western Gulf, but anglers hope for a return. Fishing is still good much farther south, along the Mexican coast.

Great Barracuda

Sphyraena barracuda

There have been hosts of swimmers and others slashed to bits, in fiction stories, by barracuda. There have even been supposedly well-authenticated stories of people who have been hurt by barracuda. Most if not all of these are at best questionable. The barracudas are certainly fierce looking, and in all rather fearless fish, long, slender, powerful, awesomely swift, and with teeth—especially the great barracuda—that look like spikes set into their jaws. But whether or not they are truly dangerous to man is still open to argument. Regardless, they are certainly excellent game fish.

Fundamentally, barracuda are tropical. However, various forms do range into northern waters. It is not especially important that anglers know the technicalities of separating them. The great barracuda is the one most fishermen catch in the Atlantic. Although it straggles north to Massachusetts, it is never abundant even to the Carolinas. It is caught mainly around Florida, the Keys, and throughout the West Indies, and occasionally in the western Gulf.

The guaguanche is a small species of barracuda whose range is about like that of the great barracuda. Few anglers properly identify it, thinking it to be young of the larger species. There is also the northern barracuda, which gets as far north as Cape Cod. Both of these are fish about the size of small pickerel, great fun on very light tackle using small lures, but not very important to anglers. Both are sometimes called "sennet." There is also a European barracuda that occasionally strays to our northern Atlantic waters. It is unimportant to anglers also, except for the knowledge that it may appear on our coast.

Besides the great barracuda, the only other well-known game fish of the clan is the Pacific barracuda, or California barracuda, *Sphyraena argentea*, which will be dealt with later on in this section.

The great barracuda, or simply barracuda, or 'cuda, as it is called throughout the southern waters of the Atlantic, averages anywhere from 5 to 20 pounds in weight, but it is known to weigh 100 and more. Specimens of 50 pounds are not especially uncommon. This is a fish blue-gray or green-gray above, silvery below. Some individuals have the sides marked, usually about midway back and below the lateral line, with dark uneven spots or blotches.

These barracuda are likely to be almost anywhere that food is abundant. The inshore channels, bays, inlets, and lagoons, even where salt- and freshwater mix around the coastal rivers, may harbor barracudas. The shallows around mangrove islands, the coral reefs of the Keys often seem alive with them. The outside reefs are excellent barracuda territory. These are fish mainly of reasonably shallow areas and are found much of the time near the surface. This is because they are exceedingly savage and voracious, and thus hang out where the smaller fish teem.

A common barracuda habit is to lie motionless for long periods. Not in hiding, but simply lying in wait for whatever may pass. As a rule such a fish is alone. In fact, barracuda are lone wolves to a great degree. There may be a number of them in the same area, but they seldom purposely operate together or act at all in the manner of school fish. Out where the deeper reefs lie, the outside reefs along the Florida coast, the largest of the barracudas are usually caught. These fish may stay near bottom, or lie in wait in reef holes. Whether one is fishing inside or outside, the rising tide is the best time, as is usually the case with predaceous fish of any kind. Barracuda appear to move inshore to some extent in summer, and to offshore waters during the fall and winter. This is no definite migration, but fishing is best at the times and places thus indicated.

One of the great delights of barracuda fishing is that this fish puts up a battle with much fireworks. Its runs are very swift, and it may leap repeatedly and violently, hurling its long body high and far. Because of the truly terrible teeth, steel leaders several feet long are invariably used. In the inshore waters and the bays and coves, a great many barracuda are caught on light tackle. During recent seasons spinning tackle has replaced much of the standard plugging tackle formerly used. Where large barracuda are likely to be caught, however, most anglers like fairly heavy tackle with 200 or more yards of line testing 30 pounds or more. Needless to say, a good angler using a saltwater spinning outfit can whip any barracuda going, and again, heavy spin tackle is an excellent rig for fishing such as this.

Most barracuda are taken trolling, usually while trolling for other species. Of course, purposely trolling for them in their known hangouts is an excellent method. But more sport is to be had by locating a good place and then casting for them. Various plugs and spoons are effective, as well as feathered jigs, either when trolling or casting.

Saltwater fly fishing has made such strides during past years that nowadays numerous anglers have taken up fly fishing for barracuda. The smaller ones are usually sought, because casting a streamer or bucktail is best accomplished in the waters where these fish of average size are likely to be lying. A barracuda of 5 or 10 pounds on a fly rod is indeed an experience.

Stillfishing with bait also accounts for a good many barracuda. It is a simple way to catch them. Almost any variety of bait in local abundance will do. Live baits are best. Trollers use strip-cut bait such as mullet.

Anglers who wade the flats along the Keys and elsewhere off Florida are often startled to find that several barracuda are following along behind them in the roil left from their tracks. These fish are probably only curious, or else feeding on crustaceans and other delicacies kicked up by the commotion. They will not necessarily strike anything that moves, and may in fact only make a swift dash to have a look. On the other hand, caution may not be amiss. Certainly these fish are at least physically equipped and capable of inflicting serious lacerations. There have been instances of barracuda slashing at hooked fish as an angler, wading or in a boat, lifts one from the water. A string of fish trailing close to a wading angler may encourage attack, and movement of the fishermen's feet and legs might get him into trouble.

The **Pacific barracuda** is in several ways a quite different fish from its eastern cousin. For one thing it is smaller. Fish anywhere from 5 to 15 pounds are caught, with the average in between. But there are no monsters, such as off Florida. A fish of 12 to 14 pounds is usually about 3 1/2 to 4 feet long. This barracuda is slender, and the head is exceedingly tapered, with the snout long and thin, and the lower jaw greatly undershot. It is also a schooling fish, often found in large gatherings. It ranges the length of our Pacific coast, clear to Alaska, but only incidentally north of Morro Bay or Monterey.

The color is gray-black above, often with a hint of bluish, with the lower parts silvery. There is little danger of mistaking this for any other Pacific species in the range under consideration. Although the great barracuda of Florida is good enough eating, it has no solid reputation as a food fish, and indeed large specimens are suspect of causing cases of fish poisoning. The Pacific species, however, was long an important market fish, and is also one of the foremost of the California sport fishes.

The good barracuda fishing generally begins off California about April. It gets better and better as the weeks go on, with the peak during May and June or a bit later. The fish are then present through until fall in varying numbers, at which time they drift southward. Those who fish below the border catch barracuda all year.

Pier anglers catch some barracuda, but most of this California variety are taken from barges and party boats operating anywhere from just offshore to several miles out. During the summer the party boats from most southern California ports consider the barracuda schools their mainstay for surefire fishing. Some of the fish are caught trolling with plugs, jigs, or spoons, either with or without added strip bait. Others are caught by casting, and a great many—probably most—by stillfishing with bait, or jigging with a feathered jig, from the boats.

Tackle can be of angler's choice. Light tackle of course gives the most sport. Saltwater spinning tackle is a perfect rig, and is used by many west-coast barracuda fans. It is especially good for fishing live anchovies, a preferred bait for barracuda. The bait fish is let down after some chumming near kelp beds, where barracuda like to hide, and allowed to swim free. Or, in lieu of this kind of bait, minnows or squid jigged from pier or boat deck will often attract barracuda schools. Regardless, the spinning rod allows gentle movement and easy handling of bait.

The Pacific barracuda in particular has become something of a tourist's fish, as well as a local standby, because in the spring and summer it is as dependable as any fish will ever be. The great barracuda of the Southeast, however, should also be considered by tourist anglers. It makes a striking trophy, and the sport on light tackle is of rare quality indeed.

Channel Bass

Sciaenops ocellata

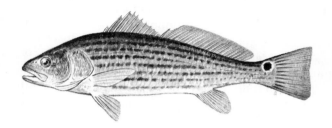

The American Fisheries Society lists this fish as the red drum. Fishermen call it "channel bass" and "redfish," and probably always will. However, it is not a bass and not even very closely related to the basses, but it is one of the most important of all game fish of the Atlantic and Gulf coasts.

It belongs to a large family of fishes, many of which are held in just as high esteem. These are the croakers, the family Sciaenidae, and all of them known as game fish are inhabitants of sandy beaches. For the most part, too, they inhabit the shallows. All but a few of our game croakers are caught in the warmer climes, from the Carolinas to Texas, and along the California coast.

Examples are the weakfishes or seatrout, the California white sea bass, the spotfin and yellowfin croakers of the Pacific coast, the game corbina also of the west coast, the black drum, the several whitings, and many more. All of these will be covered in following sections. But in beginning the croakers here with this king of the lot, it is well to know a few facts about the group as a whole.

The name "croaker" arose because of the sound many of these fish are capable of producing. Those that have air bladders (a few have none) usually have that organ so modified that it acts as a kind of resonator, and they are thus able to produce a "croaking" noise. A good distinguishing characteristic of croakers is that they have but two anal fin spines. This is a handy tag sometimes for the angler. For example, there is one small species, not especially important but often caught, that looks at a glance exactly like the white perch of fresh (and brackish) water. It is called a silver perch (*see* Saltwater Panfish section), which might be further confusing. However, a check of the anal spines proves its identity—it has two, the white perch three. Another tag of the croakers which helps spot them, although it does occur in some other fishes, is the extension of the lateral line right on through the tail fin, usually clear to its posterior edge. Tongue and roof of mouth are toothless in the croakers, but they have crusher-type teeth in the throat.

Because the croakers are fish of the surf, the bays, coves, and beaches, the shallow grass flats and the sandy reefs, they become easily accessible to almost anyone, and are caught from piers, from the beach, from small boats, and by wading anglers. Most of this family are also abundant, gather in large groups, are willing biters, and excellent eating. All this makes them as a class most desirable prey of the average fisherman. And most of the game members of the family are also important market fish.

Channel-bass fishermen line the beaches from eastern

Mexico clear around the Gulf and right on up to New York. They may catch what some of them call "puppy drum" or "rat reds," terms applying to small specimens, and they will also catch fish weighing anywhere from 40 to over 80 pounds.

Channel bass are not actually red, but in most of them a reddish or copper shading overlays the gray and silver and brownish that is their overall body color. The effect at a glance is of a definitely reddish fish. At the upper base of the tail there is at least one fairly good-sized black spot. There may be more than one. It is very noticeable, and a good identifying tag.

This fish is not a jumper. None of the croakers leap. It makes hard runs, and is a very powerful fighter, although there is an individual difference among channel bass in their apparent fighting ability. Some may strike hard. This happens mostly when one trolls for them, or casts with artificials. Others may—and usually do—pick up or nudge a bait very cautiously before finally accepting it. If the angler tries to hook a fish at this first gentle announcement of its presence, he usually succeeds only in frightening it away. Once the bait is seized, the redfish generally starts to run with it. Then is the time to snap up the rod tip.

These fish are strictly bottom feeders. As the tide moves in, they come with it, grubbing most of the time well back of the surf line, and finally, if possible, moving in over the soggy flats and into the deep holes where all kinds of bottom food such as crabs and crustaceans of numerous kinds, small fish, and marine worms are abundant. The dropoff behind a sandbar, the mouths, and sometimes far upstream waters, of coastal rivers, a deep quiet hole in the lee of a protected mangrove island, the sloughs and channels, the salt and brackish bayous—all are excellent for channel bass.

Sometimes the flats will seem to be alive with them. At others only small groups are found, or there may be but singles cruising here and there. In other words, they are not school fish in the sense of the compact schools such as mackerel often form, but they are exceedingly gregarious among their own kind.

There are many ways to catch redfish, and tackle nowadays in use is extremely varied. The standard surf outfit is the favorite of many east-coasters, especially to the north. The traditional boat rod stiff and heavy enough for comfortable trolling is a standby of the skiff fishermen. Hundreds of anglers use regular casting rods, either salt- or freshwater type, for redfish. Many employ spinning tackle, which is an excellent rig for reds. And even a few are having fun, especially with smaller channel bass, using fly rods. Although some anglers use wire leaders because of the presence of other species, monofil is perfectly adequate for redfish for they do not have biting teeth.

Happily, the fish take both lures and baits readily. It may be that generally bait does the best and most consistent job. A great variety of it can be successfully used. Shrimp, various worms, small crabs, cut bait—redfish are willing to pick almost any of it up when hungry. Sometimes it is fished still, just lying on bottom, and sometimes it is moved slowly along the bottom. Where one has the opportunity to fish deep holes, the best method is to cast a bait to a spot where it can be gently retrieved so that it appears to be creeping from the shallows to the protection of deeper water. This is especially intriguing to most channel bass. It is a common fishing method in the surf along the Carolinas and northward. The anglers anchor their boats offshore, and cast toward the surf from the outside.

Chumming works well with these fish, either from boat or beach. Stillfishing the deeper holes from a boat, a bridge, or a pier is also productive. Boat fishermen often drift-fish too. At times this is a very telling method, especially with live bait. Although fishing the moving tides, either way, is usually best, reds in quiet deep holes often hit at any time. They will also strike after dark as well as by day.

The variety of lures used for channel bass is as wide as that of bait. Plugs, both surface and underwater, depending on the depth and visibility, various wobbling spoons, feathered jigs, many of the smaller spinning lures, and streamer flies and bucktails all are good. There are no specialized tricks in the use of lures, except to remember to keep them down where the fish will spot them, and to make the retrieve interesting but at only modest speed. Of course there is no wait, when one is using artificials, before setting the hook. The fish slam into a moving artificial hard, once they have decided to strike it.

When stillfishing with bait, it is a good idea to move the bait every little while, if strikes fail to occur. Often this will attract the attention of redfish nearby. Also, if one has opportunity to fish the same area frequently, it pays to seek the precise hangouts of the fish. They are finicky at times about selecting certain holes or sloughs, or depressions behind the rips, or expanses or shell beds.

They will be there time after time when tide is right, but may scorn other spots that appear to the angler just as good. If a prolonged storm strikes a piece of beach that is prime redfish territory, fishing the high tide just as soon as calm weather returns often results in spectacular clean-ups. The fish have been driven from their feeding haunts by rough water, and when they return they usually are ravenous.

Along the Texas and upper Gulf coasts, and around Florida, channel-bass fishing is good throughout the year. However, as a rule winter is best, anywhere from October or November through March and April. Farther north on the Atlantic, the redfish appear with the progress of the season. They come swarming in along the Carolinas in spring. From May on through to October—often with very good fall as well as spring fishing—the fish are caught from here on throughout Chesapeake Bay and the New York vicinity.

So fond of the "reds" are many anglers that they eagerly await their appearance, and fish for little else during the year. Because channel bass can be caught in so many ways, they have become, along the entire coastline, something of an everyman's species. Both on a hook and on the table, they justify their reputation.

A most delightful fishing method that had its origin in force along the Texas coast is wading the grass flats for reds. Though now practiced elsewhere, the immense stretches of shallows behind the long islands that barricade the Texas coast made the method a natural for popularity there. It is done with fly rod, spinning gear or casting outfit, using a streamer fly, a spoon, a plug, or the peeled tail of a large shrimp. Wearing Polaroid glasses, an angler carefully stalks the shallows hunting his prey. The fish are awesomely shy here. When one is spotted, sometimes in only a foot or two of water, the cast is made far past and ahead, so the lure can be retrieved across before the feeding or slowly cruising fish. The slightest noise or motion of the angler heard or seen by the fish will send it, or them, flying.

When feeding, nose down, in such shallow water, redfish commonly show their tails above water. Tailing reds are easy to spot. Oddly, the tail with its "eye" spot looks pale powder blue when waving above water. The battle of a good-sized redfish in such shallow water is an astonishing experience. Large fish often surprise the tyro by feeding in water barely deep enough—and not even always deep enough—to cover their backs. A redfish of 10 to 15 pounds hooked under such conditions is seldom landed. It cuts the line on oyster or other shells. The thrill may not last long, but it is pure drama while it does.

One of the most interesting aspects of redfish fishing in our modern world is the successful transplant of them to freshwater in a few instances. Texas launched such a program in the late 1950s. It was purely experimental, an attempt to transplant certain inshore and bay species of saltwater to highly saline impoundments in western Texas, where native game fish did poorly and could barely survive.

Redfish placed for example in Imperial Reservoir south of Monahans in far western Texas grew with amazing swiftness. Flounders, and spotted weakfish also were placed there, and evidenced phenomenal growth. No spawning was ever evident. Later on further transplant experiments with redfish were tried in a number of Texas freshwater lakes, with the hope the fish would grow to become large predators helping to control shad and other roughfish populations. Although there was no spawning, the reds grew swiftly and seemed adaptable to a freshwater existence. Some were still being tried, particularly in some of the "hot" lakes with warmwater power-plant discharges, in 1980. Other saltwater game fish—black drum, flounders, trout (spotted weakfish)— all proved nearly as adaptable, though the rousing success of the landlocked striped bass dampened enthusiasm for further freshwater manipulation of reds and others.

However, during the late 1970s it became evident that the channel bass, one of the most important game and commercial species of the western Gulf, was in difficulty in its favorite bays and Gulf home. Traditionally, anglers and even some scientists have believed saltwater species just could not be "fished out." Studies proved without question that reds along Texas were being far overharvested. This led to some of the most intriguing and important experiments in mariculture ever conceived.

Redfish were placed in an enormous tank of saltwater at a coastal experiment station in which a proper environment for them had been prepared. Biologists learned in due time to induce spawning, not by injections, the usual method, but by manipulation of light and water temperature. One large female channel bass, nicknamed Ruby Red, produced millions of eggs for several years running, by being fooled into repeated spawning. Successful culture processes for eggs and fry were devised, and presently fry and fingerling redfish began to be available for replenishing and adding to natural stocks in the coastal bays. It is believed that these experiments may be the forerunners of broadly expanded efforts in mariculture with numerous species on all our coasts.

Weakfish

Cynoscion regalis

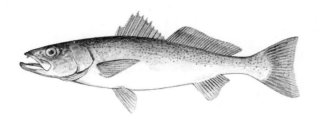

Anglers have every reason to object to the stupidity of whoever was responsible, long ago, for tacking such an undeserved name on this member of the croaker clan. The name by no means refers to the character of the fish, but rather to the softness of the mouth tissues, which allows them to tear easily. A hooked weakfish must be handled gingerly for this reason, and especially so because these fish are excellent fighters.

In fact, the weakfishes are probably the most popular, considering all facets of coastal sport fishing, of all the game fishes of the Atlantic and the Gulf. They form a kind of standard, in many sections, for the measurement of how good or how poor the fishing. They are most abundant, voracious, and worthy both at the end of a line and in the skillet.

There are several species within our range, and it is not necessary to cover them in separate sections, for all are much alike in general habits. The two best known are the common weakfish and the spotted weakfish. The other two, sometimes not recognized by those who catch them, are the sand weakfish and silver weakfish. The California white sea bass is also one of the weakfishes and is covered separately in the following section. These weakfishes while of the croaker tribe are in many ways much different and are classified in some older references in a separate family of their own. Only the male weakfish is capable of making the "croaker" sound.

The **common weakfish,** *Cynoscion regalis*, is a northern variety, ranging abundantly from lower New England down to about South Carolina. It reaches farther south, overlapping the range of the spotted variety, but it is predominantly a northern fish. Weight averages from 1 to 5 or 6 pounds, with a maximum of 18 or 20. It is a grayish and silvery fish, dark above and paler below, with some orange in the lower fins, and with dark irregular spots or blotches making slanted lines along the sides.

The **spotted weakfish,** *Cynoscion nebulosus*, is the southern variety, with its chief range from about Virginia south and on through the Gulf. It reaches occasionally much farther north, but primarily this fish is a Florida and Gulf Coast species, with the Texas and eastern Mexico coasts as well supplied as Florida. Its maximum size is a bit smaller than that of the common weakfish, with 12 to 15 pounds an average top. Fish of 1 to 3 or 4 pounds are most common, with those of 5 to 10 not at all rare. This is a beautifully colored fish, even though the shades are subdued hues of gray and silver with the back darker. It is spotted with many dark dots along the upper sides, the dorsal fin, and the tail. It is usually iridescent with shining overtones when fresh caught. On large, old fish, the inside of the mouth may be yellow.

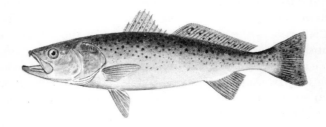

Spotted Weakfish

The other two species, the **sand weakfish,** *Cynoscion arenarius*, and the **silver weakfish,** *Cynoscion nothus*, are confusing even to scientists. The sand weakfish is a Gulf Coast species, has either no spots or very indistinct ones, a tail so shaped that the center rays are longest, and at least ten anal fin rays. The silver weakfish is an Atlantic coast species, has few or no spots, and usually only eight or nine anal rays. These fish are difficult for the layman to positively identify, and it is not especially important that he do so.

All the weakfishes have long been called by a number of common names. The most popular are "seatrout," "speckled trout," or simply "trout" or "specks." Of course they are not at all closely related to the trouts, but their general shape and the spots on them undoubtedly gave rise to the names. They are also called "squeteague." In fact, some quarters use this as an official name for the sand and silver varieties. It is a name not likely to stick very well with the average angler, and should therefore not be insisted upon by fisheries people.

Quite a few anglers somehow manage to confuse the weakfishes with other members of the croaker group. This is easy to avoid in most instances. The other croakers, such as the common croaker, the black drum, the channel bass, all have blunt snouts that overhang the lower jaw. The weakfishes have the lower jaw projecting. They also have a pair of large canine teeth at the tip of the upper jaw. These are especially noticeable in large specimens.

The most lovable characteristic of these species is that they can be taken by just about any method one selects. Trolling, stillfishing, casting with plugs, with wobbling spoons, with feathered jigs, with flies are all productive. In the North the common weakfish is found consistently in the surf and the areas where surf fishermen like to operate, while the southern spotted weakfish is more likely to be in the bays and on the grass flats. A most effective and popular method used in many areas is to bait with a live shrimp, then use a large float, or a "popping cork," which is simply a big float with a hollow head. By jerking the float a commotion is made on the surface, and weakfish coming to investigate see the moving shrimp close to the cork and seize it.

It is difficult to pinpoint exactly where the seatrout may swarm. But it is safe to say that any bay, lagoon, inlet, channel, any deep hole edged by a flat of underwater grass, or just any deep hole along a shallow shoreline may turn up hordes of them, especially on a high or a running tide. It won't make any difference whether the tide arrives at night or by day. The weaks hit as avidly one time as another. The smaller and medium-sized ones are school fish. Often the schools may be very large. They may come well up into the brackish water of large river mouths, and sometimes far up the streams. They may be spread out over a flat for miles. The very large ones, however, usually are lone wanderers. There are always special areas famous as hangouts for these large solitary fellows, and when a fisherman locates one, he can often keep going back to it with satisfying success.

In northern waters weakfishing begins to get good about the first of May and usually continues so until fall. By October it is about finished. The latter part of the season, however, is likely to be very good, especially for big fish on the tides. Chumming with live shrimp, from anchored charter boats, is a common method used at this time. The chum runs back on the tidal current and brings the fish up toward where baited hooks are waiting. This of course requires either an incoming or ebbing tide, to furnish a good current. In fact, both are good times for weakfish. All manner of baits do well, from crabs to sea worms to small fish. Artificials also take fish when cast into the chum stream and worked enticingly.

Night fishing is also very popular in northern waters, and especially so on the tidal flats during bright summer nights. Most of it is done by stillfishing with a bobber, and with the bait only a short distance below the surface. It is drifted on tidal current into deep holes, then picked up and drifted again, until struck by a roving fish.

Southern fishing for spotted weakfish is a year-round affair. Weather affects it, of course, but there are few times when fish cannot be located somewhere and induced to strike. The sheltered bays and inside flats, as well as brackish bayous and streams are the spots where most of the trout hang out. In some ways it is not as specialized in method as the northern variety of weakfishing. A great many anglers cast plugs, either surface or diving plugs, many use feathered jigs and various spoons. Lately short plastic worms with weighted heads have become popular and most effective. Spinning tackle is nowadays the popular gear, with freshwater plug rods and heavier saltwater plugging rods still used, too.

Of course bait fishing is also done, from pier, from boats, by wading and casting into the deep holes, or by using the popping cork method, which is deadly. Shrimp is the favored bait, but weakfish can be caught with almost any good natural regional bait. With either bait or lures most anglers use a wire leader, although nylon monofil will do just as well.

When hooked, the seatrout very seldom leaps. But it runs and bores down and battles so stubbornly that unless handled with some care it easily tears itself loose from the hook. Large individuals are extremely strong and stubborn. The angler who is used to handling them keeps a steady but gentle pressure, tiring them as quickly as possible, to make certain the mouth doesn't have time to tear enough for them to get away, yet never putting on enough pressure to damage it himself.

Surf fishermen use heavier outfits and must be still more gentle. Some even wrap the hook shank with soft line to avoid damaging the mouth of the fish. The type of tackle used, however, is dictated completely by the whim of the angler, since the average fish is not large enough to require anything heavy. When the popping cork is used, a rod stiff enough to pop it well is mandatory. Also, most anglers use a reel, jerk, reel, jerk retrieve, regardless of type of lure, and this is best accomplished by a fairly stiff rod. When trolling, the method is still employed, by continually giving short, quick jerks of the tip. Trolling, incidentally, is an excellent way to locate schools of weaks. Skiff anglers in bays often troll until they hit pay dirt, then cast with spinning tackle and yellow or white feathered jigs. In shallow, clear water one must be careful, of course, not to spook the fish. In such environments they are very skittish.

For the visitor to saltwater anywhere along the Atlantic or the Gulf, the weakfish is almost certain to be one of the mainstays of his introduction. It is a good propagandist for marine angling. And one of its most persuasive arguments is that most of those who were brought up on it still think the "seatrout" is the best of all.

California White Sea Bass

Cynoscion nobilis

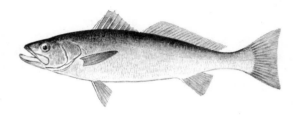

This handsome species of the Pacific coast is not a bass, but one of the largest, gamest, and most delicious of the croakers. Called "sea bass," "white sea bass," and "croaker," it is very popular with California saltwater anglers. It is a very good surface fighter, making hard, dogged runs and wallowing stubbornly. It is of good size, the average going up to 15 or even 25 pounds and the maximum 60 to 80 or more.

Thus, this fish has much to offer, and to top it, the California white sea bass is readily available to anglers of all classes. It is a species of the kelp beds and the sandy shores and the surf line. It is not often found at any distance offshore, and this makes it accessible to surf fishermen, to anglers with skiffs, and to those who frequent the large party boats.

This croaker is related rather closely to the weakfish of the Atlantic coast. Like the weakfish, it is an important commercial as well as sport species. Occasionally west-coast anglers confuse it with some of the basses that also hang out around kelp beds, and even with other croakers. There is little reason for this. The shape and size of the white sea bass are distinctive, and its fairly uniform bluish and gray and silver coloring should readily identify it. No other species in the somewhat restricted range of this fish looks especially similar. Officially its range extends from coastal British Columbia on south into Mexican waters, but not many are taken above San Francisco. From Santa Barbara southward is the range of abundance, with the concentration well into the southern portions of California waters.

Here the white sea bass is caught to some extent throughout the year. It is in summer, however, that the kelp beds in many places swarm with these big fellows. They begin to show in April, and the fishing success for them builds throughout the warm months, then tapers off into September and October.

The tyro is likely to get into difficulty when he first fishes the big California kelp beds. Beneath them in fairly shallow areas the white bass lie about, gobbling up all manner of small fish, crabs, shrimp, mollusks, and squids. Or they lie in the kelp, heads out, watching for food. A line put down too close, or a fish hooked and allowed to get back into the kelp, usually means terminal tackle lost. The kelp is very tough and heavy and thick. Experienced anglers using boats around kelp beds chum the white sea bass, to coax them out of hiding.

When chumming, anglers either stillfish or troll. Trolling is done at slow speed. White sea bass are not inclined to chase a swiftly moving lure. A hooked fish is played away from the kelp if at all possible. It must also be played with care, and a sensibly gentle hand. Like many other croakers, especially the eastern weakfishes, the white sea bass has a rather tender mouth.

To locate these big gamesters, one must of course first locate the kelp beds. These will be off the beaches, stretching through channels and around rocky areas, and just offshore from islands. Some charter-boat skippers locate large white sea bass simply by cruising or drifting slowly and looking down for them.

Although sporty tackle such as saltwater spinning rigs and average trolling and boat rods put out plenty of thrills with white sea bass, one has to know when to use them, and where. Too light an outfit won't turn a big specimen. It is better in the long run to use tackle heavy enough to keep the fish away from rocks and kelp. There is no specific tackle, however. A 9-ounce tip, a 30- to 40-pound-test line is reasonable, with hooks of 4/0 or a bit larger. Strip bait or live bait may be used. Sinkers and wire leaders are necessary.

Trollers using chum often follow up with slow-moving artificials, such as feathered jigs, spoons, tin squids, or even plugs. A large red-and-white plug has been popular and successful. Many white sea bass, incidentally, are taken at night by trollers. For pier fishing, such as at Newport, California, where white sea bass gather after dark in spring to chase bait fish, stillfishing is done with live bait, mainly small fish such as sardines and anchovies. The large charter boats anchor and use this same method, day or night.

Surf fishermen use the standard surf tackle, and standard croaker procedure. They simply cast out a bait and let it lie until the quarry picks it up. In bringing a heavy white sea bass in through surf, the angler should make certain that he utilizes incoming waves, then slacks off between waves. Otherwise he may tear the hook free.

Very occasionally white sea bass move into lagoons of brackish water, and even into the mouths of freshwater streams emptying into the Pacific. By and large, however, the kelp beds will be the payoff locations for this excellent fish, and the southern waters and warm months the best places and times.

Small white sea bass, incidentally, often have several bars, more or less distinct, of a dusky coloring running from the back down and forward. These are young fish, and should not be confused, because of the markings, with any other species.

Spotfin Croaker

Roncador stearnsi

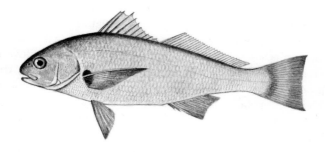

The spotfin croaker is easily identified throughout its restricted Pacific coast range from Point Conception southward by the large distinct black spot at the base of its pectoral fins. This is one of the gamest of the smaller croakers, and one of the best on the table. It averages in size from 1 to 3 pounds, commonly goes to 5, may go as high as 8, and even 10 or 12.

Like most croakers, this popular species is invariably found along the surf line of sandy shores, usually lying beyond the point where the breakers form, in depressions in the sandy bottom. Such holes draw many croakers, and when an angler locates one he is in business from then on until such time as a hard blow may make changes in the bottom. The spotfin is a dark-backed, gray-silver fish, with most individuals exhibiting a golden sheen.

In the section on the channel bass (red drum, redfish), also a member of the croaker family, a few characteristics of this large family of fishes were given. Because there

405

are several other species bearing the name "croaker" that are comparable in size to the spotfin, and because all these varieties are fished alike and have habits much alike, a few of the most popular are listed below with a scattering of the important facts about each. The Pacific coast has (besides the spotfin croaker) the yellowfin croaker, the black croaker, the white croaker, and the queenfish, the last included simply for completeness. (The California white sea bass, also a croaker, is covered in the preceding section, and the California corbina, another important croaker, is covered in the section following this one.) The Atlantic croaker represents the group on the east coast. There are several small croakers that go by other names, and they will be touched upon in the following sections, or in the section on saltwater panfish.

The **yellowfin croaker,** *Umbrina roncador,* is a gray, greenish, and golden fish of the Pacific coast with numerous dark, wavy lines slanting obliquely upward and backward along the scale rows. The lower fins and tail are yellow, the dorsal may have some yellow. It is sometimes called the "yellowtailed croaker." The range is like that of the spotfin croaker. Size averages smaller. Maximum size is about 3 to 5 pounds.

The **black croaker,** *Cheilotrema saturnum,* is a deeper-bodied fish than the others, dusky bluish to blackish above, shading lighter below. It can be distinguished by the black patch on the rear edge of the gill cover. It has many common names, such as Chinese croaker, black perch, blue bass. Its range is also like those above. Its weight generally averages from 1 to 3 pounds.

The **white croaker,** *Genyonemus lineatus,* is often known as the kingfish, or California kingfish. It is a silvery fish, often with a sheen of gold. Its shape is croakerlike, and it has a small black spot inside the upper corner of the base of the pectoral, not prominent as in the spotfin croaker. This species ranges north to Vancouver, but is abundant only over roughly the range of the other Pacific croakers, and perhaps a bit farther north. It is small, weighing from 1 to 3 pounds, the average around the lower figure.

The **queenfish,** *Seriphus politus,* is a bluish and silvery fish with yellowish fins, not highly regarded by anglers but caught to some extent. It is often utilized as a bait fish. It grows to about 12 inches, and its range is like that of the other Pacific croakers.

The **Atlantic croaker,** *Micropogon undulatus,* is in the East often called simply "croaker," or "hardhead." But on the Texas coast it is invariably called the golden croaker. It is a brassy-hued golden and silvery fish with dark dots on the upper half, these commonly forming bars that run in a forward slant from the dorsal down about midway on the side. There are small barbels on the chin. The range is from Cape Cod southward and clear around the Gulf to eastern Mexico. Average size is from less than a pound to 3 pounds, with occasional specimens running 5 pounds.

This is an important fish here and there because of the fantastic "runs" that suddenly materialize seemingly from nowhere. For example, along the Texas coast during summer only occasional catches of golden croakers are made. But after the first cool fall nights there is a movement of these fish apparently from coastal bays out into the Gulf. Passes and channels swarm with them. Anglers gather from far inland in swarms almost as dense. Employing every variety of tackle from cane poles to light spinning rigs, they catch tons of the fish. Fishing is done with dead shrimp, which is allowed to lie on bottom until seized by a croaker. This fish is a strong fighter, and as delicious a table fish as its larger relative, the channel bass. Tremendous quantities are taken commercially on the Atlantic coast.

All the croakers, as noted, like to hang out along sandy shores, over shallow shell beds, in sloughs, bays, lagoons, and flats where the bottoms are dotted with patches of weeds. Shallow water is where ninety percent of them are caught. Most species like the Atlantic croaker retreat to deeper water when cold snaps strike.

As a whole, croaker fishing is surf fishing, or stillfishing from skiffs, or from piers, party boats, and barges. A great variety of baits comes into use, depending on the locality. Anything from sea worms, mussels, and clams, to crabs, sand fleas, shrimp, and simple cut baits will catch croakers. As a rule, for any of the species the bait is cast and left on bottom to be picked up by a roving croaker. No heavy tackle is needed. Surf fishermen often use rather heavy tackle, because of the presence of larger species, or because it is easier to handle in a tall surf, but any sort of light tackle will do for croaker fishing, and the lighter the better, wherever possible, for more sport is gained thus.

Many use light wire leaders, but nylon will do just as well. Hooks of about 2/0 are standard, although sizes a bit larger or smaller are all right. In other words, it doesn't really make much difference what tackle is used, throughout, just so it is light enough to give the fish a chance. Most croakers are hard biters, seizing the bait and running with it, and most put up a good solid scrap. The spotfin, because it may come in fairly large size, is considered the ace of the group covered in this section.

Some croakers are caught around the year on most coasts. But by and large, the spring and summer months and on into early fall are best. Tidal movements enhance opportunity, because they move food and allow the fish to feed on fresh grounds. Incoming tides are generally liked best by anglers, although ebb tides occasionally produce good results, especially on the Atlantic.

California Corbina

Menticirrhus undulatus

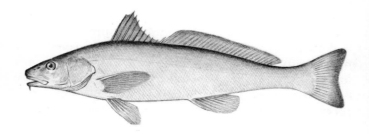

This long and fairly slender croaker with the projecting upper jaw appears to wear a rather stupid expression fixed upon its countenance. It belies a most wary, skittish, and whimsical personality. Of all Pacific fish of southern inshore waters, the corbina, or "corvina" as it is often called, is the most popular.

This does not mean it is always taken in greatest numbers. Corbina, also colloquially named "whiting" and "seatrout," are difficult fish. They are sought after diligently, but success with them is not always forthcoming, and therefore they are greatly prized.

The range of the corbina is from Point Conception southward. Like other croakers, it inhabits the shallows along sandy shores, and cruises about in shallow bays. It is primarily a target of surf fishermen. That is where almost all are caught, invariably on an incoming tide. Because it is more slender than most other croakers, it may be long for its weight. The average weight is from 2 to 3 pounds, with fish above that very special prizes, and the maximum probably 7 or 8 pounds. The color is blue-gray or varied shades thereof, with metallic hues, and various indistinct spots along the scale rows.

Because of the inherent wariness of the corbina, some anglers fish it at night. It bites well then. It also bites as well during daylight. Summer months are best, although an occasional corbina may be taken any time of year. The fish sometimes simply refuse to take a bait (they are not fished with artificials), and then suddenly, as in fresh-water trout fishing, there may come a time when all wariness ceases and they strike almost any offering with abandon. This is one of the exasperating traits that endear them to surf anglers.

Once hooked, a corbina is an excellent fighter. It will make hard runs, bore into the surf and away from it, or follow the outside of the surf line at surprising speed. Clams, mussels, soft crabs, pileworms all make good baits. Many anglers prefer live crabs, a favorite natural food of the corbina.

Although corbina do not school compactly or in great numbers, they often travel in small, loose groups. Because they are so whimsical at times about taking a hook, chumming is occasionally employed. In some ways, fishing corbina is reminiscent of bonefish angling on the Florida Keys. One's approach should be just as cautious.

Tackle can be of numerous varieties. Standard light marine outfits are used. But spinning tackle has worked wonders for corbina fishing because with it light hooks and sinkers and especially lines may be employed. When using standard saltwater tackle, fairly fine and long monofil leaders should be attached. With spinning gear, the line of course acts as leader. Even then, a finer strand at the end is a good idea. Sinkers should be used in such a way that as little pull as possible is exerted when a fish picks up the bait. A slip sinker, or a dropper with hook and bait tied on above the sinker, are both effective. A live bait, or one very gently crawled along by reel movement, will tempt corbina at times.

By and large, fishing for corbina is a specialized endeavor, and requires that an angler be a good deal more expert than for the other croakers. But the result is worth the craft, when success smiles, or the fish suddenly forget caution, for the fight is an admirable one and the menu well complemented by corbina broiled or fried.

Black Drum

Pogonias cromis

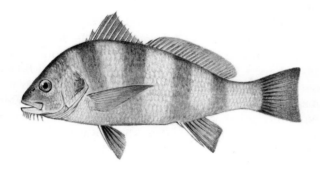

One of the most delightful aspects of angling is that tastes among participants are precisely as diverse as there are species of catchable fish. The black drum is by no stretch of the imagination one of our top-ranking game fish—as far as the majority of experienced saltwater fishermen are concerned. Nonetheless, there are black drum enthusiasts to whom this species is angling's big thrill.

It is true that the average-sized black drum is a rather sluggish, slow-moving individual, but really large specimens put up a stout argument on behalf of their boosters, and are quite likely to convince a detractor. This fish belongs to the large family of croakers and drums. It is plentiful throughout the Gulf of Mexico and all along the Atlantic coast as far north as New York. Its average weight is from 2 to 8 pounds, but it may run from there on up, with 30-pounders fairly common, those of 50 pounds not rare, and occasional ones going as high as 150. The smaller ones usually show distinct broad vertical bands of brownish to black on the sides, against a ground color of gray-silver. These are younger fish. Large black drum are a fairly uniform gray, some of them—probably simply a color phase—overlaid with a reddish or coppery sheen.

Black drum cruise in schools as a rule, inshore over sandy bottoms, especially in bays, lagoons, around channels, wharves, bridges, and in the surf. They are bottom feeders. They have crusher-type teeth with which they smash the shells of various mollusks, such as oysters. Sometimes a black drum, when opened, will be found to have a large amount of crushed oyster shells in its gullet. Commercial oystermen, needless to say, are not exactly fond of this fish.

It is called a sea drum, and also is known colloquially as "channel bass," an especially poor appellation because of the fact that the so-called "red drum," which is the channel bass to a majority of anglers, is often found in the same areas. The name "drum" originates, as with the related freshwater drum, from the sound the species is capable of making with muscles of the air bladder. Schools of croaking drum can be heard above water at times.

The best general coastal sections for taking large black drum are southward in their range: coastal North Carolina, Florida, Louisiana, and Texas. At times when schools are working mollusk beds in shallow water their tails protrude and fan the surface much like tailing bonefish. Fishing piers and ship channels along sandy shores in Florida and Texas are especially good places to hang large black drum. Large ones are not especially good eating, but the smaller ones are not bad.

Tackle for average drum fishing is not specialized. Any rod and reel will do. Artificials seldom are successful. Bait fishing right on bottom is best. The bait—cut fish, clam meat, oysters, shrimp, crab—is simply cast out and allowed to lie until the drum picks it up. Those of a few pounds come in without much resistance. For the larger specimens, or where large ones are likely to be caught, stout tackle is necessary. Surf anglers will automatically use gear tough enough to hold large black drum. Pier anglers using light freshwater plug rods will be all right on the small ones but will have a real battle with a black drum of 25 to 50 pounds.

The numerous chin barbels, the long spines of the dorsal fin, the color and general shape of the black drum will readily identify it. Once in a while a rank amateur fishing in Florida or on around the Gulf confuses a small drum with a sheepshead because of the dark vertical bars. The two species, when compared, are radically different. But lacking opportunity for comparison, the teeth alone will separate them. The drum has a modestly ample mouth, with heavy paved throat teeth; the sheepshead has a small mouth set with fused-typed teeth just inside the lips that can bite a weak-shanked hook in two.

Northern Whiting

Menticirrhus saxatilis

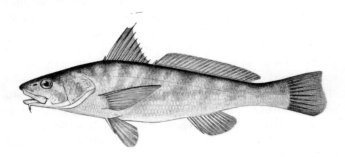

The whitings are members of the large family containing the croakers and the drums. There are three of them: the **northern whiting,** named above; the **southern whiting,** *Menticirrhus americanus;* the **Gulf** or **silver whiting,** *Menticirrhus littoralis.*

Some anglers call these fishes "kingfish." The American Fisheries Society has even adopted that name as an official common name. This is unfortunate. Today with transport moving fishermen everywhere for their sport, and communications disseminating information nationally, the king mackerel, one of the top saltwater game fish, is well known to almost all anglers as the "kingfish." There is no sound reason for calling the whitings kingfish, and even in the markets both fresh and frozen fish of these species are tagged whiting.

The three species are all much alike in habits, and rather similar in appearance. They are found along sandy shores, feeding on bottom on various small crustaceans, small fish, worms, etc. They grow to about 18 inches maximum, seldom weigh over 2 or 3 pounds, and average about 1. Their ranges are partially indicated by their names, but these ranges overlap.

The southern species is not quite so distinctly marked as its northern cousin. It may have faint dark bars, or none. Or, in some cases, it is very similar. The Gulf variety is plain silver-gray. Identity of each is simple to arrive at by the length of the third dorsal, although there is no important reason for anglers to separate them. The third dorsal spine of the Gulf species when laid flat just reaches the beginning of the soft portion of the dorsal. In the southern variety it does not quite reach the soft dorsal. In the northern it reaches well past the beginning of this soft fin.

The whitings are not strikingly important as game fish, but they are caught in great numbers by fishermen along the beaches who fish bait in shallow water. Whiting may be in the surf, or in the shallow sloughs and lagoons. They bite almost any small bait with alacrity, but ordinarily are not considered as strikers on artificials. However, they will pick up small feathered jigs that are moved gently in the surf line where they are feeding. And occasionally they will do likewise with small streamer flies. Nonetheless, there is little point in using artificials for them. Their reactions are not consistent in this field, but they will almost always willingly seize a bait.

Very light tackle, such as a light spinning or freshwater casting rod, is best for whiting fishing if one wishes to have good sport. In the North they are more abundant and willing inshore during the warm months. In the South they bite all year. They are fairly good eating fish, and are of some commercial importance. Although there is nothing whatever spectacular about them, they are certainly better than nothing. Thus, whiting fishing often attracts those who are not expert anglers but only casual operators of rod and reel, and it also fills a dire need at times for the avid angler who finds himself shunned by the gamier denizens of inlet, lagoon, or surf.

Mangrove Snapper

Lutjanus griseus

The fish above is used to head this section not because there is anything special about it as snappers go, but because it is a typical member of a group of fishes so large and varied and difficult to distinguish and classify that the casual angler is better off not wading too deeply. There are well over 200 known species of snappers scattered along the coastlines of warm seas throughout the world. How many species we have in our range, no one is positive, for several that seem to differ may be one and the same. The American Fisheries Society lists sixteen members of the Lutjanidae.

Just to give a hint of how hard it is to know precisely what you have caught, unless you are a well-schooled ichthyologist, the mangrove snapper may be mahogany in color, or close to purple. Or it may be golden to red to green, or combinations of all. Or it may be just plain gray. It is, in fact, officially called the gray snapper by the American Fisheries Society. However, the snapper shape is not difficult to distinguish, and most of the ones U.S anglers are most likely to encounter will be easily recognized as snappers by the following characteristics.

They are bottom fishes. All are Atlantic and Gulf species. They are also school fishes, and abundant. Most are found close to shore in water of only modest depth, or in bayous and tidal streams, or about bridges and pilings, wharves, piers, and rocks, or on reefs. A few are found near the surf, but as a group they cannot be thus tagged. Some, such as the red snappper of commercial importance, are found ordinarily in very deep offshore waters. Snapper banks off Texas, for example, lie in general about 30-odd miles out. They are much farther out in other areas of the Gulf. Depths of 50 fathoms are not unusual.

Snappers have rather large mouths and prominent eyes. They are voracious, active fish, with strong teeth. The teeth are in the jaws and the roof of the mouth, and also on the tongue. There are two nostrils on each side. The head looks large. The tail is either forked or concave. Most snappers are brightly colored, and many are capable of color changes. Although some species range northward on our east coast to the New York area, generally speaking the snappers are southern fish. The Florida area, and the Gulf, are the main concentration points. In the Pacific there are no true snappers within U.S. range. The fish called "snappers" in our waters there, and often brightly colored as well, are members of the rockfish family.

Probably the snappers are somewhere along the line related as distant cousins to the various sea basses and groupers. They hit hard, like a bass, and they battle savagely for their size. That may be very small, or of considerable proportion. The average snapper, regardless of species, probably could be pegged at from 1 to 5 pounds. But there are some species that commonly come in king-size, 15 to 25 or more pounds. And at least one has been reported as running over 100. All the snappers are good food fish, although the dog snapper has been tagged on occasion as not fit to eat.

Common names for the various snappers are as abundant as the fish themselves. It would be impossible to give them all. Further, many of the same names are used for different varieties. Below, briefly, are listed the species U.S. anglers will most commonly catch.

The **mangrove snapper,** *Lutjanus griseus,* already partly described, is as noted often called gray snapper. That color and greenish may predominate. It is most abundant around Florida and the Gulf coast. This is a most wary fish. It bites better at night than by day possibly for that reason, is usually taken on bait, but within recent seasons high sport has been had with this snapper by fishing it with flies, and with small lures, either with fly or spinning rod. Fine leaders are necessary, and so is fine and careful fishing in the clear water. When one does take, the battle is startling, but getting them to hit is a tricky business, and once they have "found the angler out," the deal is off. Most specimens run under 5 pounds, but some are larger.

The fish takes a bait very deliberately as a rule. And in fishing lures for them a slow retrieve—but with some action—is usually most effective. When stillfishing, which is done over reefs and in the mangrove bayous of south Florida also, numerous baits will work. A piece of blue crab, if it can be kept on the hook, is an excellent bait.

The **schoolmaster,** *Lutjanus apodus,* may range to Cape Cod, but is definitely a southern fish, common about south Florida and the Keys. It is brightly colored, from gray to red-brown with bands of pale greenish, and with the fins usually yellow and orange. It hangs out in the same general places as the mangrove snapper and bites about the same, with the hours of darkness easing its caution. This fish is not as interested in lures as the mangrove snapper, but does occasionally strike one. Bait is the usual method, with shrimp or cut bait preferred. Size will run on the average about like the mangrove snapper.

The **lane snapper,** *Lutjanus synagris,* is also a southern species, caught mainly about Florida. This also is a brilliantly hued species. It is pink to rose above, gray-silver to olive-silver below. There are usually indistinct longitudinal stripes of yellow, and also interlacing vertical bands. But these vary in distinctness. The lower fins are yellow, the dorsal and tail red, from which comes the common name, red-tailed snapper. The clincher for distinguishing this fish is a fairly large and very distinct dark spot, usually dark red, on the upper side just below the soft dorsal. Colors may all be different from those described, but the blotch remains.

The lane snapper is smaller than those so far described. It may run to 3 or 4 pounds, but averages about 1. Its habits are much the same as the others, and it is abundant, both inshore in such places as stream mouths and other snapper hangouts, and offshore on reefs and

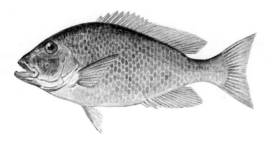

Red Snapper

shallow banks. It also may occasionally strike a small lure, but is predominantly a bait anlger's fish.

The **muttonfish,** or mutton snapper, *Lutjanus analis*, is a larger snapper, averaging several pounds as a rule and running to over 20. It is a species of Florida and Texas waters, found in fairly deep water on outside reefs, and sometimes closer in, over the rocks, in shallows. It is of some commercial importance. The color is drab greenish-white above, shading into reddish on the sides. There may be blue spots forming slanted lines as they follow the scale rows. However, the colors and the patterns change radically. The small scales help identify this snapper. It may have a dark spot on the side, rather similar to that of the lane snapper, but smaller. Best tag: the fins, which are red, except the dorsal, which is yellow with red edging. This snapper occasionally strikes trolled or cast lures, but is generally caught stillfishing with cut bait or other regional standard bait.

The **red snapper,** *Lutjanus blackfordi* (some references *L. aya*), is the commercial species caught on the deep banks chiefly in the Gulf. It is a red fish practically overall, deep bodied, with heavy head. Size runs from 5 pounds on up to 30 or more. Handlining is the standard method or else taking the fish on rod and reel and pumping them up from great depths. They are in general considered more important as commercial than as game fish, but many persons do enjoy going out on snapper boats from various Gulf ports. On most boats the trip is for overnight. This has become big business in several places. The fish, when located, bite readily, and hundreds of pounds are usually taken in a short time.

The **dog snapper,** *Lutjanus jocu*, may weigh better than 20 pounds, but averages under 2 as a rule. It is predominantly a species of the Keys and the Gulf. Its haunts are similar to those of most snappers. It may be found deep, or over the shallower reefs. It is a reddish fish with olive shading overlaid. Generally there is a blue stripe below the eye. This is also found in other snappers, especially young specimens, but the dog snapper carries it through life. A good identifying tag is the patch of whitish set in a triangle below the eye. The dog snapper is taken still-fishing, and as an incidental by reef trollers using strip baits.

The **yellowtail snapper,** *Ocyurus chrysurus*, is not to be confused with the fish of the Pacific called yellowtail. The latter is a large game species covered in another section. The snapper called yellowtail is most abundant about the Florida Keys, where bottom fishermen catch it by hundreds. The fish may be in close to shore, in the shallows, or out over the reefs. It is generally small, to a pound or 2, with a maximum of about 5. This fish has a deeply forked tail, which is canary yellow. A yellow swath runs from the eye back, broadening as it reaches the tail and finally including it. There are also yellow spots on a gray to gray-blue and pinkish ground, and yellow in the fins. It is usually stillfished.

Tackle for all of the snappers can be whatever the angler wishes. Obviously the lightest of tackle will give the best sport, for seldom will an individual over 5 pounds be brought in. Fly rods, spinning outfits, freshwater-weight plugging rigs, or any kind of stillfishing pole will do. Short lengths of wire leader are commonly used but are not always necessary by any means. Hard monofil in reasonably heavy test, changed frequently at the tip, does nicely. Of course, boat rods and surf rods and saltwater casting rods of various weights are so commonly owned by anglers in snapper territory that most of the time the fish are caught on tackle far stouter than is needed.

As a group, the snappers are not only excellent eating, but they are very much worthwhile, especially to the winter visitor to the South. At times, without snappers there would be no action at all.

It should be mentioned here that the bright-hued snappers are sometimes confused by anglers with the grunts, which range abundantly in the same area and are indeed often found hanging around with the snappers. For information about the grunts, see the section on saltwater panfish and the northern porgy.

Tautog

Tautoga onitis

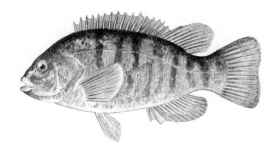

This is the blackfish, or oysterfish, so well loved by coastal anglers from Cape Cod to the Carolinas. Its range spreads past those points to some extent, but within the modest stretch noted it is most abundant. The tautog is a member of the wrasse family, all of which have powerful crushing teeth which they utilize in breaking the shells of mollusks, their favorite food.

Most wrasses are tropical. The tautog is an exception. Most are very brightly colored. Again the tautog is an exception. It is a drab gray fish splotched with irregular charcoal patches and broad mottlings. It is chunky, with a blunt nose, has a long stoutly spined portion of the dorsal fin, usually with sixteen spines, a straight rear tail margin with upper and lower corners very much rounded. The average tautog weighs from 3 to 8 pounds, with 10 fairly common and those on up to 20 or a bit more not rare. This is a most delicious table fish.

The tautog, like many of its relatives, is known as a stealer of bait. It is hard-mouthed, able to snatch the bait and be away so swiftly that schooled tautog fishermen have learned to ram the hook home—hard—at the first tug. It is strictly a bait angler's fish, and is almost always caught on bottom by stillfishing, although some are taken by surf fishermen.

The rocks and rocky bottoms in bays and coves where there is a fairly good depth of water are favorite places of tautog. Here they lie on their sides, in rocky hideouts, a curious tautog habit, or they may hang around beneath piers and docks, or take up residence in numbers by a sunken ship. The time of year dictates what depth the fish will select. From about late April or early May through until mid-October tautog will be found in shoreside waters. After that they retire to deeper offshore spots. They can still be taken, but the fishing is harder because of the depth.

Because they have such hard mouths, heavy hooks are essential, and sharp ones, so they may be properly set. The tautog is a very strong fighter and is exceedingly sporty when taken on medium spinning gear or light saltwater outfits. However, over rough and rocky bottoms, or when fishing deep, most tautog fans use rather stout gear. The fish must be turned before they get into rock holes, or snag or cut off the line. The setup for such fishing is generally made with sinker on the bottom and hook or hooks a few inches above, so the hooks are kept away from obstructions and the bite can be felt.

Crabs are a favorite bait, fiddler crabs, or green crabs, or any that are handy. Fiddlers, because they are small and likely to be seized in one bite, offer a good chance of hooking the fish. However, all of the usual saltwater baits of the area will take fish, and local anglers generally have favorite baits for each portion of the season. One who knows the coast will find spots where tautog can be caught from shore. The best fishing, however, is from skiffs anchored over good spots not far out. Chumming works very well on tautog when they are sluggish. Chopped mollusks or crabs make a good chum. As with most of the inshore species that feed near bottom or in the surf, tautog usually are most active on high and incoming tides, although any moving tide may arouse them.

The **hogfish,** *Lachnolaimus maximus*, is a relative of the tautog that is taken occasionally around Key West. It may straggle northward to the Carolinas. It is considered a good game and food fish, and is worth mentioning because of its peculiar looks. It is reddish, mottled, with a deep body, a much more pointed snout than the tautog, and with buck teeth. Upper and lower lobes of the tail are much elongated, and the first three dorsal spines are long and sweep up over its back and are not joined by membrane for more than a minor distance.

Among average anglers, perhaps most unsuspected as a relative of the tautog is the so-called **California sheep-head,** *Pimelometopon pulchrum*. This fish is of course not related to the convict-striped common sheepshead of the Atlantic and the Gulf. Note that the spelling differs. It is a wrasse. It may weigh as much as 20 or 30 pounds, and male and female are quite different. The head of the male is black, with a white chin. The rear half of its body, plus its tail and its anal and most of its dorsal are also black. The mid-section of the body is pink, magenta, or red. The female is generally rose colored all over, or sometimes black.

This is a fish of the rocky shores and the kelp beds of the lower third of the California coast. Waters around Santa Catalina Island seem to be the main headquarters for the species. It is not an especially desirable sport fish, although a number are caught, and the larger ones put up a stiff fight. It is caught by stillfishing with clams, crabs, or shrimp and is sometimes taken by surf anglers.

The **cunner,** *Tautogolabrus adspersus,* is a relative of the tautog that inhabits most of its main range, from New Jersey on north. It is a small wrasse, seldom weighing more than 2 pounds, and usually much less. It is very common, and not always held in esteem. It looks rather similar to the tautog but has a snout much less blunt, and the body is not quite so chunky. Cunner hang out with tautog, and in the same types of hideout even in deep water. They steal bait and exasperate anglers after larger species. The colloquial name for this fish over its native range is "sea perch," a poor one to use because there are no less than a hundred other fish so called by native anglers over the vast length of our coastlines.

The cunner is not a bad table fish, and is actually a very gamy little species on light tackle. It is a standby of party-boat fishermen and inshore anglers out for whatever they can catch, and furnishes an ample amount of fishing fun. It is caught by stillfishing with any of the standard local baits. There is nothing difficult about fishing for it. In fact, the difficulty at times is to keep from catching cunner.

Sheepshead

Archosargus probatocephalus

This fish—actually a kind of porgy—is a most abundant and common bottom and inshore species of the Atlantic and the Gulf. Although it ranges from lower New England clear around and throughout the Texas Gulf coast, it is undoubtedly most concentrated throughout its southern range. How many tons of sheepshead have been caught by tourists from Florida bridges and Texas piers is anybody's guess.

The sheepshead is something of an old standby. But it is no dunce. It is a most wary species, and has caused trouble for thousands of beginners because it is capable of taking a fiddler crab, one of its favorite baits, off a hook without so much as once jiggling a bobber or tugging a line. Probably this is because it has a small mouth set with close-fitted buck teeth that are hard as rock. It can swim up to a dangling fiddler crab and snip, snip, snip until the crab just simply disappears.

This dark gray-silver fish with its seven broad, dark bands—very boldly in evidence in small, young specimens but less distinct in large, old ones—should not be confused with the California sheephead of the Pacific, which is a totally different fish. Nor should it be lumped with the freshwater sheepshead, to which it is not related. It is a fish that hangs out in bays and channels, around wharves, piers, and pilings, where it feeds mainly on crabs, crustaceans, and mollusks, which it is quite capable of crushing or cutting up. The black drum, when young, also has dark bands, but this also is a quite different fish, as a look at the teeth will quickly establish.

Sheepsheads are excellent eating. They put up a very stiff underwater fight. They even give a bit of trouble after they are caught, for the spines of the dorsal are very large, tough, and sharp, and the scales are large and coarse. The easiest and best way to clean them is to cut the skin along the fillets, and then pull the skin away with pliers and cut away the fillets, without removing either head or entrails. Or they can be scaled and gutted, leaving the fins on. When broiled thus, the delicious meat can easily be eaten from between the stiff rib bones.

Tackle used for sheepshead fishing can be of any kind, even to a handline. The hook, however, must not be too large but it must certainly be strong. A large sheepshead can actually bite through a thin wire hook with ease. Lures are not used. Stillfishing is the method, and the best spot as a rule will be a place where a piling or rocks or other obstruction will concentrate the food on which this fish thrives.

The bait is simply let down and from there on nature takes its course. The most difficult part of this fishing is knowing when, and how, to set the hook. With large sheepshead—they average 1 to 5 or 6 pounds, and may go to 15 or 20—a good tug is felt when they take the bait. But unless one turns the trick just right, an empty hook comes up. It is a technique that must be learned by trial and error. The fish will give one plenty of practice, for ordinarily they are not at all scarce or unwilling to bite.

Probably the sheepshead should not be classed as a school fish. It is, however, a species that congregates, moving with the tides wherever the feed is good. An excellent way to assure success with them is to crush a collection of various mollusks or crabs and dribble this chum into the water near bridge pilings, a jetty, or a pier, or in a tidal channel or bayou or sluggish tidewater creek. A wire leader must be used when the fishing begins, of course, else the fish will simply snip off the line. And when the baited hook is let down, unless fish are in evidence feeding at a particular level it is best to have it just barely off bottom, or else lying right on bottom. The line must be held snug to feel the bite. From 6 to 15 or 20 feet of water will be about normal for this species. And it won't have to be chased from place to place. It stays put rather well. Find some today, and next week or month or year the spot will often be just as good.

Although Florida tourists catch this fish all winter, and the natives catch it all summer, along the somewhat colder Texas coast, and farther north along the Atlantic coast, from early spring throughout summer are in general the most productive times. Nonetheless, good catches are often made in cold weather along Texas, if one finds a congregation of fish around deep-set pilings. Shrimp is a common bait in Texas, fiddlers more common eastward. Steady tides seem to yield the most fish, whether they are high, low, or slack. In other words, during periods of still water the sheepshead seem to feel most like feeding.

Fishing for sheepshead is one of those endeavors not calculated to make the heart of the true game-fisherman thump wildly. But it is certainly a fine casual pastime. The pull of the fish is rugged, its nibbling habit exasperating enough to force an angler to concentrate, and the table qualities of the fillets leave nothing to be desired. Incidentally, the lining of the body cavity is black. There are timid souls who consider this a sign of something perhaps not edible. It is nothing of the sort.

Black Grouper

Mycteroperca bonaci

This particular species is used here to head this section simply as a matter of convenience in introducing a large group of fishes very important in some areas to anglers, but rather difficult for the layman to distinguish one from another without a healthy margin of error. The groupers belong to the sea bass family, a large and most diversified family of fishes, the majority of them "bass-like" in general form, and with well-developed spines in the forward portions of both dorsal and anal fins. The family includes the striped bass, even the white perch of brackish and freshwater, and the white bass of freshwater.

The true groupers have broad heads. Others of their relatives such as the hinds (some of which are called cabrillas) have narrower heads. Three other divisions of the family contain extra-large species, two in the Atlantic and one in the Pacific, within our ranges. These three will be dealt with in the section following this one. There are also several sea basses on our Pacific coast, not of the grouper and hind clans, but still members of the same large family. These, too, are covered in a later section. True groupers of the Pacific are south of U.S. range, except as stragglers near San Diego.

The groupers and hinds of our east coast are big marine basses that live around rocks and reefs and sunken wrecks. They are powerful fish, and when one is hooked, although there is nothing spectacular about the sporting qualities of its fight, it battles deep and most stubbornly. These are not school fish in the true sense, like the mackerels, which cruise and wander. Groupers ordinarily lie near or on bottom, hovering among the rocks or other obstructions or living in holes in the deep reefs, feeding on almost anything that comes their way. Their large mouths are well adapted to engulfing a variety of bottom foods.

Some of these fish are drab in color, some are beautifully blotched, mottled, and speckled. One of their characteristics that makes identification difficult, however, is that this whole group is capable of swift color changes. A great many kinds of fish exhibit this phenomenon. But few do it more confusingly than the groupers and hinds. These color changes are caused by sudden rearrangement of color pigments within cells of the skin, due to some nerve stimulus. Various basic emotions commonly appear to give impetus to the changes. In experiments done in this field, fish kept in a tank and fed in a certain manner were found to switch patterns as the food appeared. Others did likewise when the aeration device in their tank was in operation. The groupers, whose colors and patterns you may think you know very precisely, are likely to change while fighting on the hook, and then switch again when pulled out of the water, and again as they die.

Following are listed the groupers most likely to be encountered, with a few facts about each.

The **black grouper,** *Mycteroperca bonaci,* averages to 10 pounds, grows to 50 or more, is mainly a species of Florida and the Gulf. It is usually dark gray with a few black horizontal barlike blotches on its sides. But it may be white, greenish, reddish. The dark color is most common. There are supposed to be two forms, shallow water and deep water. The tail margin helps identify this fish. It dips inward slightly from center in both directions, thus having the outer rays on both extremities, and the center rays longer than those of the two concavities. This black grouper is considered by many to be the best sport fish of the tribe.

The **yellow grouper,** *Mycteroperca venenosa,* and the rock grouper are thought to be one and the same fish, or else one a subspecies of the other. The yellow is a phase of shallow water, a fish colored generally light clay color with black and red markings, the rock a deep-water fish, red and gray, with dark markings. These fish are caught mainly about the Florida Keys, and are not very important sport species. They are also vastly confusing because color switches may run from mottled scarlet to almost pure white. Size of these groupers is seldom over 8 or 10 pounds, averages smaller.

The **gag,** *Mycteroperca microlepis,* is a grouper of some importance to sport fishermen, mostly around the Florida Keys. It averages small, around 3 to 5 pounds, but is suspected to grow much larger. It is a brown fish,

Nassau Grouper

with a blue-blotched black tail. The edge of the tail is light to white, and is concave.

The **red grouper,** *Epinephelus morio*, is commonly caught, and it's a good food fish but not much of a fighter. It is a reddish-brown or reddish-gray fish mottled extensively with paler hues. It has, however, many color changes and phases, one of which is entirely black. Probably the best identification of this species is made locally by anglers who know it. This fish may be fairly large, from 8 to 25 or 30 pounds, or even more. It is common about Florida and the Gulf, even to Texas. And it reaches well northward along the Atlantic, in fact, probably in greater numbers in the northern range than any of the other groupers.

The **Nassau grouper,** *Epinephelus striatus*, is an important sport fish in this clan, and a good fighter. It is a confusing member as to color phases, however, and is likely to change pattern more swiftly and drastically than other groupers and hinds. Ordinarily it is a gray and brown well-mottled fish with several fairly distinct broad dark bands on the sides, these bands themselves broken by mottlings. A rather distinctive mark is the broad dark stripe beginning at the back of the eye and running back and up to the dorsal. The margin of the tail is mildly convex. This grouper is mostly caught around Florida, and averages to 8 or 10 pounds, with a maximum of 40 or 50.

The **rock hind,** *Epinephelus adscensionis*, is another species of most variable color, but it can usually be identified by the amount of definite green in tail and fins, and scattered here and there over the body, and by the round red or orange spots, or dots, that in some completely cover the body and head, even to the roof of the mouth, and reach out onto the lower fins and at least the spinous portion of the dorsal. This is not a large fish, probably seldom reaching or exceeding 10 pounds. It is predominantly a species of the Florida Keys.

There are numerous other species, none of them very important to us here. The red hind is a small species mostly abundant south of our Florida waters, and throughout the West Indies. The coney and the grasby are of minor importance around the Keys.

Groupers will strike artificial lures rather well. Plugs and wobbling spoons are ordinarily used for them, and in Florida bays and around shallow reefs and rock piles either casting or trolling will take fish. Most of the fish taken in the bays and close inshore, in the shallows, run small. Of course, they are taken by thousands on bait, too. It can be just about anything. Chunks of fish are a common bait. Crabs, shrimp, or small live fish also are effective.

The larger groupers are taken as a general rule by trolling deep over known reefs or rocky areas that lie at least a short distance offshore. These "grouper beds," as they are commonly known, are sought out by charter-boat captains. The grouper is a good "tourist fish" because it is usually willing, once its deep hangouts are located and a trolled lure or bait placed at the proper level. Also, they usually may be taken in numbers, and of a size to give the client a good thrill.

For such trolling a popular lure is a large wobbling spoon with a strip of cut mullet attached. Heavy weights are necessary to get the lure deep enough. This requires that fairly heavy tackle be used. In fact, even for stillfishing over such grouper beds (which is not usual) stout tackle is needed. Pumping fish, and lead, up from deep water is assisted by a solid rod and large reel. Wire leaders are used in grouper fishing, because the fish try their best to dive among rocks and cut off. Also, the lure and lower line is often likely to strike jagged rock as it is fished. Hooks are always of good size, for the mouth of a grouper is large and hard.

The beginner who trolls coastal waters will soon find that any rocky point that juts out beneath the water and appears to be surrounded on each side by sand beach invariably forms a haven for the larger groupers. They may not be up among rocks which can be seen in the water, but rather will be out a bit deeper. Drifting across such places gets strikes. So does casting or stillfishing.

Trolling for groupers should be done more slowly than for surface species. The fish should be able to lunge from their deep hiding places and engulf the lure or bait without chasing far. Tides are not ordinarily important in grouper fishing. Nor is time of day. In fact, the whole clan of these rough and sturdy sea basses fills an important spot for local and visiting southeastern anglers because groupers can usually be caught whether or not anything else can. In addition, most of them are exceptionally good table fish when skinned and filleted.

It should be well noted that all the groupers go by a wide variety of names. Also, in one port the name used for one species may be the same as that used for another species not many miles away. From calico hind, rockfish to snapper, the names are as confusing as the color phases of the fish. The best thing to do about it is just to catch them and not worry.

Spotted Jewfish

Epinephelus itajara

Whether or not this huge fish is a game species, it always attracts a great deal of attention when caught, and quite a number of anglers make a specialized hobby of fishing for it. Although it ranges in the warm waters of both Atlantic and Pacific, it does not reach our range on the west, but is quite common about Florida and the Keys, and some portions of the Texas Gulf coast. In some references it appears as giant sea bass, with the scientific name *Promicrops itajara*.

A so-called jewfish may weigh anywhere from 30 to 40 pounds on up. Those of 200 to 400 are not unusual, and the species grows maximum to at least 750. Small ones are not caught regularly. The average is probably from 75 to 300 pounds.

The best places to fish for these huge gray-brown and black mottled hulks is around bridge pilings, in deep channels between open water and a bay, or in the deeper rocky holes along fairly protected coasts. Sometimes an outsize specially made hook is used, and on it a whole sheepshead of possibly 6 pounds is placed. Or, the same hook is baited with several large crabs. The hook may be secured by a rope, and the rope tethered to a cruiser or a bridge stanchion, or the piling of a pier.

Such set-line fishing has little to do with sport, but it must be admitted that catching a fish of this size regardless of method has a certain appeal. Now and then a big jewfish is taken by trolling, but ordinarily stillfishing on bottom is the method. When rod and reel are used, obviously these need to be very heavy and strong. The fish fights somewhat sluggishly. Nonetheless, its sheer weight must be considered. Steel cable leaders are requisite.

This giant is at home around deep outside reefs as well as in the shallows and inlets. Skin divers get high adventure from stalking large ones around the bridges and the shallower reefs, accounting for quite a few. Sometimes the shaft is shot into place, then the fish played down from a rope running to a boat above. This fish and some of its outsized relatives are popular with specialists working around oil rigs in the Gulf. Several fish of 100 to 200 pounds often are boated in a single session. The flesh is good, but rather coarse. For years it has been a popular market item, partly because it sold cheaply.

A relative, the warsaw grouper, sometimes called the black jewfish, or black grouper, *Epinephelus nigritus*, is occasionally confused with the spotted jewfish. It is usually found in much deeper water, however, often several hundred feet down. This species seldom has any mottling, but is a solid dark color overall. It has a much higher forward portion of the dorsal fin than the spotted jewfish. It is caught by stillfishing, with baits much the same. The range where most are taken is also the same, and the size of this fish matches that of the spotted jewfish.

The **California black sea bass,** which is also called giant black sea bass or simply giant sea bass in some books, *Stereolepis gigas,* gets mixed up quite regularly with the Florida species. It does take the place, in the Pacific, of the outsize eastern sea basses. It is a big, black or brownish-black fish unmistakable in its own range, going up to 500 pounds in weight, with those of 100 to 200 most common, but small ones seldom are hooked.

These also are bottom fish, with habits similar to those of their relatives. They take large baits and fight powerfully, but display little flare for real fireworks. They range north about to central California, and are quite popular with fishermen, simply because they are a large prize and good eating. On occasion one is hooked while trolling for other fish with a feathered spoon or a spoon and bait combination. But stillfishing is traditional, or else drifting with a large bait down near bottom, usually close to a rocky shore. Summer is the best time.

Black Sea Bass

Centropristes striatus

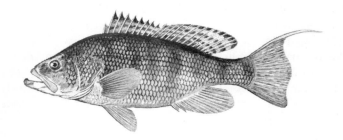

This is one of those fish that is not very important over the greater share of its range, but extremely important to a great many people over a particular section of that range. It straggles north in the Atlantic as far as Maine, and reaches south clear around into the Gulf of Mexico. From Cape Hatteras to Cape Cod is its point of concentration, and shoreside anglers between those two Capes would be just about lost without their "blackfish," or "humpback," or "black will," or just plain sea bass.

Very small ones may be found in shallow water right around the shores, in quiet places such as bays. But most of the big fellows seek the offshore reefs, where they lie on bottom among the rocks, in water from 10 feet on down to as much as a couple of hundred. "Big" means sea bass of from 3 to 8 pounds. The last is about maximum. The average will be from 1 to 3.

A great many anglers in the New York area go after these sea bass from small boats during the summer when many of the fish stay within easy range of shore. Ledges under water and rocky heads are good places. Others go out on party boats to fish the deep offshore banks. Of course a great many casual fishermen also catch sea bass of this variety right around the pilings of piers. A common bait among steadies is the skimmer clam. Bloodworms, shrimp, and crabs are also good baits. On occasion a black sea bass can be induced to strike a spoon retrieved along bottom, but there is little reason to fish for this species by any other method than stillfishing with bait. With few exceptions, the fish are eager to bite.

Tackle for shallow inshore fishing can be of any sort. A light freshwater plug rod or spinning rod is fine. For deep fishing, however, where larger specimens are taken, heavy tackle is just about mandatory. Not that the bass puts up more than a good solid fight, but bringing a fish of even a few pounds up from such deep water is a hard job. It is hard on light tackle and wearing on the angler. And it is slow. When the fish are biting and things are lively, the best thing to do is get one cranked up so the bait can go down after another. Steel leaders are used with hooks of modest size.

Although summer and early fall cover the good black sea bass fishing over the upper portion of its range, farther south these fish are caught around the entire year. Most anglers believe that neither a high nor a low tide, but rather the quiet period between tidal disturbance, is the best part of the day for this fishing.

The chunky little bass is good eating, and well worth fishing just for good fun. It is not difficult to distinguish the quarry from others, even though there are a lot of different basses and basslike fishes in the sea. It is a drab-colored customer, black to gray or brownish-gray. Spots on the dorsal fin, in rows, make that fin appear to be striped with lighter hues. The sides also appear to be narrowly striped, and in some specimens broad vertical bands overlay these indistinctly. The tag that most quickly identifies this fish, however, is the elongated upper ray of the tail. It sticks out past the rest of the tail and makes that member look sometimes as if a bite had been taken out right below the long ray. The remainder of the tail is very noticeably rounded.

There are at least two other sea bass species at times confused with this one. These are the **rock sea bass** and the **Gulf sea bass.** The first ranges south from the Carolinas, is a drab olive color with indistinct bars slanting forward over the upper portions. The latter has long middle rays in the tail also, and that part of the tail spotted with black. Both these fish are usually small, and separating them is not very important to the casual angler, because both are outside the range where the black sea bass gets the most attention.

California Kelp Bass

Paralabrax clathratus

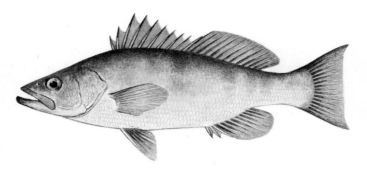

The inland angler fond of freshwater black bass, and fishing the Pacific for the first time, might be startled to see this fish, or one of its close relatives, come aboard. At a casual glance the California kelp bass looks strikingly like a freshwater black bass. However, its dorsal spines are longer and much heavier, and it is a much rougher-appearing fish in every respect, fitted for its life among the rocks and the kelp.

This is a fish of green, brown, and gray shades, more or less mottled and barred above and pale to silvery below. It ranges from central California south, but is most abundant southward. It is very popular with anglers, because it is willing and abundant, and easily accessible. A few years ago, according to California surveys it was first in numbers among California coastal game fish caught. Most sportsmen call it a "rock" bass. Because of its large, basslike mouth and its typical bass shape, it is not likely to be confused with other marine fishes, except possibly two of its own relatives.

These two are also commonly called "rock" bass, and most anglers lump all three together without bothering to distinguish among them. They are often found together. But neither is as abundant or as important as the kelp bass.

One of them is the **sand bass,** *Paralabrax nebulifer.* It looks very much like the kelp bass, but its body is deeper in the broadest portion, general color is usually darker, and it has some small spots of gold or yellow below the eye. The easiest means of quick casual identification is to look at the third spine of the dorsal. It is very noticeably much longer than the spines immediately following, whereas the kelp bass has the third, fourth, and fifth spines about the same length. Although the range and habitat of the sand and kelp bass are about the same, farther south in Mexican waters the sand bass outnumbers the kelp bass, while the opposite is true along southern California.

The **spotted bass,** *Paralabrax maculatofasciatus*, is the third of these inshore basses. It is unmistakable because its olive-colored body, and most of the head as well, are covered with small, rounded, brown spots. It ranges from about San Pedro on south, inhabits the bays and lagoons more than open shore waters. It is the least important to anglers of these three "rock" basses.

All of these fish seldom weigh more than 5 pounds. They are good scrappers on light tackle. They are not jumpers. Indeed, when they are taken among the rocks and the kelp it is a good idea to use tackle stout enough to turn them. Otherwise they get into the kelp, or cut the line on rocks. The sand bass, as its name indicates, is often found over sand bottoms. These are fish for the pier anglers, for those fishing from rocky heads, from barges and party boats, and for all inshore anglers who try here and there from the beach or from a skiff in the bays. Bait of many kinds will catch them. The most common are chunks of fish or small live fish, but almost anything at hand will do.

Often the bottom-fishing boats take these bass along with the various rockfish (*see* ROSY ROCKFISH). On occasion one is hooked by a troller, or taken on a cast artificial lure. But normally the rock basses are fish that hide in areas not suitable for trolling or casting. Stillfishing accounts for almost all of them, and there are no specialized techniques other than to get the bait to the fish. As with most California fish, summertime offers the best fishing for the various rock basses. Of the three, the kelp bass is by far the best eating. It is, in fact, a very good table fish.

Tripletail

Lobotes surinamensis

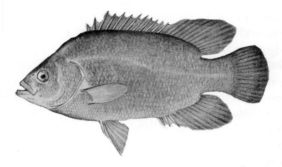

Because saltwater contains such a tremendous variety of fish species, with many of them only spottily distributed, almost as many angling specialists have evolved as there are species for their specialization. Among the most dedicated are those few Atlantic and Gulf fishermen who concentrate on locating and catching the tripletail, a fish not even known to many marine anglers. Of the two endeavors—locating and catching—the former is likely to be as difficult as the latter.

The average tripletail is a deep, compressed fish of about 5 pounds, in shape a bit reminiscent of the freshwater bluegill. Ordinarily it is black-green, but is able to change shades through to yellowish tan. At full maturity the tripletail may weigh as much as 30 pounds, and because of its deep, flat body it is able to put up a phenomenal battle. It does not, of course, have three tails, but the rear, soft portion of the dorsal fin, and the anal fin, both extend backward so far that they appear at a glance almost like extra tails.

With few exceptions, an angler must find a patch of shade or cover in open water in order to locate a tripletail. This means scouting old wrecks, floating weed rafts, channel buoys, driftwood, or any other object beneath or near which the fish may hide, and it also means fishing strictly for this species and nothing else. It is truly a specialist's game. Undoubtedly the tripletail hangs around such objects because its food—small fish, shrimp, and crabs—are likely to be found there, too. Often only a single fish will be at each location. Occasionally two or three will stay together. Oddly, when lazing about just under the surface, the tripletail habitually lies on its side, head down.

By going from marker to marker and drift to drift in a small boat, watching closely, an angler can spot the fish at a fair distance. No close approach with motor should be made. The trick is to get on the side from which it is possible to drift a bait to the fish, and do it quietly. When a fish is hooked, the boat should be moved back, and the fish played away from its hiding place. This avoids frightening into deep water its companions, if any are present.

The strike is often a severe one, and the fish will dive instantly to try to snag the line if possible. Cut bait, shrimp, and crabs will take tripletails readily, and now and then feathered jigs, wobbling spoons, or plugs do well. Tackle should be fairly sturdy, if it is to hold the dives and runs of the larger specimens, and a wire leader and stout hook should be employed.

Although this fish ranges from Mexico clear to Cape Cod, there are only scattered spots where it is abundant enough to encourage a prospective local specialist. The Carolina and Florida coasts have intermittent sizable populations. But the best area lies along the coasts of Alabama and Mississippi, where the tripletail can be caught all year, with second choice coastal Louisiana and Texas.

Some tripletail enthusiasts go from buoy to buoy along a ship channel, or from oil rig to oil rig, seeking fish. Among the most ingenious schemes ever evolved by anglers is the trick of setting up "traps" for tripletail by placing floating objects in known tripletail territory, to attract them. One angler even conceived the idea of utilizing old newspapers. Newspaper sheets will float on calm water for a long time, and they are no hazard to boat traffic. The tripletail are attracted to the shade they offer, and the angler in this instance simply set his "traps" and then went from paper to paper to try his luck. The trick has since proved successful in several locations.

Rosy Rockfish

Sebastodes rosaceus

There is nothing so very difficult about catching a rockfish. What is puzzling is how to tell which rockfish you
have after you've caught it. The rockfish family Scor-
paenidae, is a large one. Some few of its members are
found along our Atlantic coast, but are not important as
sport species. The ocean perch, or rosefish, whose fillets
have become so common in the frozen-food departments
of supermarkets, is one. It is a typical rockfish. It lives in
deep water and is seldom caught by hook and line.

It is on the Pacific coast that rockfish are really abundant and varied and of substantial importance as sport
fish. There are sixty-odd species ranging from Alaska to
Mexico. Some are found hiding in holes formed by piles
of inshore rocks. Others are found in slightly deeper
water where kelp beds or rock cover is available. Many
inhabit deep offshore waters. All are bottom fishes. Along

the California coast alone there are fifty or more species of rockfish. At certain times of year the market counters are highly colorful with stacks of them in several gaudy hues. Party boats out of Morro Bay, Monterey, Eureka, and on north along the Oregon and Washington coasts take people out bottom fishing and come in loaded with varied kinds of rockfish. The catch is especially good in winter and spring, although rockfish are caught all year.

The rosy rockfish which heads this chapter is not the most important. It was selected simply because in appearance it is typical of the rockfishes. All have a bony cheek plate extending from beneath the eye, running down and backward. In some the face looks more armored than in others. The bocaccio, for example, a rather important sport species, looks quite reminiscent of the sand and kelp basses. This and several other less exotic-appearing rockfish are often confused with the several basses, which belong to a different family. However, all rockfish do have armored heads, all have exceedingly strong dorsal fin spines, usually thirteen in number (the basses in question have ten), and three anal fin spines. The lips on all are thick and heavy. All rockfish bear their young, rather than depositing eggs.

The color variation among rockfish is tremendously broad. The blue rockfish, sometimes erroneously also called black rockfish, one of the most important hook-and-line varieties, is conservative in hue, splotched bluish black shading lighter downward to a whitish belly. But others run the gamut from bright orange and brick red with or without varied spots, dots, and blotches, to mottled black and canary yellow. Size is also varied. The bocaccio grows to a maximum yard in length and a weight past 20 pounds. Likewise for the orange rockfish and the vermillion rockfish. Others grow maximum to 12 to 15 inches, and a weight of 5 to 6 pounds. On the average, rockfish of all varieties run from 1 to 10 pounds.

There is danger of confusing the "rockfish" name with other species. On the east coast the striped bass is commonly called "rock" or "rockfish" in several areas. Several of the groupers, especially in Florida waters, are colloquially called "rockfish." And on the Pacific coast the true rockfish are sometimes called "rock cod," a name passed out indiscriminately to various fishes from different families. Some of the true rockfish are also called "bass" here and there. The greenlings of the Pacific also go by "cod" and "rockfish" names occasionally.

It is difficult to identify the various rockfish specifically, but it is fairly simple to set any of them apart from other families if the points noted here are observed, and the other species referred to here are carefully studied. All are covered in separate sections. For positive identification of each and every rockfish, technical bulletins are needed. A good one, and one that will serve most average purposes, can be obtained from the Marine Fisheries Branch, California Department of Fish and Game.

Rockfish live on small forage fish and on all kinds of food they scrounge from the bottom and from among the rocks. They are taken now and then by trollers, but mainly the rockfishes are prizes of the stillfisherman, whether he drops a line overside from an anchored party boat somewhere offshore, or casts into the surf in rocky areas, or drops a hook from a jumble of rocks down into cracks and crevices below water. It is possible to catch rockfish with artificial lures such as spoons and metal jigs. These are trolled deep, or jigged near bottom by stationary anglers. However, old-fashioned cut bait, or live bait fish, chunks of crab or clam account for most of the rockfish caught.

Tackle of any sort, light to heavy, will do. In deep water a reasonably stiff rod is needed to let the heavy sinker down and to work a long line. A unique tactic occasionally indulged by old hands at rockfish angling from shore is as follows. A stiff metal rod of small diameter, such as a length of welding rod, about a yard long is fitted with a small ring or swivel at one end for attaching the line, and at the other for attaching a stout hook. The fisherman ties this to the end of his line. With hook baited, he stands on rocks and drops it down among other submerged ones. The metal rod slides down among the crevices. When a rockfish bites it cannot run off and foul the line, but can easily be hauled up. This curious rig is even cast out into kelp or rocks at a distance from the angler. It is awkward in some ways, but does the trick.

All of the rockfishes are fair fighters, and, depending on the species, from fair to excellent on the table. They serve mainly as a good pastime in the slow winter months for thousands of anglers who otherwise would have little else to catch. A day's bottom-fishing trip on a party boat after rockfish out of northern California, or Oregon or Washington, is a lot of good garden-variety fun and is likely to turn up some fast action and a bagful of fish for everyone aboard. Rockfishing is also an inexpensive activity, in tackle (handlining for rockfish is popular), in bait, in boat fees. It is one of those fishing endeavors possible for everybody, and perhaps this is what lends this large family of fishes its greatest importance.

Here are the species most likely to be caught, with general ranges where the angler is most likely to catch them. To avoid confusing the casual angler, scientific names of these are not given.

Bocaccio	Mexico to British Columbia, progressively more abundant southward.
Yellowtail Rockfish	Length of U.S. Pacific coast.
Olive Rockfish	Length of U.S. Pacific coast.
Chilipepper	California coast, most common in southern half.
Black Rockfish	Point Conception, Calif., northward.
Blue Rockfish	Southern California northward, shallow water.
Whitebelly Rockfish	California coast.
Orange Rockfish	British Columbia southward, most abundant from northern California northward.
Vermillion Rockfish	U.S. Pacific coast, progressively abundant southward.
Widow Rockfish	Southern half of California coast.
Speckled Rockfish	Southern half of California coast.
Rosy Rockfish	Oregon south.
Greenspotted Rockfish	Northern California southward, deep water.
Starry Rockfish	Central California southward, deep water.

Other species the angler may possibly catch, or hear of, are: pink rockfish, flag rockfish, honeycomb rockfish, greenstriped rockfish, black-and-yellow rockfish, red-striped, gopher, china, and halfbanded rockfishes.

There is another true rockfish not so far mentioned, but of solid importance to southern California still-fishermen. This is the **sculpin,** left here until last to avoid any further confusion than that already caused by its official misnomer. It is of course not a sculpin at all, and since there are several members of the authentic sculpin family along the California coast (*see* CABEZON) it is of interest here to properly place it. The sculpin, sometimes called scorpionfish or bullhead, grows to about 15 inches, is typical of the rockfishes in general appearance. There are twelve spines in the dorsal fin. The color is reddish above, pink below, with much mottling and speckling, even over the tail. Its scientific name is *Scorpaena guttata*. It is caught from piers, barges, and party bottom-fishing boats and is highly esteemed by bottom-angling addicts.

Cabezon

Scorpaenichthys marmoratus

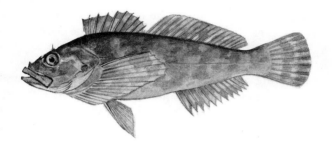

This is a true sculpin, the only member of the sculpin family on either of our coasts that is considered a game fish. It is a Pacific species. Its relatives are small and inconsequential, and a nuisance to stillfishermen. There are diminutive freshwater sculpins, too. These are the so-called "muddlers," often used as trout bait.

The cabezon is a very odd fish, but it is easily caught, a fair battler, good eating, and accessible because it is commonly found inshore in shallow water. Thus it has for years been a popular sport fish along the entire Pacific coast, and especially so off central California. Monterey and Santa Barbara are hot spots for cabezon fishing.

This big sculpin grows to 2 1/2 feet long and a weight of 25 pounds or more. It averages much smaller, from 2 to 5 pounds. The scaleless, wrinkled skin, the fleshy skin flaps over the eyes and on the snout, the spines over the eyes, the large, well-toothed mouth quickly place this species in the sculpin family, and separate it from the rockfish called "sculpin." The color is reddish to gray to green or brown, and quite variable. It is always mottled, however, and is sometimes called the "marbled sculpin."

It is also known as "blue cod," a poor name because the Pacific cultus, another game fish (see that heading) is sometimes called by the same colloquial name. "Bull cod" and "bullhead" are other confusing names, both also used for other species.

The lining of the cabezon's mouth is most peculiar. It looks translucent, and is blue-green in color. Although the table qualities of this sculpin's greenish or blue-tinged fillets are esteemed, there is evidence that the roe is poisonous.

The cabezon feeds principally on crabs and various mollusks. The fish roam over rocky or sandy bottoms, and stay right on bottom. They are mainly found in shallow water. Quiet tidal waters and kelp beds are favorite scrounging places for cabezon. Some very large specimens, however, are taken in rather deep water, occasionally by trollers.

The main catch comes from shore waters, and goes to the stillfishermen. A few use metal jigs, dancing them near bottom. Bait is more popular. Almost any bait will take the cabezon. Mussels, sea worms, crabs, cut bait, live bait fish are all good. Tackle isn't especially important. Even handlines are used by many. Because of the cabezon's teeth a steel leader is mandatory. Hooks of fair size are indicated by the size of the fish's mouth.

These fish can be caught at any time during the year. The larger specimens put up a fair scrap. They should be handled carefully when landed. They can bite, and their spines are sharp.

Lingcod

Ophiodon elongatus

This popular west-coast sport fish is neither a ling nor a cod, nor is it closely related to either. It is probably related to the rockfishes and sculpins, and belongs to a family of fishes called the greenlings. The name "cultus" is a puzzler. This comes from an Indian word meaning "without any value," which is hardly true of the tough-battling, excellent-tasting lingcod.

It is perhaps unfortunate that this fish was not given some more individualistic name, for both "ling" and "cod" have been colloquially attached to so many different species that are neither. This species is also called "greenling." At one time certain references placed it as a lone member in a family of its own, while others placed it with the greenlings. The American Fisheries Society subscribes to the greenling classification. Sport fishermen in California and on up the west coast nearly always use the name lingcod, which has become an official common name.

It seems as if almost everything about this species, from name to size and color, is highly variable. Lingcod may average from 1 to 5 pounds, but they commonly are caught in the 10- to 25-pound class, and specimens of 50 to 70 are not unusual. These are presumably always females. The coloring may be dark greenish or blue, or brown to reddish, with much mottling of reds, yellows, and darker blotches and spots. This variable color scheme is related both to environment and emotions. The individual fish tend to assume protective coloration of habitat, and they also switch colors very swiftly when hooked, or fighting on the hook, or when brought aboard. Even the flesh color is variable, and sometimes downright startling. It may be whitish, but is just as likely to be blue or green. Color of flesh has no bearing whatever on its taste, however, and all shades are edible.

The range of the lingcod is from very shallow to very deep water, and the entire length of our Pacific coast. However, below mid-California it is not abundant. It is extremely popular with fishermen of central California, and it is also taken in numbers on up the coast, in Puget Sound and along British Columbia. Rocky shores where both rocks and kelp beds are found, where tidal currents swirl and small fish such as herring and flounders, as well as shrimps, crabs, and squid abound—these are the hangouts of the lingcod.

They are fished both from shore and from boats. Some anglers make a practice of drifting offshore from rocky places, fishing with cut sardines, or jigging metal lures, or casting with plugs and spoons. Trolling at modest speed in such places, keeping the lure or bait well down, is also effective. The type of tackle is not important except that it should be selected to match the size of the fish most likely to be caught, and the method of fishing. Wire leaders and heavy hooks should be used. The lingcod has canine-type teeth and is a rough customer if of a good size. It is also a voracious feeder and vicious striker, all told a good game fish that fights a rugged underwater battle.

It is interesting to note that the lingcod has both the bony cheek support just beneath the skin that is found in the rockfishes, and the fleshy flaps above the eyes that are found in the sculpins. It has a shape mildly reminiscent of the cod, and mottling, eye flaps, and fin shape strikingly similar to the true greenlings. To separate it from other genera of the greenling family, it is only necessary to look at the lateral line: the lingcod has one, as do most fish; some greenlings have five.

In places where lingcod are commonly found, they are usually in exciting abundance. They are taken all year, but the best fishing occurs from early spring through until about October.

Greenling

Hexagrammos decagrammus

This is the game fish of the Pacific coast commonly called seatrout, greenling seatrout, rock trout, rockfish, bluefish, and kelp greenling. Of these names, seatrout is the most commonly used on the California coast, and greenling northward. The species is of course not even remotely related to the trouts. It is a true greenling.

This fish is highly esteemed by anglers, but it is not abundantly taken. There are several other greenlings more common in scattered locations. Examples are the whitespotted greenling with a range of greatest abundance along the northwest coast, and the rock greenling rather common off north California.

The authentic seatrout greenling is a colorful species, and an odd one. Male and female differ drastically in coloration. The female is slate blue to reddish brown in varying shades, with several distinct dark blotches along the back and sides, and a mass of red-brown speckles over the entire body. The male lacks the speckles. It is iridescent blue above, or coppery and blue, with dark, stripelike, vertical blotches, shading to blue-gray beneath. The head and shoulders have blue patches etched in darker lines and spots. The species has five lateral lines, instead of the single one of most fish. Occasionally the bones are green.

Greenlings are not large. Two or 3 pounds is about average. They inhabit dense kelp beds and rocky areas in bays, places of heavy algae growth around reefs and rocky headlands, and along island coasts. At times they are in the surf near rocks and reefs. They are more abundant northward in their range than southward. They are, in fact, fairly rare in southern California waters. Quite a number are taken near San Francisco. In general they are fish of rather shallow water.

The greenling is not difficult to catch. It feeds avidly on many kinds of crustaceans, worms, crabs, and small fishes in its favorite habitats. It is seldom fished for with artificial lures, and seldom taken on them. Stillfishing is the proven and popular method, with the bait a piece of fish, a chunk of clam, or a marine worm of some variety. Neither time of year nor of tide is vitally important.

Tackle can be any outfit from handline to freshwater plug rod to boat rod, and the fishing can be done either from shore or from a small boat. No specialized tricks are necessary. Once good greenling "holes" are located, and a bait lowered, the angler is likely to be in business, with one or another of the species. They are good fighters. A hook size on the average of 2/0 is practical, and a wire leader should be used. The greenling may not cut a line, but something else may.

All told, the greenlings are eagerly sought by inshore fishermen and are properly classed as game. They are also good table fish.

Ocean Whitefish

Caulolatilus princeps

The ocean whitefish isn't a whitefish at all. It is a member
of the tilefish family, most of which are marine fishes of
warm water with long, low dorsal and anal fins. They are
not even remotely related to the freshwater whitefishes,
and how the name originated is not known. Certainly it
had nothing to do with color. The ocean whitefish is
brown, shading lighter below, and with the fins tinged
with yellow, green, or bluish. Now and then a specimen
is taken that is yellow rather than brown.

This is a species of the Pacific, within our range along
and off the California coast, from central California southward. It frequents rocky coasts and rocky bottoms. There
is nothing very special about it as a game fish, but it is
a very good food fish. It does give a good account of itself,
and a great many are taken either incidentally or purposely by California anglers, who often call them "bottom
yellowtail." It is noted here chiefly to make sure it is
properly identified by those who catch it.

Ocean whitefish grow to very respectable size, averaging anywhere up to 10 or 15 pounds, with the maxi-

mum somewhat larger. They are commonly caught over the rocks along with various species of rockfish which are covered in the section under Rosy Rockfish.

In fact, these are fish strictly for bottom fishermen. When one goes out on a live-bait boat some ocean whitefish usually come aboard, especially if the boat plies the vicinity of the offshore islands such as the Coronados, Catalina, and the coast near Santa Barbara and those islands, and the Channels. Fall and winter and on through until spring seem to bring better fishing for this species than does the warm weather.

It is doubtful that ocean whitefish ever strike artificial lures. Or it may be that none are ever presented to them. They are caught by stillfishing on or near bottom, over rocks, with live or cut bait. Tackle should be fairly stout: standard bottom-fishing boat rod, with line of possibly 36-pound test, and wire leader. Quite a number of fishermen catch ocean whitefish to use as bait for the outsize California black sea bass, which seems especially fond of them whole.

Caution should be used in taking ocean whitefish off the hook. They have gill covers with knifelike edges that can do serious damage.

Barred Surfperch

Amphistichus argenteus

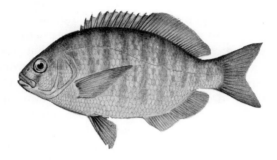

The barred surfperch is a member of a large family of
Pacific surf fish. By all traditional fishing standards it
should be called a saltwater panfish. That word "panfish"
is a hard one to define, but it undoubtedly means about
the same to all anglers. It is a way of giving credit to
smaller species not especially consequential as game fish
but nonetheless much sought by anglers because they
are fun to catch and good to eat. Just where one should
draw the line between "pan" and "game" is impossible
to say. Certainly the terms overlap, and probably in the
last analysis all "panfish" means is a small fish that will
fit in a frying pan, for a great many highly touted game
fish are small.

These west-coast surf fishes are stubborn fighters, and
some of them come in sizes too large for the average
skillet. They are caught by the thousands along the Pacific
coast, are rather important in the markets, and have been
the subject of fishing derbies in California. The section

following this one is given over to saltwater panfish as a means of rounding up numerous small marine species not covered elsewhere. The only reason the surfperch are allotted a separate space is that they are very specialized fish and seem to deserve special treatment.

The surfperches, of which there are at least twenty species along our west coast, are not perch, but of the family Embiotocidae, the surf-fish or surfperch family. They do not deposit eggs, but bear their young live. In general outline they remind freshwater anglers of the sunfishes. Their bodies are deep and compressed. Some of them stay in or near the surf, over sandy bottoms, others over rocky bottoms. All these species are spoken of by anglers as "surfperch." Some of them are found farther out, in deeper water, and are dubbed "seaperch." The rest are simply lumped together as "perch."

All are caught with various kinds of bait, from pieces of fish to small minnows, live and cut crustaceans—just about any natural shoreline food. On light tackle they are reminiscent of the freshwater sunfish. They lay a flat side against the pull of the rod and give a most satisfactory short battle. But unlike the freshwater varieties of sunfish, some of these surf fish may be of 2 or 3 pounds in weight, and up to 18 inches long. The average is about 8 to 14 inches, and 1/2 to 1 1/2 pounds. Light spinning tackle is highly recommended for them, although in the surf it is often necessary to use standard surf tackle, to overcome the problems of the breakers.

The reproduction process in these fish is worth noting. Breeding is accomplished in summer, and the eggs develop within a highly specialized uterus, each embryo enfolded within layers of uterus tissue. For almost seven months following, the mother fish carries her young. At the end of this astonishing gestation period, the young, which may number upwards of a hundred, have formed much-elongated fins. Through these, oddly, they absorb oxygen. Meanwhile they are bathed in a liquid within the uterus that is literally their food, which they also absorb. At birth the young may be as much as 2 inches long. They are born ready to swim and feed just like the adults.

Following are a few of the chief species of surfperch most likely to be caught:

The **barred surfperch,** *Amphistichus argenteus,* that heads this section ranges from central California southward along sandy shores. It is silvery and blue-gray, usually with dark bars and spots. It grows to about 16 inches, is one of the most important sporting species. Surf fishermen catch most of them.

The **rubberlip perch,** *Rhacochilus toxotes,* has the same range, but is generally found along rocky coasts. It is a whitish or coppery fish, often with a smoky overcast. It grows to about 18 inches, is caught from jetties, piers, in bays, along rocky shores, is an excellent food fish.

The **striped seaperch,** *Embiotoca lateralis,* ranges from Alaska to central California, also along rocky shores. It grows to about 15 inches, is unmistakable because of its narrow longitudinal striping in orange and blue. Still-fishermen take it from rocky areas and from piers and near pilings.

The **walleye surfperch,** *Hyperprosopon argenteum,* ranges from Vancouver southward along sandy shores.

It grows to about 12 inches, is bluish above, silvery below, and has its ventral fins black tipped. Anglers catch it in the surf and from piers, by stillfishing.

The **white seaperch,** *Phanerodon furcatus,* ranges from Vancouver southward along sandy shores, grows to about 12 inches, is whitish with a black line along the base of the soft dorsal. It is a very important commercial species, and one also much sought by anglers.

The **rainbow seaperch,** *Hypsurus caryi,* ranges from north-California to Los Angeles, is caught off rocky coasts. It grows to about a foot, has gaudy horizontal stripes of red, orange, blue, and streaks of orange and blue on the head.

The **redtail surfperch,** *Amphisticus rhodoterus,* ranges from Washington to mid-California along sandy shores, grows to 14 inches. It looks much like the barred perch but has ventral fins and tail reddish. This is an important angler's species, caught mostly by surf fishermen. It is the "porgy" of the Northwest.

There are many more—the **pile perch,** a silvery to smoky 16-incher ranging along the entire coast, caught mainly with small crabs around pilings or rocks, and sometimes over sand; the **black perch,** usually a brown fish tinged with numerous brighter colors, but with color patterns varying, a 14-incher of central-California's rocky coasts. Then there are the **calico surfperch,** the **pink seaperch,** the **kelp perch,** and a few more.

The reason brief details are given on so many species is that anyone who fishes inshore along the Pacific at all is certain to catch one or more varieties. In some areas at particular seasons when fishing is otherwise poor these fish make up almost the total catch.

When fishing sandy areas, the bait is simply cast out past the surf line and allowed to lie until a perch picks it up. No wire leader is necessary. In rocky places a leader may be used, simply to keep from fraying line, although monofil works well. Here the fish may hang around just at the lip of a submarine ledge, and are often caught swiftly in great numbers when the precise spot is found for the bait. Hooks should be small or of only moderate size. There is nothing difficult about fishing for these surf fishes, and anyone who makes a hobby of it with very light tackle will be well rewarded in sport. In fact, then it will be easy for an angler to understand how difficult it is to separate the "game" from the "pan." Spritely small species like these are certainly both.

Northern Porgy

Stenotomus chrysops

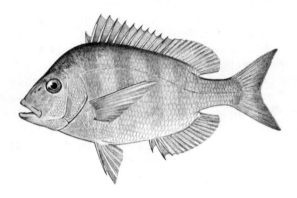

Anglers almost anywhere might protest that the northern porgy improperly heads the round-up of small saltwater fish of hook-and-line importance not covered elsewhere in this book. They are legion, and one man's favorite may be scoffed at by another, or not even known by him. In fact, no serious attempt can be made here to give a complete list of the scores of species, of many families totally unrelated, that are of very real importance to saltwater fishermen along our thousands of miles of coastlines. However, a number of them are so common and abundant and worthy that they must be touched, even if lightly. Probably more of the smaller species along our shores are taken every year by the hordes of anglers than of all larger game fish lumped together. Because the porgy often appears in astonishing swarms along the upper Atlantic coast, and is caught by thousands of average fishermen who greatly relish it both on the table and on the hook, it seems typical enough to start the list.

The porgies in our range are Atlantic and Gulf fish. Those called "porgy" in our Pacific range are actually surf fishes. The sheepshead of the Atlantic and Gulf is a porgy, but it, being fairly large, is covered elsewhere. Porgies are rather ovate, compressed fish, high-backed, with small mouths set with strong jaw teeth. Most of them weigh from 1/2 pound to 2 pounds, a few grow somewhat larger, to several pounds.

The northern porgy ranges from the Carolinas to Maine, is silvery and brown, mottled, feeds on crabs and crustaceans, on bottom. It is abundant in summer and fall off New England and New York, and is taken by still-fishing. It is often called "scup."

The southern porgy, also called "scup," looks much like the northern species, ranges from Virginia to Texas, is not usually common.

The jolthead porgy, grass porgy, littlehead porgy, and saucer-eye porgy all are more or less common about the Florida Keys, are variously and brightly colored. They are good little scrappers on dainty tackle. Occasionally one may strike a small lure but primarily they are panfish for the bait anglers.

The pinfish, one of the porgy group, must be mentioned because it is extremely common especially on the Gulf coast of Florida and Texas, where it is not only casual fun to catch, but a prime tarpon bait. It is bluish-silver, with golden stripes, and with the dorsal and anal blue and yellow. Its identifying tag is a dark spot on the "shoulder."

The **grunts** are another most important family of Atlantic and Gulf panfish. These average a pound, go to 3 or 4. They are related to the snappers. They do not have teeth on the roof of the mouth, which separates them from the snappers. Also, the scales along the lateral line do not run parallel with it. Many of the grunts have the inside of the mouth bright red. Most of them are tropical, or at least favor warmer waters. Ordinarily the grunts hang out in schools or small groups, inshore and over shallow reefs, around the mangroves, under bridges and near pilings, in bays, inlets, and all such protected waters. Their mouths are comparably larger than those of the porgies, and without the strong "buck" teeth or jaw teeth so evident in some of these fish.

The grunts as a group are gaily and beautifully colored, with canary yellow and bright aqua and blue in stripes and streaks, spots and spangles their stock in trade. Along the Florida coasts and about the Keys, and in one or two cases on around the Gulf to Texas these fish are caught by hundreds of stillfishermen and beginning anglers. They bite readily and are excellent eating. The sailor's choice, the French (or yellow) grunt, the blue striped grunt, white grunt, and margate grunt are good examples. Although reported to be night feeders almost exclusively, they seldom cling entirely to this habit. The porkfish of the Keys, a yellow-and-silver striped dandy with a black face and collar is one of the grunts. So also is the common

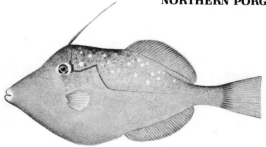

Yellow Filefish

pigfish of the Gulf and Atlantic coasts. All the grunts are fished on or near bottom, with any standard regional bait.

In our Pacific range there is but one member of the grunt family commonly caught. This is the sargo, "china croaker," or "blue bass." It is a gray-silver fish with indistinct darker markings, and is a minor sport fish, especially in Newport Bay.

The **blowfish,** or **swellfish,** of which there are several species, some of them known in the markets as "sea squab" are commonly caught on bottom all the way from the New York area on south around Florida and the Gulf. By no means game fish, they take baits readily, puff up their bellies to amazing size, grunting away meanwhile, when pulled from the water. Although there have been persistent tales of "poisonous" flesh of these fish, the backstrap and tail, about all there is on them, are eaten with relish and are considered a delicacy by numerous persons.

The **filefishes** also are so common hanging around bridge pilings and elsewhere in similar situations in Florida that no visiting angler can avoid seeing them, and having them steal bait meant for sheepshead and other fish. They are good eating when skinned. The skin is rough, and the deep, angular shape of the fish, with its preposterously small mouth and single stout spine sticking up on the back, is unmistakable.

The **mullet** (there are several species) so common everywhere has been intensely researched by sport fishermen for some years, to try to find out how to make it take a hook. A few southern coastal anglers have discovered the trick, by using very small baits, and very small flies, and even bits of moss. A mullet, beautiful leaper and active fish that it is, certainly leaves nothing to be desired as a game fish. If the time ever comes that techniques are perfected in surefire manner, so that anyone can turn the trick, undoubtedly these fish will move up from the bait and pan and commercial categories to become prime game fish.

Among the croakers there is a small member not mentioned elsewhere here, the **spot,** that is a fine panfish. It sometimes appears in vast numbers especially along the Gulf Coast. Its range is from Texas to Cape Cod. It is a gray and silver fish that takes its name from the yellow spot on the shoulder. There are dark bars, very narrow, running down from the back, slanting slightly forward and reaching just below the lateral line. Like other croakers, it takes worms, mollusks and crustaceans, fished on bottom over hard or sandy areas. It seldom weighs a pound. It has all the typical croaker features.

Then there is the **silver perch** of the Atlantic and Gulf coasts. It, too, is one of the croaker clan. But in appearance it is very similar to the white perch of fresh and brackish water, and easily confused with it. The lateral line runs to the end of the tail, however, and there are two anal spines instead of the three found on the white perch. The silver perch frequents sandy shores, enters northern bays in summer. It is caught stillfishing with baits suitable for other croakers, grows to about a foot long, and is fairly good table fish.

The little **moonfish** and the **lookdown,** both members of the jack family and both curious-looking species, are good panfish. Both are predominantly tropical, although both reach northward as far as New York. They are very deep, short-coupled, compressed species, the moonfish with a strikingly concave head, the lookdown with long streamer-like anterior dorsal and anal rays. Both are silvery, iridescent and pearly colored, with greens intermingled. The lookdown especially is a game little creature, and can be caught with tiny hooks baited with bits of fish or mollusk. It is excellent eating.

Among the jacks and pompanos there is a small species quite unlike the others in general outline. It is the **leatherjacket,** *Oligoplites saurus*, or skipjack. The scientific name is given because both common names are indiscriminately applied to several other species. This fish, about a foot long, is shaped much like a mackerel or bonito, pale blue-green above and silvery below. Oddly, it is often confused by Florida Spanish mackerel fishermen as a young mackerel. It will strike lures and take baits and is an excellent little fighter, as well as a fine

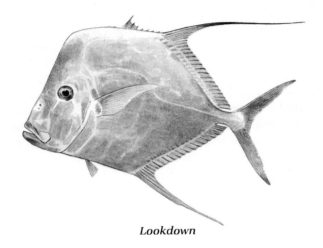

Lookdown

eating fish, even though small. When one can locate schools of these fish, and take them on small streamer flies, they are especially good sport.

On the Pacific coast, from Monterey southward, the **opaleye** is an important species of modest size taken mainly by surf fishermen. It may grow to 4 or 5 pounds but is usually smaller. It is found along both sandy and rocky shores, is a deep-bodied fish with a somewhat blunt snout and two bands of teeth in the jaws. It is greenish blue with a peculiarly opalescent blue eye and a light spot on either side of its back. This fish feeds mainly on seaweeds, and the small sea life that abounds in them.

The **halfmoon,** another Pacific species, ranges southward from central California, is a blue-black, long-oval shaped fish that also eats seaweeds. Both it and the opaleye are commonly called Catalina perch, and other "perch" names.

The **spadefish** is an almost round species with tiny mouth and long fins. It is pale gray with striking vertical bands of black, one of which runs through the eye. It is commonly confused with the angelfish. It is found along all of the Gulf coast and the lower Atlantic, is a fantastic fighter even when very small, and a delicious table fish. It averages from less than 1/2 pound to about 2 pounds, but grows much larger. Specimens of 15 or 20 pounds are occasionally taken. These are tremendously powerful sport fish. Because so many small ones are caught, the spadefish is dealt with here as a panfish. About May as a rule it swarms around places such as pilings of fishing piers along the open Gulf, is caught by using extremely small hooks with a tiny bait.

The list of these less consequential and usually small species caught here and there in U.S. coastal waters could go on and on. Each variety, if and when one catches them, can be identified, if necessary, from standard scientific reference books. It may be said that these panfish as a motley group should be not less respected as sport fish for being gathered together here. Their abundance, their willingness, their variety are what lend one of the brightest faces to saltwater fishing. Their color and the curious forms of many keep anglers asking questions, and in that way one is spurred to seek further knowledge, and to learn, and in turn to enhance the first delight of catching something that, even though not rare, was to the angler until then unknown.

Codfish

Gadus morhua

The codfish of the Atlantic, which ranges over rock and sand bottoms from the Carolinas northward but is mainly a fish of the New England and east-Canadian coasts, is better known in cod liver oil and as salt codfish than as a game fish. Nonetheless, it has its enthusiastic following, and though a cod's battle on the hook may not be startling, it is still a powerful and voracious fish, and he who catches it is assured of excellent eating.

The flesh of the cod keeps well when salted. Because of this the cod was one of the most important of fishes during early settlement of this country. It still is, even though nowadays comparatively little is salted. It is not an especially handsome fish. It is pot bellied, and sports a chin whisker, or barbel, on the lower jaw.

Cod fins are rather unique. The dorsal is spineless and split into three separate portions. The anal is also spineless, and in two sections. Cod color may range from yellow or brown to reddish to greenish, but is usually some yellowish cast, with darker spots scattered over most of the body and head. The lateral line running down the side is much lighter colored than the rest of the fish. This is a good point of identification.

Cod fishing has not changed a great deal over the centuries. Some of our early colonists were attracted to America because of the abundance of cod on the northern offshore banks. The schooling cod, predominantly a bottom feeder, was taken in nets, of course, but was also commonly caught on a handline. That is how most fish are still caught.

The reason is that codfish are deep-water fish. They inhabit waters down to well over 1000 feet deep, but are most often caught by sports anglers at the 50 to 300 foot levels. Occasionally when feeding on schooling bait fish, they are caught near surface. Cod are migratory fish, trading back and forth from near shore to offshore, and migrating vertically, too, from near surface to great depths. Numerous colloquial names are used for this fish, but almost all of them include the word "cod." Occasionally the cod and the pollock are confused by tyros at this fishing. The easiest way to distinguish one from another is by looking at the jaw. A cod's upper jaw projects a bit past its lower jaw, while the reverse is true of the rather similar pollock, often found in the same waters.

The average size of cod caught by anglers is from 3 or 4 pounds up to 25 pounds. They grow much bigger, occasionally weighing 175 or more pounds and being as long as a tall man. They eat crabs, mollusks, various marine worms, and of course seize whatever small fishes happen to come handy. There are few items, in fact, that cod will turn down.

Clams, cut baits, squid, live smelt or other small fish are used for bait by handliners, or by others using conventional rod-and-reel outfits when cod are in water shallow enough to make such rigs practical. A fairly stout line and a good-sized hook are requisite. So is a sinker of 3/4 pound or more, when the cod lie deep, so the line will be taken down to them swiftly. In more shallow water a smaller sinker may be used. If a rod is used, it must be stiff for deep water and heavy sinker.

Like most other marine species, cod are most susceptible inshore when the tide is rising and rolling in. When they are very deep, tides have little effect on how well they bite. From late summer on through the winter months is the best time for codfishing in the more southerly portions of their range. They are cold-water fish. They are taken all year farther north, with the comfort of the fisherman, and the whimsy of cod migrations, dictating when the fishing will be done.

Off Newfoundland, Nova Scotia, and New Brunswick, throughout the Gulf of Maine, and around such areas as Cape Cod, many docks rent boats for bottom fishing. If one intends to try the open water, special and very substantial skiffs purposely built to take rough water are needed. These are available over most of the northern area where cod fishing is most popular.

The **haddock,** a member of the cod family with which nearly everyone is familiar at least in restaurants or markets, sometimes furnishes sport to bottom fishermen. It is not large, usually from 1 to 3 pounds, with the maximum 10 to 15. A black lateral line and a black area on the shoulder sets it apart from the cod. This is a deep-water fish ranging south about to North Carolina, usually found over hard but smooth bottoms.

The various **hakes,** too, are often taken by sport fishermen in the general cod fishing areas, and often by those after cod and haddock. Hakes resemble cod superficially. They are not of the same family, however, but are fairly close relatives. They run in large schools in both very deep and very shallow water, depending on the time of year. They are good fighters, and hard strikers, but are short on staying power. Average size is about 2 pounds. There is some fly fishing for them when they are in the shallows, and in this respect they are a good diversion. Bucktails and streamers on about a 1/0 hook are used. The sport is not at all bad. Dusk is a good time, and in summer, around Cape Cod and northward. There is also a Pacific hake, but it is not very popular with either sport or commercial fishermen.

It must be mentioned here that there are two species in our Pacific waters spoken of as "cods" that are not even closely related to the true cods, nor even very closely related to each other. One is the sablefish, coal cod, or blackcod. This is an important commercial species, and is also taken especially along the Washington coast and its bays to some extent by sport fishermen. The other is the blue cod, or more properly lingcod, also called Pacific cultus, which is covered in another section. There is a

Pacific cod, *Gadus macrocephalus*, which ranges from Oregon northward and is a close relative of the Atlantic cod. It is caught casually by stillfishing, but is primarily a commercial species, and one so far rather neglected even in that field because of lack of demand.

Pollock

Pallachius virens

The pollock is a fish of northern Atlantic waters, ranging south to Cape Cod. Boston bluefish, green cod, and coalfish are common names for it, and within its restricted range it is a rather important sport fish. It is dark green or black-green on the upper portions, with gray and silvery lower sides. The lateral line is distinct and light colored. There is not very much danger within its range of confusing it with any other fish. Although it resembles the cod superficially, it is not spotted, its tail is somewhat forked while that of the cod is straight-edged, its lower jaw projects past the upper while that of the cod is just opposite. There are three portions of the dorsal fin and two of the anal, as in the codfish.

Pollock average anywhere from 4 to 10 pounds, but very commonly are taken in the 15- to 30-pound category, and grow even larger. They are a good food fish, and are an important commercial species especially along the Maine coast.

Some anglers fish pollock in deep water. When taken thus they are simply stillfished, with cut bait or small fish, clams or squid. They are not very good fighters at such times because they are brought up from deep water. However, what has made the pollock especially important during the past few years as a game fish is the inshore movement during May, at which time, anglers have discovered, pollock on or near surface take lures readily and are striking battlers.

At such places as Race Point Rip on Cape Cod, and other areas over the general vicinity of the coast, pollock come up from deep water and begin to move inshore about the last of April. By mid-May the movement is usually at its peak. In certain areas, such as the one mentioned on Cape Cod, they feed almost within casting distance of shore, and indeed the smaller ones do come in that close. Anglers swarm to the beaches with surf rods, or out in small boats to clean up. The same phenomenon occurs all along the coast within pollock range.

Some fishermen troll, some stillfish with bait drifted into the schools of surfacing pollock. The fish come to or near the surface to feed on schools of forage fish. But the anglers who have the highest sport are those using artificial lures such as yellow or white feathered jigs, metal squids, and other standard upper-coast lures. Saltwater spinning rigs are also in wide use for this fishing.

The pollock take a lure with a rush and give an altogether different account of themselves from that which ensues when they are caught deep. They make a swift, powerful run and then bore down and battle grimly. It is not unusual for a 15-pounder to put up a fight of fifteen or more minutes on light tackle.

Some pollock enthusiasts chum for them, but most select the places known to be spring hangouts and wait for the fish to boil on the surface. Or they simply cast, let their lures sink and run down through the rip, or over a dropoff, then retrieve in an attractive manner. Some use wire leaders, some do not. On light tackle such as spinning gear, a sufficient amount of line is mandatory, for it is difficult to stop a large pollock. A few anglers have taken to fishing during this spring spree with saltwater fly rods and large streamers. It is a most successful, interesting, and sporty method. The streamer is simply cast to places where fish are boiling, allowed to sink, and stripped back in.

This fashioning of the somewhat lethargic pollock into a fine game fish is a prime instance of the clever utilization of less attractive species for top sport. Farther north, pollock fishing is popular all during the summer and on into early fall, around Nova Scotia and the upper New England coast. Much of this fishing, however, is bottom fishing, although a good many are still taken in shallow water or near the surface or close inshore through until about October, when they slip back out to the depths.

Most pollock fishermen prefer the moving tides, especially the incoming tide, and most also feel that early and late in the day are the best times. However, when pollock first swarm inshore in spring they may feed wildly at any time. Often the birds give an indication of when this feeding may begin, by diving from above on schools of harassed bait fish.

Atlantic Halibut

Hippoglossus hippoglossus

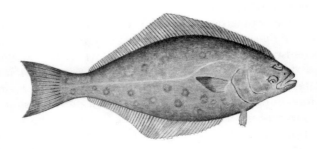

The odd flatfishes are among the world's most abundant, most diverse, and most important food fish. While they put up a very good struggle on the hook, and are sought by anglers, they are on the fringe as far as the term "game" is concerned. For the most part they are caught for the plain fishing fun of it, and to eat. There are hundreds of fishermen along the New England coast and on south for some distance who would rather miss Christmas than miss the arrival inshore of the summer flounders. There are others along the Pacific who diligently fish for halibut, would rather catch one good one than all the sails and marlin in the seas. Happily, such are the varied tastes of fishermen. For that matter, as far as the eating is concerned, it would be difficult to argue with a flatfish enthusiast.

There are some 500 known species of flatfish in the world's waters. These are grouped into at least fifty genera. While most exhibit some of the standard flatfish characteristics, the vast group as a whole is most difficult and confusing. Therefore, we will not try in this brief space to do much with identity of species, which might be only more confusing, but will stick, rather, to generalities. The entire flatfish clan is composed of fish that, as adults, lie and swim on one side. As young they begin life in an upright position with each eye normally placed. But as they develop each fish begins to tilt to one side or the other, some right, some left. Finally a most amazing phenomenon occurs: one eye begins to "migrate." Presently the eye has assumed a position beside its mate, so that both are now on one side of the head, and fish now spends all its time on its side.

Most of the flatfishes have been classified according to the eye position: the right-eyed flatfishes, the left-eyed flatfishes. But there are occasional specimens that do not fit as they are supposed to. They somehow begin to tip the wrong way, and a right-eyed flounder becomes a "freak" left-eyed one. While all begin life with both sides pigmented in the various drab colors worn by flatfishes, after becoming adult and lying flat, they lose pigment below, and become whitish on the underside. There are minor exceptions to this.

The drab colors of the flatfishes are for the purpose of camouflage. Most of the species lie on bottom, in sand or mud. With the pale, unpigmented side down, the upper side matches the bottom. One classification difficulty stems, however, from the fact that many species are capable of switching pigmentation to match their surroundings. As they lie flat with both eyes weirdly staring up, they are in an excellent position to seize any food that comes along.

The flatfishes are composed of the flounders, flukes, halibuts, turbots, soles, and dabs. Very generally speaking, the turbots, soles, and dabs are the smallest, weighing from 1 to 10 pounds, the flukes and flounders may be of that size, or up to 20. There is of course much overlapping here. The halibuts, while often of nominal size such as 10 or 15 pounds, are commonly taken at 50, 100, 200, and in some species to 500 or more.

Here are the chief species known along the Atlantic and Gulf coasts, common names only (these common names may differ from region to region, colloquially). Greenland halibut, common halibut, sanddab, northern fluke, southern fluke, Florida fluke, Gulf fluke, four-spotted fluke, ocellated fluke, rusty dab, winter flounder, smooth flounder, sundial, eyed flounder, peacock flounder, smallmouth flounder, fringed flounder, striped sole, naked sole, scrawled sole.

The Pacific species most common are: The Pacific sanddab, speckled sanddab, fantail sole, bigmouth sole, California halibut, Pacific halibut, arrowtooth halibut, slender sole, petrale sole, sand sole, scaly-fin sole, English sole, rock sole, Dover sole, rex sole, starry flounder, diamond turbot, curl-fin turbot, hornyhead turbot.

Of all these, the winter flounder, summer flounder, Gulf flounder, and halibut on the Atlantic side, and the starry flounder and halibut on the Pacific are probably the most important to anglers, although a great many of the others are caught. The winter flounder ranges from Labrador to South Carolina, is most abundant along the New England coast and a bit south late in winter and through spring. It is right-eyed, has a small mouth, weighs seldom more than 4 or 5 pounds. The summer

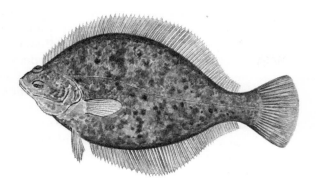

Flounder

flounder is left-eyed, has a large mouth, has its range of greatest abundance similar to that of the other, is most abundant in summer, weighs commonly to 5 pounds and may go much larger, to 20 or more. The starry flounder of the Pacific is predominantly right-eyed, has black and orange-tinged bars on the dorsal and anal. It ranges from Point Conception north and weighs about like the eastern summer flounder. Halibuts are larger, can seldom be mistaken because both their jaws bear well developed teeth, while the teeth of flounders are usually best developed on the blind side. Many of the soles and dabs are all but toothless.

Stillfishing is the traditional method of catching the flounders, although sometimes small feathered jigs and wobbling spoons retrieved slowly and enticingly along bottom will elicit strikes. Baits used are the various marine worms, pieces of clam, crab or shrimp, small live fish or cut bait. The bays, the inlets, the sloughs, the sandy bottoms and the muddy ones, boat basins and harbors and tidal flats are all good flounder habitat. The starry species of the west coast also likes brackish to fresh tidal waters of rivers. It is seldom necessary to fish any of the flounders far from shore. In fact, a great many are caught from shore, and sometimes the largest ones are taken right in the surf.

Hooks should be of nominal size. For large flounders a short wire leader is often employed, but is not really necessary. Rods, reels, and lines are the choice of the fisherman. Here again, spinning gear has become popular as a method simple to use for stillfishing and a way to get the most sport out of the fish. The sinker is usually rigged at the end of the line, with the hooks above it, to keep the bait just off bottom. One of the best ways to catch flounders is to get the depth exactly right, then drift, letting the light sinker barely bump along bottom. This is also a good way to catch flounders on certain artificial lures that are active at slow speeds. The rising tide is considered best, but sometimes it makes little difference. Commonly the outgoing tide is just as good.

Some fishermen like bobbers for floundering. They adjust the depth, using a very light sinker, so the running tide drifts the bobber along. Others use no bobber, only a split shot or two, and drift a bait thus from shore, pier, or boat. Because the flatfishes lie watching for passing food, a moving bait is generally more productive than a still one.

On party boats along the west coast, and occasionally behind the surf, the California halibut is caught by still- or drift-fishing, and sometimes on lures. The halibuts are more active in pursuit of their forage than are the other flatfish. This halibut may weigh as much as 50 or more pounds. The largest specimens (Pacific and Atlantic) are seldom caught by sport fishermen because they live at such great depths offshore.

An interesting use of the flatfishes as sport fish occurs in numerous regions, from the Texas and upper Gulf coasts on around Florida and the Carolinas. At times the inshore movement of the smaller flatfish of various species into very shallow water is astonishing. They literally swarm. At night, with a low tide, one can wade the flats with a light and spot them everywhere, their eyes protruding from the sand. A small gig is carried and the fish are impaled and popped into sacks carried for the purpose. This activity has become extremely popular in areas of great flatfish abundance.

Gaff-Topsail Catfish

Bagre marinus

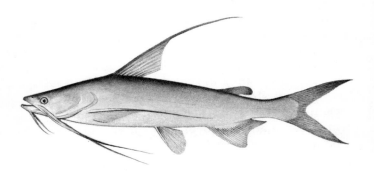

The catfishes of saltwater are not generally considered game species. However, the gaff-topsail, so named because of the extra-long anterior dorsal spine that raises the narrow filamentous portion of the dorsal like a small sail, is something of an exception.

This catfish grows to good size, averaging from 2 to 5 pounds with a maximum weight around 10. It is for the most part a clean-water fish, inhabiting open waters and feeding chiefly on living food such as small fish, crabs, and crustaceans, not scavenging as do the smaller sea catfishes.

It is a heavy-bodied, dark to medium gray fish with a deeply forked tail. Only a single pair of barbels on the lower jaw, long narrow spines on the pectorals, and the curious dorsal distinguish this catfish unmistakably from its relative the sea catfish, which may be caught in the same areas. The common sea catfish has four barbels, and lacks the filaments on pectorals and dorsal.

Many gaff-topsail cats are caught around Florida and westward through the Gulf, from the surf, from docks, in channels, bays, and sometimes in water of moderate depth offshore. They range on north in the Atlantic about to New England, but are less abundant the farther north they reach.

Most "gaff-tops," which are good eating, are taken by stillfishermen, surf fishermen, and casters using bait. Rather consistently they also strike artificial lures such as plugs, jigs, and spoons. They hit very hard, and they fight a strong, dogged battle, much faster than one would imagine. They should of course be handled carefully when being removed from the hook, to avoid the spines.

Fishing is usually best in the spring and summer months, when the catfish move inshore. Winter generally finds them in deeper water, excepting in the South, where they are often taken all year, both commercially, and by sport fishermen.

The spawning habits of this catfish are unique. The male catfish takes the freshly extruded eggs into his mouth and they are incubated there. He must carry them for at least two months, after which he continues to carry in his mouth the young, until such time as they are able to care for themselves.

Although many anglers despise the saltwater cats because they are a nuisance while one is fishing for something gamier, this species in particular should be respected. Nowadays a number of fishermen are discovering that it is good sport fish, better in many respects than some others considered above it in sporting stature.

A Sampling from Mexico

Because immense numbers of American fishermen travel more and farther and faster than the fishermen of any other nation, this book ends with a brief preview of what is to be had—what in fact a sizable number of our anglers are already having—in some places at the fringes of our range.

On our eastern coast and in the Gulf a great many of our species are tropical or subtropical. Thus, we are able to fish, off Florida or along its Keys or eastward out among the islands, for a number of species that are the same as those inhabiting coastal and offshore waters of South America. But on the Pacific side the ocean within U.S. range is colder, and therefore the fishes from farther south do not come into it to as great an extent. However, just to the south of California lies Baja California, with its warm offshore waters and bays, and its great Gulf of California.

A great many western-U.S. anglers, and many from other parts of the country now make pilgrimages to this area, which is ever being serviced better by roads and airlines. This great southern region contains what is unquestionably some of the world's best fishing. The Gulf of California is a veritable fish trap, catching and concentrating millions of fish of numerous species that come into it from the open Pacific.

A number of the species found here are foreign to U.S. waters. They are too numerous to cover in detail, but several of the outstanding and more unusual game species are worth noting, as a kind of "bait" to lure anglers into trying the region. Because it can now be so easily fished, and because it so teems with game fish, it has become for all practical purposes a part of fishing in the United States. Much the same is true for Mexico's east coast, and of course for all of Canada and the Far North, which have been better explored by the average angler.

Some of the species visitors will catch will seem strikingly exotic. A classic example is the **roosterfish,** *Nematistius pectoralis*, of Baja and the Gulf of California. Called by the Mexicans *papagalio*, which means literally the head rooster or the papa rooster, this striking species is a sensational game fish. In general conformity it resembles the jacks and pompanos, and indeed it does belong to the same family. But the anterior spines of the dorsal are much elongated, like a rooster's comb. It is a gray-blue fish with metallic sheen. Roosterfish come in all sizes up to 75 or more pounds, with the average 5 to 20.

Roosterfish are caught by trolling, and they are also taken in inshore bays by casting plugs and other artificials. They are furious fighters, extremely strong and with great stamina. They are excellent game fish as well as delicious on the table. Adding to its game qualities is the mystery of its comings and goings. A certain sandy bay may be full of roosterfish today, and they will strike anything that moves. On the next day not one can be found.

This is only one of the many surprises which will bait the angler who probes the great fishing hole of the Gulf of California and the Baja coast. Of course many of our own Pacific game fish are found there, too. But the ones with which we are not familiar are the species that add the spice.

For example, there is the **totuava,** *Cynoscion macdonaldi.* This is a kind of croaker. But it is a king-sized croaker, the largest of the lot. For those many enthusiasts of croaker fishing, the totuava, which ranges abundantly through the Gulf of California, with its heaviest concentration in the upper portions, is a kind of jackpot prize, a super-croaker. The fish commonly weighs from 50 to 80 pounds, and may weigh well over 200.

With the exception of early spring, when it is difficult or impossible to locate, the totuava can be taken all year. The traditional method is slow deep trolling, either with a strip or live bait, or a large wobbling spoon. This great silvery fish may be 5 or 6 feet long. It is an important commercial species, as well as a target of sportsmen.

The **golden grouper,** a color phase of the leopard grouper, is a Gulf of California denizen that grows to about 3 feet maximum. It is yellow-orange overall, black or spotted with black along the back. The **orangemouth corbina** is another 3-footer, a croaker with a bright orange-yellow mouth. Along the Mexican Pacific and in the Gulf of California there is also a special sport fish found nowhere else in the world. This is the **striped pargo,** a dynamic battler averaging 5 pounds but at maximum up to 100. It is closely related to the snappers. These species are a sampling of what is below our borders in saltwater.

Index